THE CHIEF'S
CHIEF

THE CHIEF'S
CHIEF

MARK MEADOWS

Former chief of staff to President Donald J. Trump

All Seasons Press
6800 Gulfport Blvd. Suite 201-355
St. Petersburg, FL 33707

Interior design by Timothy Shaner

FIRST EDITION: NOVEMBER 2021

Library of Congress Cataloging-in-Publication Data has been applied for.

ISBNs: 978-1-7374785-2-2 (hardcover), 978-1-7374785-3-9 (ebook)

Printed in the USA

10   9   8   7   6   5   4   3   2   1

Dedicated to my family who has always
lovingly supported me.

And to the millions of forgotten men and women
who President Trump always remembered.

CONTENTS

THE CHIEF'S
CHIEF

"Hanging Around"

AS I WRITE this, President Donald J. Trump has been out of office for around nine months. In that time, I've had the privilege of traveling with him all over the country. We've been to state GOP conventions, CPAC events and fundraisers for the America First movement. Occasionally, these trips occur because some down-ballot candidate in a tough state is holding a rally and has requested—or, in most cases, *begged for*—an appearance from the forty-fifth president of the United States. These candidates know that no matter what the Fake News tells us, an endorsement from President Trump is about as close to a guarantee of victory as you can get in these dark, confusing times. The liberal media tries to portray that the Trump magic is a thing of the past.

So, whenever President Trump gets one of these requests, provided the candidate hasn't committed any felonies or dragged him through the mud in the past, he tries his best to get on a plane and head over. When my schedule allows it, I'll go with him. I do this, in part, simply because I enjoy his company. President Trump, or "the boss," as we always called him in the White House, has a wicked sense of humor, and traveling with him is never boring. But I also do it because I truly believe he is the leader of the conservative movement in this country, and whatever he does next, I will be there to support him.

Which brings me, of course, to the eight-hundred-pound elephant in the room—the question that President Trump gets asked more than any other. As of this writing, I have never seen him enter a room without having to hear it at least ten times.

What's next?

Many of the people who ask him this question are casual supporters. They're business associates and old friends, all genuinely curious about what the future holds for our forty-fifth president. Sometimes, these people are journalists looking for a few lines for their books, always smiling and throwing out compliments while they're in the room, secretly hoping all the while that during their conversation, President Trump will slip up and say something that they can use against him—something that they can put forward in their newspapers and Twitter feeds as further proof that he is evil, racist, sexist, bigoted, or whatever new liberal buzzword happens to be in vogue that day.

In both cases, President Trump doesn't quite answer the question. He equivocates, delays, says he can't say anything due to election laws and basic decorum. Most people are willing to take that non-answer for the moment, though not always happily.

But every once in a while, I'll hear the question come from someone who *needs* an answer. Needs it, it seems, like they need food, water, and air. These people are die-hard Trump supporters, the ones who sent him to the White House in November

2016. They are the "forgotten men and women" that President Trump served so well for four years in the White House, overcoming staggering odds to pass an historic agenda on their behalf. According to the latest totals, there are more than 70 million of these people, all of whom believe they were cheated out of another four years of President Trump. In the seconds between the question and the answer, these people often look as if they won't be able to breathe another few minutes without knowing whether it's really going to happen—whether our president is going to come back, throw on his bright red MAGA 2024 hat, and save us from the horrible mess that the United States of America has become in his absence. For these people, the question comes from deep in their soul, sounding more like a desperate prayer than a simple inquiry.

I understand this third kind of person very well.

In fact, I'm beginning to think that I might be one of them.

In the months since we left the White House together in January 2021, President Trump and I have watched the country fall into the kind of disrepair that hasn't existed since . . . well, since the last time we put Sleepy Joe Biden in charge of anything. The integrity of our elections is in jeopardy, our enemies are laughing at us, Americans have been left behind in Afghanistan in a botched withdrawal that cost the lives of thirteen US military, and a pack of deranged, incompetent socialists has taken over our government.

In March, President Biden's secretary of state stood by while China told us that the United States is not operating from "a position of strength." This spring, the administration shut down President Trump's inquiry into the (extremely likely) possibility that the Wuhan Coronavirus did, in fact, leak from the Wuhan Institute of Virology. It seems that everyone, from our leftist politicians to our celebrities, has made sucking up to the Chinese Communist Party part of the United States' official foreign policy platform. If things get any worse, a struggling Joe Biden is going to be sending his son Hunter over to Beijing with a white flag (and maybe some of his horrible art) to negotiate the terms of our abject surrender.

Down at the Mexican border, hundreds of thousands of migrants are pouring into our country. The border wall that President Trump began building during his presidency—spending millions of dollars for the best technology around—is laying, unassembled and unpainted, on the sand. When I spoke with President Trump in July, he seemed particularly outraged by the incompetence of Democrats when it came to the border.

"They have now spent two billion dollars guarding the unused materials for a new five hundred mile portion of the wall," he says. "All because they didn't want to put up the wall. We could have had it built for five hundred million. Now all the contractors are asking for five times more. I know contractors better than anyone. They are smart. They want five times what they asked for, but they're asking for money for *not* building the wall. They're saying that their businesses are destroyed. The Democrats are putting us out of business."

Nearly every time we speak, President Trump expresses profound sadness and worry for the American people, especially those in our major cities. This is understandable. In the months since he's been out of office, ideas that once sat at the fringes of the Democratic Party's platform have gone mainstream. Phrases like "defund the police" are not only taken seriously, they are standard talking points for anyone running in this country as a Democrat. Critical Race Theory is being taught in our schools, and it is on the verge of overrunning the United States military as well. Along with President Trump, I shudder at the thought that our soldiers, once the fear of every army in the world, might soon be required to ask the enemy for his preferred pronouns before executing a strike in a foreign land; maybe they'll have to hold diversity seminars for blood-thirsty members of ISIS to make the caliphate "woke" before eradicating it from the face of the earth.

Some days, it seems like too much to take.

Thanks to these horrific and shortsighted policies, all designed to appease the most unhinged members of a party already gone off its rails, life in the United States is on the decline. Crime is up in nearly every major city. In Chicago, as President Trump recently pointed out to me, there is one police officer for every fifteen gang members. New York City, President Trump's hometown, has seen its murder rate skyrocket. Inflation is running wild, and the average cost of consumer goods is soaring. The government has been giving out so much money to people that many don't want to come to work. This is a problem that goes far beyond Joe Biden himself, but it is something that we have seen coming for some time.

Still, President Trump has not announced that he will run again in 2024. I've asked him, of course, and I usually get the same answer that he gives to most people.

"There's a term in golf," says President Trump, sitting in his office at Bedminster in July. He's holding the front page of a newspaper in his hand, eyeing a stack of new, bright red MAGA hats on the corner of his desk. "It's called *hanging around*."

The sound of children laughing drifts into the room from the club's pool, which sits just outside of the president's new office. The boss leans back in his chair, dressed in a sport coat and a crisp white shirt that's open at the neck. He looks at least twenty pounds lighter than he was in office. It also seems like he might have slept for a few hours last night, which was a rare occurrence during our time in the White House.

In the past week, dozens of news articles have come out about the final days of the Trump administration, all claiming to have the "inside scoop" on what really occurred. Most of these stories quote aggrieved former officials like General Mark Milley, the president's chairman of the Joint Chiefs of Staff. In interviews for the many books that have been released, Milley has said that he tried to stop President Trump from instituting a "coup," comparing him explicitly to Adolf Hitler. In one article in *The New Yorker,* he is quoted as saying that President Trump was going to strike Iran as a way to maintain his grip on power, and that he, General Milley, put a stop to this dastardly plan as soon as he could—something that, conveniently, made him a hero to liberals and Trump haters everywhere, just in time for him to hit the speaking circuit with Generals Mattis, McMaster, McChrystal, and the rest of the McLosers who've found that there's money to be made by dumping on President Trump in public.

The president recalls a four-page report typed up by Mark Milley himself. It contained the general's own plan to attack Iran, deploying massive numbers of troops, something he urged President Trump to do more than once during his presidency. President Trump denied those requests every time. In the months since he's been out of the White House, President

Trump has grown much calmer, less concerned about the routine matters and petty squabbles of politics.

There's an expression for it, he says.

"When a guy is hanging around, he's just watching everyone scoring. Great golfers put themselves behind, then they come back. That's what I'm doing. We'll see what happens."

Just up the road, a few dozen guests sit on a wooden deck overlooking the golf course, all hoping that President Trump will come up and dine among them that evening. When he does, they'll all get on their feet and applaud. Most of them will ask the inevitable question, and they'll probably get some variation of the answer that I'm getting right now.

We're going to do great things; we're going to be back; it's going to be great.

In other words, just "hanging around."

But anyone who thinks that this means President Trump has given up the fight is sorely mistaken.

"The worst thing these people did," he says, "is they stole the election. I have these guys come in here all the time, and they tell me to stop. They say, 'we'll get 'em in three years, sir!' I love these guys. Honestly, we're not going to have a country in three years. . . . We are living in a Communist country. I call it the Radical Left Democrat Communist Party . . . The way I see it, there are two phases. First, find the fraud. The second phase is okay, we found it. We caught you. How do you say that? You know, when a diamond thief steals a bunch of diamonds from Tiffany, he doesn't get to keep the diamonds. But we'll worry about that later. If all Republicans fought, this thing would be over. But they don't . . . They say I'm wasting my time. But I am fighting that fight."

When you mention the various books and articles that have come out about him, he doesn't mince words.

"It's all false," he says. "All of it. These people come in, and they don't even ask me about the things that are supposedly controversial. It's a waste of time, doing these interviews."

When President Trump learned I was writing my own book about the time we had spent working together in the White House, I offered to come up to Bedminster and get his side of these one-sided stories, just to make sure I could print the truth in my own book. But it soon became clear that doing so would be pointless. I did not ask the president, for instance, if he ever said that Hitler did great things, as was printed in Michael C. Bender's book *Frankly, We Did Win This Election*. I knew that he hadn't. I did not ask whether he had ever balled up a newspaper and tossed it at Mike Pence, knowing that the answer would be an emphatic no.

A few minutes in, I realized that refuting these lies would have taken almost as much time as he had been in the White House in the first place. There were so many, and their origins were so obscure—and, in all likelihood, fictional—that there was no point in giving them any attention.

President Trump did, however, reserve special scorn for General Mark Milley, who, as of this writing, is still on his apology tour of the country, trashing the president.

"He was a dopey guy," he said. "Not a good leader. I guess he was 'woke.' When I first realized, I went to the church, and he was with me, along with many other people. They were moving people back respectfully. But not for me! It all came out that I was one hundred percent right . . . But then, all of a sudden, I see this guy making a speech and apologizing. And from that moment on, I never liked him. I just never liked him."

But in the end, we always returned to the futility of coming out against these lies.

"I could read all of these books," he said. "But I would have to retire and sit down for years to do it."

The president asked only that I get the truth out with this book. That's what I'm attempting to do. As for whether President Trump is going to come back in three years, I have a strong feeling that the answer is yes.

When I see him these days, I don't see a man who is "hanging around" and planning to fade into the sunset. I see someone who is coming back. This is a man who has the best years of his life ahead of him, and he is more than willing to use those years, once again, in service of the American people who need him.

"I've heard from many people," he says, "that I am the only one who can save us."

He is sitting back, planning, and waiting for his moment.

And when that moment comes, I don't envy anyone who dares stand against him.

ONE

Trending

"CONGRATULATIONS," said President Trump. "You're now the most powerful man in the world."

It was around nine o'clock on the evening of Friday, March 6, 2020. I was standing in my kitchen talking to the president of the United States on my cell phone. A few minutes earlier, President Trump had set the political world on fire, as he often did, with this tweet, delivered in an instant to his nearly 90 million followers:

> **@realDonaldTrump:** I am pleased to announce that Congressman Mark Meadows will become White House Chief of Staff. I have long known and worked with Mark, and the relationship is a very good one . . .*

---

* This fragment, incredibly, is all that remains of the president's tweet. When Twitter banned President Trump, they removed not only his ability to tweet but also the full archive of his past tweets, which contained about 50,000 pieces of presidential correspondence with the public. As of this writing, they are not available in full anywhere on the internet. It is almost as if Big Tech is trying, and succeeding, to erase him from history.

When the tweet first hit the web, I was finishing dinner at a local restaurant with my wife, Debbie, and two of our good friends, John and Cindy Fleming. John had been one of my closest colleagues in the House of Representatives. We had been founding members of the Freedom Caucus together. Over dinner, I had asked him if he would consider coming to the White House as one of my deputies, and I was honored that he had said yes right away. John was a principled conservative and also a medical doctor, which were two attributes that would serve him well during the harrowing ten months ahead.

By the time Debbie and I were outside and walking back to our condo, I had around two hundred notifications on the home screen of my iPhone. Most of these were from people who wanted to wish me well. Others were from people who wanted access to President Trump.

Walking up the steps of our condo, I noticed the caller ID code that typically signals the White House switchboard—UNKNOWN, displayed in all capital letters—and picked up the call. President Trump was on the line. He said he was calling from Mar-a-Lago, his palatial resort in Florida, known to his staff as the "Winter White House." He had spent that morning, March 6, 2020, surveying parts of Tennessee that had been damaged by tornados, then headed up to Atlanta for an afternoon briefing at the Centers for Disease Control, which was dealing with something that we—along with just about every news network in the country, try as they might to cover it up—were then calling the "Wuhan Virus."

I told the president that I would be honored to take the job, and that I was excited to get to work on behalf of the American people.

"That's great to hear, Mark," he said. "Whether you're excited or not, we need to get started soon." He told me that this was an important time for the United States—more important than any other era in our nation's history, including the Great Depression and both world wars—and the West Wing was in dire need of some direction.

I understood what he meant.

Just a few months earlier, in January 2020, we had begun receiving reports from China that a new virus was spreading through the wet markets of a city called Wuhan. President Trump had immediately inquired about the origins of the virus, believing that it had probably leaked from the nearby Wuhan Institute of Virology. At the time, we knew that scientists there had become sick with a mysterious flu-like illness in November 2019, and that they had conducted extensive "gain of function" research, intended to take simple coronaviruses and make them more deadly, infectious, and transmissible.

That was public knowledge at the time. Anyone who cared to know could have dug up the records and found out. But every time someone reported it to the media, they were ignored. To those of us in government, however, the mystery didn't seem all that hard to solve.

President Trump had also assembled a team of our nation's top experts in infectious disease (or, at least, a group of people who referred to themselves that way whenever you gave them the chance). This group included Dr. Anthony Fauci, who'd done work with HIV/AIDS in the 1980s and spent the rest of his career as a bureaucrat at the National Institute of Health, an organization that was responsible for organizing funding for research—often dangerous gain-of-function research—into viruses. Also included was Dr. Deborah Birx, who'd spent most of her career studying viruses and vaccines at Walter Reed Medical Center in Bethesda, Maryland, and also played a major role in trying to fight the AIDS epidemic. These people weren't famous (yet), but they were well respected in their fields. The president had no choice but to trust them.

Over the past few weeks, while I was still in Congress, fighting the Democratic impeachment efforts, these two experts and their teams had been meeting with the White House Task Force on a daily basis. They claimed that we had no alternative but to shut down the country to stop the spread of the virus. Because of the lofty titles they had earned no one dared question these people, especially not about when we would reopen.

In most White Houses, this would be an ideal time for the chief of staff to step up, prove his worth, and take decisive action.

This time, not so much.

Mick Mulvaney was a three-term congressman and former OMB director from South Carolina who'd been President Trump's acting chief of staff for just over a year. He'd been given the job when General John F. Kelly, a man who had tried and failed to "contain" and "manage" President Trump, had left the White House in late 2018. When Jim Jordan and I were fighting like mad to clear the president's name in Congress during the lead-up to the bogus impeachment trial in October 2019, Mick got up in front of a room full of reporters and said that yes, the president *had* engaged in a quid pro quo with the president of Ukraine, effectively undermining the Trump administration in public and embarrassing the White House he was supposed to be running. Then, on March

5, 2020 when case counts were rising rapidly in the northwest and the coronavirus outbreak was on the verge of becoming a full-blown pandemic, the president had called Mick, who should have been leading the charge against the virus, with a question about how best to implement a certain policy related to Covid-19.

No answer.

President Trump asked around and learned that Mick was out in Las Vegas for the week, on a trip that he'd scheduled before the pandemic, playing golf. Needless to say, the president was . . . well, let's just say *displeased* when he learned this news. I don't know who was in the room with him when he found out, but I certainly don't envy them. At least, I hope they were wearing ear protection at the time.

In the months to come, I would find out that the situation in the White House was worse than the whispers and leaks had suggested. There was covert insubordination and a stunning lack of coordination—not to mention that every few hours, there seemed to be a major leak to the press. For instance, the Coronavirus Task Force, which needed more direction and definitive action, had just changed from Secretary Azar's to Vice President Pence's leadership. The West Wing had to be hitting on all cylinders now that a global pandemic was threatening to upend life in the White House and life in the United States along with it.

I should say, though, that I don't think any of that makes Mick Mulvaney a bad guy. It doesn't even make him a bad chief of staff, at least if you're willing to grade him on a curve. The man had signed up for a job that's known the world over as one of the hardest gigs in government—or any industry, for that matter. Even the people who've been dying to give it a try their whole lives find that it's much, much harder than they thought once they get behind the desk.

As Rahm Emanuel, who served as Barack Obama's first chief of staff, once said, "If it's between good and bad, someone else will deal with it; everything that gets into the Oval Office is between bad and worse."

Now, Rahm and I probably don't agree on much, but when it comes to his description of the job, he was right on the money.

For decades, since President Dwight Eisenhower, the former supreme Allied commander of Europe during World War II, tapped a governor from New Hampshire named Sherman Adams to go through his mail and decide what he should and should not read, the president's chief of staff has served as the president's last line of defense against the outside world. As you might imagine, this is not an easy task, and it's not one that has historically been undertaken by timid people.

President Richard Nixon had an irascible former advertising executive named H. R. Haldeman, a man who, according to his obituary in the *Washington Post*, "kept such close guard over access to Nixon that he was accused of erecting a Berlin Wall around the Oval Office." Around the building, he was known as the president's "son of a bitch."

In the 1970s, President Gerald Ford had Dick Cheney and Donald Rumsfeld, two people who are about as tough as it gets in politics. During the Ford administration, it was Rumsfeld, and later Cheney, his replacement, who were tasked with delivering bad news to cabinet members—and, on occasion, to the president himself. Obviously, this was a job that required nerves of steel, supreme time management skills, and a willingness to tell the most powerful man in the world when you believed he was wrong.

More recently, Presidents Ronald Reagan and George H. W. Bush put their respective White Houses in the capable hands of James A. Baker III, long considered the gold standard of the position. For both presidents, Baker coordinated staff, managed thousands of foreign and domestic problems, and served as a confidant on some of the most difficult issues. He was a friend when he needed to be and an adversary when the times called for it. In the weeks leading up to my taking the job, President Trump had wondered aloud, sometimes in my presence, whether I was going to be *his* James Baker, getting his White House in shape, protecting him from the outside world, and helping him to accomplish what he promised he would for the American people.

Every day, these men fought off a million ancillary concerns and made sure that their boss, who also happened to be the leader of the free world, dealt with only the most pressing issues of the day. They oversaw every single person who worked in the White House, from the senior staff and speechwriters to the interns and assistants, making a special effort to ensure that no classified information leaked. It was the chief of staff's solemn duty to take the hit when things didn't go right, and to give the president all the credit when things *did* go right.

Due to the high-stress nature of the position, and the fact that I *really* liked being a congressman, I would have been more than happy never to have been anyone's chief of staff. But now with a global pandemic about to begin and the president's enemies reloading, it was more important than ever that he have a chief of staff he could trust.

Besides, as Debbie was fond of saying in the early days of my tenure at the White House, it wasn't up to me. It was up to God. On our walk home from dinner that evening, Debbie had gotten a call from her brother, who'd seen the announcement and was surprised.

"Is he crazy?" he said. "Is he ready to hear 'you're fired'?"

"We didn't have any choice," she'd said. "God cornered us."

I couldn't help but think of those words as I listened to President Trump speak on the phone. He outlined his expectations for me one more time and let me know that we were going to have a smooth transition process. I would serve in an acting capacity until April 1, when I would resign my seat in Congress and become chief of staff.

"And one more thing," he said, about to hang up the phone. "I noticed that your name is trending above mine on Twitter because of the announcement."

I told him that I hadn't realized that.

"Well, I'll allow it," he said, with a mischievous tone in his voice. "But just this once."

After reviewing a few more details, I hung up the phone and went to speak with Debbie. I had drafted a statement earlier in the week when I first learned that I would be offered the position, which I reviewed one more time. I said that Mick Mulvaney had done "a great job," because only a chief of staff could know how difficult the job really was. The guy had taken more than enough punishment as it was. Then I wrote about how the best was yet to come, and how honored I was to be working with the president.

It was all true.

I hit SEND on the email, which went to a few reporters who'd been asking for a comment. I decided to leave the other four hundred-some texts that I had received until the next morning.

Debbie and I sat there in the kitchen for another hour or so, dazed by the new direction that our life was taking. Toward the end of the evening, she remarked again how surreal it was that we had found ourselves here. In a million years, I said, I wouldn't have imagined that I'd be given this responsibility.

I prayed that I would be up to the challenge.

While I slept that night, my name slipped from the number-one trending spot on Twitter down to two, then to three, four, and five. By morning, it had fallen completely off the list, likely bumped by some breaking news item about a celebrity breakup or the latest poor soul to be "canceled" for a bad tweet.

That's where I hoped it was going to stay for a very long time.

Of course, that is not what ended up happening.

_____

In the months to come, I would stand by President Trump's side during what would turn out to be one of the worst years in American history. Neither of us could have known what was coming.

Together, we endured a once-in-a-lifetime pandemic that, to date, has claimed the lives of more than 600,000 of our fellow Americans. We fought together to contain that virus through cutting-edge therapeutics, and we designed Operation Warp Speed to develop several vaccines in record time, allowing us to set the economy on the road to recovery.

I was by the president's side on that fateful day in October when we learned that he had come down with Covid-19, and I flew with him to Walter Reed Hospital, where he was treated. I was also there when he emerged from Walter Reed, completely cured of the disease and in what he called "the best shape of his life." I was there during the infamous walk to St. John's Church, one of the most lied-about events of this century, and I witnessed firsthand the president's reaction to the historic George Floyd protests of that summer.

When the first round of votes came in on Election Day, I sat with the president in his Residence, and when the next round of votes came in—most of them on trucks and in computers, all under cover of darkness—I got together and talked through strategies to set the record straight.

On Inauguration Day, after it had become clear that the recount was not going to go our way, I watched President Trump board his final flight off the tarmac of Joint Base Andrews.

To this day, I speak with him nearly every day, and I know he continues to plan his next move to bring this country together again.

Throughout those ten months that I served as President Trump's chief of staff, I got a glimpse not only of a president but of a man—and what I witnessed was amazing. I saw a man who had been elected by the forgotten citizens of the United States to serve their interests for the first time in history, and he was willing to do anything—give up his business, skip holidays, sleep less than four hours a night—to make that happen. He worked harder than anyone I had ever seen in my life, and he held everyone around him to the same exacting standards. Contrary to what you might have seen on the news or read in books, there has never been a president who worked more, or accomplished more, than President Donald J. Trump.

It was the honor of my life to serve with him.

I don't claim to have done everything right, nor can I say that I have no regrets about the time I spent serving in the Trump White House. But not a single one of those regrets has to do with the man who was behind the Resolute Desk that whole time.

For the past few months, I've been inundated with requests from reporters who are writing their books about the Trump administration. Many of these writers, including Michael C. Bender of *The Wall Street Journal*, Bob Woodward, and two reporters from the *Washington Post* whose names nobody ever remembers, have contacted me for interviews, and I've declined those requests almost every time. I didn't think I had much to tell them, and I didn't see any reason to give them my account of events when they were just going to pick my words apart to make a negative story anyway.

I've been around these reporters long enough to know how things work. They talk to the people who were present for the events they want to write about, act like they're friends, get what they need, and then destroy those very same sources once the book is written. They want to add credibility to their false accounts.

I could, for example, give one of them this quote: "I thought it was an honor to work with President Trump. He was able to accomplish great things. The bad press that is coming out about him is terrible." Then, when the pages get sent to me by the author for "fact-checking," I'll find a line that says this: "Mark Meadows, President Trump's chief of staff, said recently 'I thought . . . President Trump . . . was . . . terrible.'"

So, I say nothing.

Unfortunately, when you refuse to talk to a reporter, they just go elsewhere—often to disgruntled former staffers, interns, and a whole host of other people, most of whom have abso-lutely no idea what they're talking about. They get stories about what *those* people think happened, then write them up as if they talked to the people who were in the room. What they usually get are rumors, whispers, and false accounts of secret meetings that involved only a handful of senior staff members.

In other words, they get a false narrative, at best.

But take it from someone who *was* there and who didn't lend his account of things to the Anti-Trump Publishing Industrial Complex: Do not believe everything that you read.

In short, this book contains a sampling of the stories that I feel need to be told about President Trump's turbulent final year in the White House—the ones that no one else, particularly the authors of the few dozen books that have already come out about him, have told with complete accuracy. As of this writing, the sheer volume of falsehoods that have been published about the president's time in the White House is astounding. I consider this book a small opportunity to correct the record.

All I have is my personal vantage point, and that's what you're going to get here.

— TWO —

Trump Country

I WAS BORN in 1959 at a US Army Base in Verdun, France, and spent most of my childhood in a small house in Tampa, Florida. My father worked as a draftsman, drawing up plans for phosphate tanks and my mother was a surgical nurse.

Thanks to my parents' hard work, we managed to live just inside the lower middle class. Although we were comfortable, my siblings and I grew up without a lot of the "extras" that some of our friends could afford. Family vacations were in a camper, never a fancy hotel. But the lights in our house were always on, and there was always food on the table.

Most important, we knew we were loved.

Yet somehow, by the age of fifteen, I had become what no young high school boy wants to be: a big, fat nerd. One afternoon in the spring, after I had been turned down for a date by a pretty girl in my class, I knew that I had to do something.

Later that night, I stood in front of the mirror and promised myself that I was going to lose weight, and I was going to do it by running—first a mile, then whatever I could handle after that.

I managed to finish the mile, but just barely. Then I did another one the next day, and one more the day after that. I wasn't great, but I was making progress. During those early days, you could have clocked me with a sundial. But soon the pounds fell off. Before long, I was running four miles every night, cinching my belt tighter, returning to my front door in less and less time with every loop I completed around the neighborhood.

By the end of high school, I had attracted the attention of another girl (this one much prettier) named Debbie Phillips. We were in the same SAT prep class at the time, and I got her number off the registration form on her desk. When I asked *her* out, she said yes, to my genuine surprise.

Since then, she's been with me through everything. We opened a sandwich shop in Highlands, North Carolina, called Aunt D's Place in 1987, and settled nearby in the mountains. After a few stressful years in the restaurant business, I got my real estate license and eventually opened my own firm. We had two children, Blake and Haley, in 1992 and 1993, respectively, and homeschooled them together.

When I first decided to run for Congress, it was Debbie, Blake, Haley, and a large group of their friends from college who went around with me knocking on doors in our district. Over and over again, they heard from people who said that the government didn't care about them, that their jobs had been taken from them, and that they needed someone to stand up for them in Washington.

When I won the race and went to our nation's capital for the first time, I was careful to keep those people in mind. I was also cautious. I had heard stories about representatives who'd run on exactly the same platform that I did, bemoaning the establishment in Washington and promising to bring about real change for their constituents, only to sell out and become the very establishment that they'd run against once they arrived in Washington.

If nothing else, I promised myself that it wasn't going to happen to me. Even if I had to drag myself through my first couple of bills the way I'd dragged myself through that first mile run, I was going to make sure the will of the people was done.

That, it turned out, was no easy task.

―――――――――

I arrived in Washington in 2013. The Democrat Party was ascendant, led by President Barack Obama. His signature piece of legislation, the Affordable Care Act, was now the law of the land, and conservatives all over the country were outraged about it. This complex healthcare plan was supposed to repair our broken insurance system and get care to those who needed it most. In reality, it was going to raise premiums astronomically and completely remove the ability of patients to choose their own doctors.

During my first campaign, I had heard from thousands of constituents that they wanted the law defunded. I knew that other Republicans in the House were hearing the same thing. So, I figured that priority number one for our party would be making sure that the Affordable Care Act, or "Obamacare," as we had taken to calling it, was not fully funded, at least not in its current form.

That's when I found out that the Republican Party had a leader, too, and he was not a man given to rocking the boat in Washington, DC.

John Boehner was a congressman from Ohio who had risen up the ranks by following every unwritten rule of the House of Representatives. He had given money to the right people, parroted the right talking points, and ended up as the Speaker of the House. Under his reign, power was concentrated in the hands of a few, and they served special interests rather than those who elected them. In those years, Boehner had "enforcers," not unlike a mafia don. If you didn't vote how he wanted, these enforcers—most notably his leadership team—would ban you from congressional travel, ban you from committees, and find other ways to try to ruin your career.

I'm sure that Speaker Boehner had heard the same things from his constituents about Obamacare, but he had not bothered to listen. To me, and to many other members, he seemed like the perfect example of a man who'd let Washington corrupt him. He attended the cocktail parties, spoke at the fundraisers, and cut deals with people from all across the political spectrum, never letting the opinions of the people back home sway him.

Boehner didn't agree that we should defund Obamacare right away even though every registered Republican in the country was begging for it. He didn't think that we should make *any* radical changes, even as his office fielded thousands of calls a day from people in the country desperate to keep their current plans, keep their current doctors, and to avoid the doubling and tripling of their insurance premiums.

During my early years in Congress, I had read a book called *Troublesome Young Men*, which tells the story of a few young members of the British parliament who laid the groundwork for getting rid of Neville Chamberlain, the prime minister who famously tried to "appease," rather than confront, the tyrants of Europe in the lead-up to World War II.

"They were challenging a powerful, authoritarian prime minister," writes the author, a former White House correspondent named Lynne Olson, "who equated criticism of his policies with treason and employed a full complement of dirty tricks to stamp out dissent. Opponents branded the rebels as unpatriotic . . . But in the current crisis, they believed, they owed loyalty to their country, not their party or prime minister."

As I read those words in my new, tiny apartment in Washington, DC, I felt a flash of recognition. I knew that the crisis we were dealing with in the United States bore little actual resemblance to the growing conflagration of World War II, but the themes felt chillingly familiar.

So did the characters.

My fellow Republicans and I had been elected to serve the people of our districts, but we were being told by leadership that we couldn't do that. If we went along with their style of governing—or, more accurately, *not* governing—we were told that we might get prime committee assignments, cocktail party invitations, and the chance to run for leadership ourselves someday.

I decided that I didn't want to take them up on the offer. So, when I went home to North Carolina for the Christmas break in 2014, I drew up a list of names on a yellow legal pad. These were names of true conservative members like me who were tired of putting up with being shut out, controlled, and otherwise demeaned by John Boehner and his cronies.

Around dusk a few days before Christmas, I started making some calls. My first call was to Jim Jordan. We split the list and decided that Jim should be the first chairman. In a few days, we had our own group of troublesome men (and women), which included Ron DeSantis, John Fleming, Raul Labrador, Matt Salmon, Steve Pearce, and many others.

We decided to call ourselves the Freedom Caucus.

At the door of one of our early meetings, everyone was handed a copy of Lynne Olson's book to read, just in case they hadn't grasped the severity of the situation we were facing. We took the words of Ronald Cartland, who was quoted in the book, to heart.

"No government can change men's souls," he had written. "The souls of men change governments."

During our first few months, we did our best to change the United States government so that it actually worked for the people—or, at least, we tried to nudge it in the right direction. It was our way of reminding the leadership that we were here, we existed, and we weren't going to back down.

John Boehner and the leadership fought us every step of the way. He continued to intimidate, belittle, and threaten our members.

Meanwhile, I was trying to learn as much as I could about the process of lawmaking. Every night, I would sit down with a pile of files and memos, trying to understand how we could make better laws about everything: insurance, civil rights, taxes, mortgages, and a litany of other issues. But I also read older things—including some of the first documents ever written about the United States Congress.

One afternoon I asked the House parliamentarian for a copy of Thomas Jefferson's original rules for the House of Representatives, which he managed to locate quickly in his office. Reading through my three-inch-thick, hardback copy, I came across a line that said that "privileged motions" could be brought to the floor at any time, by any member. It didn't matter how junior (or how loathed by House leadership) that member happened to be. I had already known that, of course, at least in a theoretical sense. What I didn't know was that all those years ago, Jefferson had envisioned something called a "motion to vacate the chair," designed to remove a sitting Speaker of the House if members felt that he was not executing his duties properly.

For a few months, I thought it over. I knew that if I filed a motion to remove John Boehner from his position as Speaker of the House, I could be risking political suicide. The chances of failure were incredibly high. If it didn't work, I would almost certainly look like a moron.

But I knew in my heart that it was the right thing to do. I still wanted to be able to look my constituents in the eyes when I went home to North Carolina, and I wouldn't be able to do that if I didn't give my job every ounce of energy that I had. That meant trying even crazy ideas, reading every page of material, and fighting every single provision in every single bill that I didn't believe had their best interests at heart.

After a great deal of prayer, I began telling a few other members about my plan. At dinner with our wives, John Fleming nearly fell out of his chair with excitement. Scott Perry also encouraged me. Thomas Massie, a Republican from Kentucky who'd been educated at MIT in engineering, was similarly thrilled. Thomas would even help edit the document. Although my name would be the only one at the bottom of the motion, they vowed to be supportive when the time came.

One member who didn't want me to do it was Jim Jordan, but not because he didn't want change. He was concerned for me. He knew that if I failed, I would probably not be reelected. Whenever Jim saw me walking the halls of the House of

Representatives during those few months in the spring, he would make sure I didn't have the motion in my hand. On one occasion, I caught him running at me full speed like he was about to pile drive me into the wall. Other than an angry President Trump, I don't think I've ever seen anything quite as terrifying as Jim Jordan running at me, full steam ahead, intent on stopping me in my tracks. It turned out I was just on my way to the bathroom.

But I knew I was going to submit the motion; it was just a question of when.

In early July, Debbie and I went to see a new exhibit at the Library of Congress that included a rare original Dunlap broadside of the Declaration of Independence, printed on July 4, 1776. On that day, I noticed, probably for the first time, that the only signature on the bottom of the document was that of John Hancock, the president of the Continental Congress.

I felt like I could hear God speaking in my heart, leading me to make the move. Just as John Hancock's name had been the only one at the bottom of that Dunlap broadside, mine would be the only one on the bottom of my own motion.

I submitted the motion on July 28, 2015, a day that just so happened to be my fifty-sixth birthday. Immediately, there was an uproar. Newspapers printed headlines like "Mark Meadows: Army of One." I got calls from members all over the House telling me I was insane. The name calling was voluminous.

But in the following days, Jim Jordan stood by my side. He had every right to say *I told you so* and run like hell in the other direction. But he didn't do that. In fact, he took it upon himself to gather a group of House members who'd voted for Boehner in his last election for speaker. They met with him to express that a huge majority of them did not have the political capital to support him again.

After a few glimmers of hope, including a deluge of letters from around the country—from my district and hundreds of others—expressing support for Boehner's removal, our initial effort seemed futile. Boehner managed to delay the vote. Yet only fifty-seven days later, when Boehner announced his resignation in the chamber of the House, we got some vindication. During a speech to reporters, Boehner did not admit that my effort to remove him had been his sole reason for resigning. But everyone knew that without the motion to vacate the chair, he never would have resigned.

For me, and for true conservatives everywhere, this was a victory. But it had also come at an enormous cost. In Congress, I was forever going to be known as a partisan bomb thrower who wanted to shake up the House, even shutting things down when they didn't go my way. Although that was not exactly accurate, it would become my reputation, nonetheless.

But as I had put it during a radio interview in the heat of the fight to get rid of Speaker Boehner, I would rather have the people at my back than Washington in my pocket.

If anything, the fight surrounding my motion to vacate was the thing that woke me up to a cold reality: Anyone who wanted to take on the establishment in this town, to challenge the kingmakers and backroom fundraisers who really ran our nation's capital, was going to need an iron will, nerves of steel, and a fighting spirit to rival any boxer.

At the time, I wasn't sure I had it in me. This episode had hit me hard and I knew there would be more coming. Toward the end of Obama's presidency, pundits were talking about a

Republican Party so diminished that it would cease to exist, and it felt like they might have been right. I certainly didn't ever think that our ragtag band of outsiders would be able to topple the establishment for good.

Thankfully, we didn't have to.

That's when Donald J. Trump stepped on to the scene.

— THREE —

The Fighter

ON JUNE 16, just under two months before I filed my motion to vacate the chair, a billionaire from Manhattan named Donald J. Trump had come down the golden escalator of Trump Tower, his fifty-eight-story skyscraper on Fifth Avenue, and launched the political campaign of the century. This guy, I thought, had come out of the gate hotter than the blacktop during a summer in Tampa, and he was *not* going to back down.

"Our country needs and deserves a comeback," he said. "But we are not going to get that comeback with politicians. Politicians are not the solution to our problems. They *are* the problem. They are almost completely controlled by lobbyists, donors, and the special interests . . . I am not a politician. I can't be bought. I won't be running around the country begging people for money for my campaign. I won't owe anybody anything. I won't be beholden to anyone except to you, the American people, if you elect me to serve as your president."

Early on, I was with a known commodity, Senator Ted Cruz. But it didn't take long before I realized where the country was going and who was really going to win this election and shake up the swamp.

I watched that announcement speech from my office, my mouth hanging open in amazement. So did my constituents, who began writing me letters about Trump almost as soon as he exploded onto the political scene. Clearly, this was not someone who was going to be cowed by the establishment. He was throwing punches all over the place, and he didn't care whose face he was knocking in. He went after lobbyists, corporate interests, bankers, and, of course, the media, which he would dub the Fake News.

But not everyone was on board.

In those early days, whenever Donald Trump came through North Carolina for a rally, most of the state's elected federal representatives found reasons that they couldn't make it. They would say that they had to pick up dry cleaning, get their kids to school, return library books, even have emergency surgery. Anything to get out of being seen with the guy. If elected Republicans in my state actually got as many haircuts as they said they were getting that election season, many barbers would have been able to buy themselves summer homes in the Blue Ridge Mountains.

These politicians knew that there would be an enormous upside to being on Team Trump if the man won, of course, but they didn't think that he would. And if he lost, the penalty for supporting him would be severe. So, they took the safe bet and tried to avoid him.

I, on the other hand, believed in the message that Donald Trump was trying to spread. I had never seen a candidate who spoke more clearly to the people of my district, and I had certainly never seen one that got them more excited. To this day, I've got letters from people who couldn't believe he was real, they were so thrilled. Given that I was already something of a pariah in Washington, I didn't hesitate to board the Trump Train. I expected an exhilarating ride.

So did Debbie. In fact, on the Sunday after the infamous *Access Hollywood* tapes were released, Debbie and another congressional spouse, Nancy Schulze, were boarding a bus they had organized with WOMEN FOR TRUMP emblazoned on the side. Several other congressional spouses were joining them as well. They intended to travel all around North Carolina, convincing women that Trump was the right candidate no matter what the liberal media had to say. On the side of the bus, right below WOMEN FOR TRUMP, was a small endorsement for Governor Pat McCrory, a North Carolina Republican who was running for reelection at the time. But just before the tour, having grown skittish because of the *Access Hollywood* news, someone from McCrory's office called and requested that the governor's name be removed from the bus. Even the NC GOP had tried to stop their bus. So, right after the call, Debbie ripped McCrory's name off the side of the bus, leaving nothing but WOMEN FOR TRUMP and MAKE AMERICA GREAT AGAIN. Off they went, undeterred.

On the way to one of their first stops at Appalachian State University, the bus pulled into the parking lot of a McDonald's. As soon as Debbie got outside, she was approached by a few reporters from MSNBC, who were curious about why any woman in the country would support Donald J. Trump after the *Access Hollywood* tape. The MSNBC van had been trailing the bus for miles, eager for an interview.

The answer she gave was pretty good, if I do say so myself. Although I don't remember the exact wording of it now, I know it pointed out the hypocrisy of condemning Donald Trump over a few bad words he had said eleven years ago while Hillary Clinton, just a few weeks earlier, had called conservative Americans "deplorable" and "irredeemable." Debbie also said that she shuddered to think what might come out if someone had attached a secret microphone to her—or *anyone*—for the past eleven years.

When Debbie first called me to say that she'd been interviewed by MSNBC, I thought she was making one of her funny jokes. Then I looked up the clip, and realized that it was *not* a joke. There was my wife, supporting the most embattled candidate in the country, all because she believed he was the right man for the job. I was surprised, but I was also extremely proud.

And I wasn't the only one watching.

For years after, President Trump would bring up the bus. Long after he won the election, he would remember how Debbie stood by him when almost nobody else would, never wavering for a second in her belief that he was the man who was going to lead us for the next four years. Sometimes I wonder why he didn't hire her to be chief of staff.

We did several more events for him during that election—which, as a third-term Republican congressman, I was also running in—and we celebrated along with everyone else when he won the White House on November 8, 2016. That night, after all that we had been through fighting with swamp creatures in the party, it felt like a season of change was finally beginning in Washington, DC.

It was incredible to behold.

———————————

For the next three years, change is exactly what we got. Donald Trump, now the forty-fifth president of the United States, was shaking Washington to its core. In the coming months, he signed executive orders to recognize the Golan Heights, rolled back scores of regulations, nominated hundreds of conservative judges, and set the economy ablaze. For Republicans in our nation's capital, as well as the people who had voted for us, it was an exciting time.

But President Trump's ascent had also awoken something troubling in the Democratic Party—something that we are still dealing with today.

On the morning after his election, many Democrats had flat-out refused to accept the results of the presidential election. They couldn't prove anything like fraud, of course, and they couldn't find any votes that had been miscounted in any major swing states.

Yet against all odds and all available evidence, they persisted.

In the final days of the Obama administration, when the votes were counted and the inauguration of President Trump was being planned, there was speculation in major newspapers about whether the Electoral College might enact some emergency measure and refuse to vote the new president in. If that sounds familiar, that's because the same thing happened in the year 2000, when it was determined that George W. Bush won the state of Florida, and the presidency, instead of the Democratic candidate, Al Gore.

In 2016, they said that Vladimir Putin had managed to infiltrate the Trump campaign and forced him to *collude*—there's that word that would cover the front pages of every newspaper in the country for three years—with the Russian government to steal the election for Trump. They were a little hazier on the details of exactly *how* Putin and the Russians had gone about this. After all, they couldn't prove that a single vote had been changed on Election Day, and they couldn't find any evidence of Russian agents casting millions of ballots in secret to push Trump to victory over Hillary Clinton. Still, they continued to push a narrative that President Trump was illegitimate because the Russian government had stolen the election for him.

The next time you hear one of these same Democrats, or one of the dozen media outlets that effectively serve as their public relations departments, refer to the hundreds of thousands of people in this country who have serious questions about the way the 2020 election was conducted—with the numerous credible allegations of fraud that have been unearthed since Joe Biden was sworn in—you might remind them of the absolute circus that ensued after the votes were counted in the 2016 election. You might point out that when *they* cried fraud with absolutely no evidence, the country had to endure an endless array of hearings, trials, and press conferences. The White House was forced to appoint former FBI director Robert Mueller as a special counsel to do a thorough, purposely dragged-out investigation of these baseless allegations, knowing all the while that he would find absolutely nothing. In the end, this would cost taxpayers nearly $32 million. And the House of Representatives, of which I was still a member, had to stop its business every few days to hear more testimony, more bloviating, and more lies from those who just couldn't take the fact that a guy they didn't particularly care for had won the White House instead of their handpicked candidate.

Of course, that's assuming that these people are actually willing to listen to reason—which, they have demonstrated time and time again, they are not.

Shortly before the first round of hearings, I was in Washington, DC, at Union Market with Debbie. We were eating ice cream at a place called Trickling Springs. The market was bustling, and there was noise everywhere. Suddenly, I got a call from UNKNOWN, which could mean only one thing. I picked it up, moving over to the quietest corner I could find.

It was President Trump.

He was in Sicily, he said, enjoying his first official trip abroad as president. It was about two o'clock in the morning, and he couldn't sleep, which was understandable. I wouldn't have been able to sleep either if I had to read reports about how I was an agent of Russia, an illegitimate president, or a person who hired prostitutes to urinate on my bed in Russian hotel rooms (which, in case you don't remember, was a major feature of the infamous Steele dossier, published in January 2017 by BuzzFeed).

"Mark," said the president. "I need you and Jim to defend me. You're fighters. These other guys aren't going to do it. I've been in the foxhole with them before, and they jump out."

"Yes, Mr. President," I said.

"Mark, I don't know anything about Russia. I haven't spoken to any Russians. I haven't emailed any Russians. Your wife knows more about Russia than I do!"

"We'll get out there, Mr. President."

A few weeks later, after Jim and I had done some rough questioning of witnesses in the House, the *Washington Post* published a political cartoon of the two of us. We had brass knuckles and angry scowls on our faces. The caption read "Working for Boss Trump." If the *Post* had meant that to be

an insult, it sure didn't work. The folks back in the Freedom
Caucus loved it. So did the president.

For the next few months, Jim and I did everything we could
to defend President Trump against the daily onslaught of lies
and slander that were coming his way from all sides. Whatever
happened, we weren't jumping out of the foxhole.

Of course, it wasn't all sunshine and roses.

When you're fighting the swamp, it never is.

One of the president's first initiatives when he got into office
was repealing Obamacare. He had traveled around the same
districts that I had in the lead-up to the 2016 election, and he
had heard the same complaints about the Affordable Care Act
that I had. He knew that premiums were too high, people were
losing coverage, and the insurance exchanges that the law had
set up were failing left and right. So, when he got into office, he
entrusted Speaker Paul Ryan and his staff with drafting a law
that would get rid of Obamacare.

For a man who doesn't make many mistakes, that was a
big one.

For the next few months, Ryan and his staff worked in
secret with the Republican leadership, writing a bill behind
closed doors that would modify Obamacare. Inexplicably, they
came up with something that was even worse. The new bill
would have made premiums even higher than they already
were, which was a difficult thing to achieve. It was like having
Boehner all over again, only Ryan had swapped protein shakes
and workouts for the red wine and cigarettes of his predecessor.
I made no secret about my distaste for this bill when President
Trump called to ask me about it.

By this point, President Trump and I were speaking on the phone a few times a week. I would later learn that on the approved call sheet that the White House switchboard kept for the president (so they could filter out unwanted callers), I was the fourteenth name listed.

During our phone calls on healthcare, I told him that no one knew what was in the bill, and that we probably weren't going to like it when we found out. At one point, my colleague Senator Rand Paul wheeled a copy machine over to the chamber where they were sequestering the bill so he could print it, take it back to his office, and read it.

They didn't give it to him.

When they finally revealed the bill, my worst fears were confirmed. It was a big mess, obviously written by people—or, to be more accurate, by staff members of people—who hadn't come up with a replacement plan in the eight years they had been complaining about Obamacare. It was a dark moment, not only for the Republican Party, but for the country.

It also would turn out to be the lowest point of my relationship with the president. He and I argued back and forth about whether the bill was going to be good for the American people. I said it was going to make premiums go up rather than down, and that the people who'd elected him were going to suffer if we passed it. He said that my fears weren't unfounded, but that we could fix it later with a series of amendments and other add-ons, called Bucket Two and Bucket Three. I told him that Bucket Three definitely was full of something but it wasn't health care.

He asked if he could count on the support of the Freedom Caucus.

I said no.

When President Trump learned that Jim Jordan and I actually were not going to vote for the bill, he sent out a tweet threatening to "come after us" in our own districts. I didn't think he was going to have much luck, but I figured he would cool down. When I called Sean Hannity, another favorite confidant of the president, he warned me about trying to patch things up too soon.

"Don't call him," Sean said. "Boy, is he *mad* at you."

After the bill failed (largely because the Freedom Caucus was against it), I got to work trying to write something better. I stayed up many nights reading, trying to give myself a PhD in healthcare so we could figure out something that was really going to help the American people. Along with Congressman Tom MacArthur of the moderate Tuesday Group, we came up with a workable plan that would have made a real difference. It worked for everyone, especially the American people. When this new bill passed the House by a margin of one vote, President Trump called to congratulate me. Even though that bill died in the Senate with John McCain's infamous thumbs-down vote, we could rest assured knowing that we had not given up without a fight. It was a stinging defeat, but there was a silver lining.

President Trump and I had forged (in fire) a friendship based on strength, respect, and speaking the truth. Although it might have been easier in the short run to agree with absolutely everything he said, I always tried to tell him when I believed he was being misled. The fight over the Obamacare repeal was one that put me at odds with some of my friends and allies on Capitol Hill and around the country. In fact, a number of people didn't understand why the Freedom Caucus didn't just go along with Speaker Paul Ryan's plan. I didn't understand why we didn't just pull out the repeal bill that had already passed the House and Senate dozens of times and have it waiting on President Trump's desk when he was sworn in on January 20, 2017. Jim Jordon and I, along with our Freedom Caucus members, knew that the swamp was hard at work to pervert the president's first legislative initiative. Sean Hannity found himself talking with the newly sworn in president, more like a Capitol Hill legislative director than the news show host he was. Hannity had come to understand that repealing Obamacare was a top priority for conservatives and the president as well, but he also became a de facto ambassador to reach out to the Freedom Caucus when Paul Ryan's bully tactics failed to produce results.

One evening, while the president was complaining about the impasse, Sean told him that there were only two changes that the Freedom Caucus was demanding in order to deliver the votes, if Speaker Ryan would just agree. In his signature fashion, that I would see time and time again in the future, the president went straight to the people he thought could solve the problem. Whether it was getting Valdimir Putin and the King of Saudia Arabia on a phone call to stop plummeting oil prices during the OPEC Plus meetings or getting pork and poultry processors on the phone to keep the grocery stores from running out of food during the pandemic, the president would go straight to the source.

A few minutes before midnight my phone rang with the operator merging me, Sean Hannity, Speaker Ryan, VP Pence and the forty-fifth president of the United States onto one call. Perhaps only in a Trump White House would you see a group like this assembled for a midnight problem solving phone call. Speaker Ryan was not accustomed to a president bringing everyone together to discuss policy. Ryan was largely seen as a policy expert, perhaps more suited to being chairman of Ways and Means than the Speaker of the House. With everyone on the phone call at the same time, the misdirection and blame game that often takes place on Capitol Hill was not possible.

Sean opened the call with a deferential tone and the request to see if a few amendments could be made in order to get the necessary votes to pass it in the House and move it on to the Senate. Paul Ryan started selling like a used car salesman on the last day of the month. The only problem was that a used car salesman would at least describe the car you are buying, whereas the Speaker's presentation didn't resemble reality. He was counting on the new president to just buy into his rhetoric.

But I was having none of the Speaker's current bait and switch tactics. At one point, after beginning several sentences only to have them interrupted by Paul Ryan, I made my objections clear.

"Mr. President," I said, "the Speaker of the House just lied to you!"

I laid out the Freedom Caucus's modest request for changes as we went back and forth for the better part of forty-five minutes. My wife, who was alternating between putting sticky notes on the lamp shade with recommendations and praying, was seeing for the first time (but certainly not the last), that President Trump would conduct work well into the wee hours of the morning. Paul Ryan made the political calculation that he would not budge an inch and that he would steamroll President Trump and the Freedom Caucus. His miscalculation didn't serve the president, the American people or even his own interest very well.

The healthcare battle hurt my relationship with the president temporarily, but we came back together stronger than ever. It reminds me of a proverb: "Faithful are the wounds of a friend."

From there, we enjoyed several other great victories. We passed the historic Tax Cuts and Jobs Act of 2017, which was a rewarding accomplishment after the defeat of his healthcare agenda. President Trump moved the United States embassy moved from Tel Aviv to Jerusalem. He helped to lift regulations off the backs of small businesses, and ended the individual mandate of Obamacare. Under President Trump's watch, the border was tightened, and the horrible practice of human trafficking was decreased severely.

That whole time, President Trump and I spoke often. By the time his second chief of staff, John Kelly, was getting ready to leave the West Wing in late 2018, I had moved from number fourteen to number seven on his call list. We sometimes spoke three or four times a day about issues as varied as tax policy, healthcare, and electoral strategy. I would often come to the White House for briefings and meetings on key issues that I was passionate about.

When it came time for him to find a chief of staff to replace General Kelly, he offered me the job. I let him know that I would be honored to take it, but it seemed more important at the time that I stay in Congress and defend him. At the time, the Mueller Report hadn't yet dropped, and the president needed all the defenders he could get. Little did I know that a few days after the Mueller report cleared him, he would get on a "perfect phone call" with the president of Ukraine, giving his enemies another pretense to hit him for the next year or so.

Along with the president's defense team, I did my best to clear his name during that impeachment sideshow as well. We fought daily to be sure not a single Republican House member voted for impeachment. And we succeeded.

Then, in January, the first reports about the China Virus began pouring in, and the country began to enter crisis mode. President Trump needed to act quickly, and he needed someone he could trust to be his new chief of staff. This time, when Jared Kushner called to ask if I would be interested in the job, it was not really a question. The president of the United States was asking me to serve my country, and the answer was going to have to be yes.

As my wife would put it later, God had cornered me.

On February 28, I went to the Oval Office for a meeting with other Republican lawmakers about reforming the Foreign Intelligence Surveillance Act, which the United States intelligence community had used to spy on President Trump's campaign. After the meeting was over and the other lawmakers were filing out of the room, the president called me into his private office, a midsize dining room that sits just off the Oval. When two other people tried to follow us, President Trump put his hand up and told them to stay out. During this private meeting, he asked when I wanted to start.

"Well, sir, that's up to you," I said.

"Soon," he said. "It's going to have to be soon."

By the time Debbie and I went out to dinner on March 6, the night of the announcement, I had drawn up staffing plans in my head including Ben Williamson and Eliza Thurston, who had been with me since my early days in Congress. I had written out an agenda to implement right away. Now that John Fleming had agreed to serve alongside my three other deputies, I was looking forward to getting started. Whatever happened, I was glad to have at least a few people whom I could trust.

On the morning of March 7, I got a call from a number that I didn't recognize. I assumed it was probably the president calling from one of his private lines.

It wasn't.

"Chief Meadows," said a voice on the other end. It was the first of many times that someone would address me this way.

"Yes?"

"This is the White House Situation Room. We've received word from someone who was with you on the evening of February 28, and that person has tested positive for Covid. We have reason to believe that you may have been exposed to the virus as well."

Well, that seems about right, I thought. I took a job on the eve of the worst global pandemic in the history of the country, the stock market was on the verge of crashing, and we were about to lock down the United States for the first time in history. I couldn't quite figure out what God was up to, throwing in a home quarantine before I even got into the office.

"Well," I said. "What do we do?"

The voice outlined a plan for the next few days. Before I did anything else, I would need to be tested. Depending on what the test said, we would figure out what to do from there.

"Oh," he said. "And congrats on getting the job."

— FOUR —

Questions

I SPENT MOST of Saturday morning staring at my iPhone, secretly hoping for a *just kidding* call from the Situation Room. For a split second, I thought that maybe the whole thing might have been some elaborate, tasteless White House hazing ritual.

But it wasn't.

Instead, around noon, I got a call from President Trump. He had learned a few minutes earlier that his newest employee, the one he had officially hired just a few hours earlier for the specific purpose of getting Covid-19 under control, might have come down with a surprise case of the virus himself.

"Well," he said. "How is the most powerful man in Washington, DC, doing *now?*"

I let him know that I was feeling fine, and that I'd be in the office as soon as possible. Until then, we'd be doing a whole lot more talking on the phone.

"You've gotta be kidding me with this," he said. "Just get tested and get the hell in here as soon as you can, alright? We have to get started."

And there it was: my first official order from the boss as chief.

I was determined to follow it.

———————

That afternoon, Debbie and I got into my old BMW and drove toward Walter Reed Hospital in Bethesda, Maryland. For about sixty years, the White House had used Walter Reed as its default care facility for the president and the First Family, as well of some members of senior staff and the cabinet. But it was also a world-renowned research center. Some members of the Coronavirus Task Force had spent decades studying viruses in the hospital's large, state-of-the-art facilities.

The drive to Walter Reed took Debbie and me from our front door in Alexandria toward the Maryland state line. The traffic was slightly heavy for a Saturday. As we drove, my thoughts turned to the thousands of other people in the country who might have gotten the same call that I just did—or, at least, a similar call from their doctor or a relative who'd tested positive. I was sure that at that moment, there were thousands, maybe hundreds of thousands of people who were becoming anxious. Fear, which would make the pandemic far worse, was spreading.

Driving over the Potomac River, I had a solemn feeling that soon, many others would have to make similar trips to hospitals like Walter Reed. I only hoped that before any of that happened, President Trump and his team in the White House would be able to marshal the full power of the federal government and get this pandemic under control.

His actions so far had proven that he was more than capable of doing so, but only if he had the right team around him. Early in the pandemic, for instance, the president's Coronavirus Task Force had let him down. They had relied on the CDC to design and manufacture tests for the virus, which is not something that the agency was capable of. Yet Alexander Azar, the president's Secretary of Health and Human Services, had continued to assure President Trump that everything was fine with the tests. Although smart when it came to some things, Secretary Azar was a classic example of someone who tried to please President Trump by never disagreeing with him or saying anything that he believed might upset him. This, as I had learned during my time in Congress, was not the way to go.

Eventually, President Trump discovered the CDC's horrible failings when it came to Covid-19 tests. He learned that the agency could not produce enough tests in the time that was available to them. He also learned that the tests the agency *had* managed to produce were almost entirely inconsistent and laborious, making them effectively useless. Immediately, President Trump arranged for two private companies, Abbott and Roche, to take the lead on providing readily available testing. In a matter of weeks, there were tens of thousands of workable tests in production, including the two that Debbie and I were about to take in the parking lot of Walter Reed. It demonstrated a fundamental truth about President Trump—that no matter how difficult a problem may be, it was always best to give him the facts upfront, then work with him to reach a solution. It was also a clear indication that he understood, as a businessman, that the private sector was much better suited to solving our problems than the bloated, inefficient bureaucracy of the federal government.

That, I knew, would be essential if the country was going to successfully navigate this pandemic.

Debbie and I pulled up to the hospital gates around two o'clock in the afternoon. We were directed to a parking garage, where two medical workers in full protective gear came up to our car. Watching them approach the vehicle, struggling with cotton swabs, oversize gloves, and massive face shields, I realized fully that this pandemic was not going to be over in a matter of a few weeks, as some people were claiming. It probably wasn't going to be over in a few months, either.

I don't know if I thought about President Trump as I rolled my window down for a test that afternoon, but I do know that I felt fortunate to be getting a test at all. Thanks to the president and the two private manufacturers he had enlisted to make them, I was going to be able to get into the White House in a matter of days rather than weeks.

But testing was only one piece of the puzzle.

In the next few months, we needed to make key decisions about the nation's response to the virus, including how or if we would enter a complete lockdown similar to the one that the Chinese government had instituted in Wuhan in late January. The "experts" on the task force were strongly in favor of this move. If we shut down businesses, I warned, it will be much harder to open them back up. What would be our criteria to do so? We also needed to work with businesses in the private sector to manufacture masks, ventilators, and personal protective equipment, avoiding the kind of government bungling that had occurred during our rollout of test kits. Most importantly, we needed to design and produce vaccines and therapeutic treatments for the virus, which were the only things that stood a chance of bringing this pandemic under control.

It was a daunting challenge. But if there was anyone I trusted to oversee this nation's response to a global pandemic, it was President Trump. From his vast knowledge of the private sector to the uncanny ability he had to analyze data, hear arguments, and make quick decisions, he was well suited to handling this crisis.

But he wasn't getting much help at the time, especially not from the various federal agencies who were supposed to be leading the charge against the virus. The people who had the right information were not communicating with the president, and the people who were communicating with the president did not have the right information.

With those forces aligned against him, there was only so much that President Trump could do.

Thanks to my required quarantine, I spent the next few days working from home, a phrase that would become all too common in the months ahead. I filled out my HR forms and dialed into meetings from my kitchen and my living room couch, trying to gain an understanding of what was going on at the White House. For the most part, this wasn't so bad. But the lack of connection, especially at the beginning of a new job, was almost enough to drive me crazy. I hoped that if we were forced to make people all over the country do this, it wouldn't be for long.

It did, however, give me a chance to sit back and gain an understanding of what was going on in the media. On Sunday night, I saw an interview with Dr. Anthony Fauci, who seemed to have designated himself the nation's primary source for information about the Wuhan Virus. (It would be a few weeks before calling it that was deemed "racist" by the mainstream media.) Normally, I wouldn't have had time to watch the interviews and public appearances that the members of our task force were doing, but the time at home gave me an extra couple of hours every day.

Asked about whether people in the United States should think about wearing masks to stop themselves from catching the virus, Dr. Fauci responded dismissively, using the sage, all-knowing voice we would all come to know and despise.

"Right now," he said, "in the United States, people should not be walking around with masks. When you're in the middle of an outbreak, wearing a mask might make people feel a little bit better and it might even block a droplet, but it's not providing the perfect protection that people think it is."

That didn't mean much to me at the time. In fact, it sounded reasonable. So I was shocked when I heard him talking a few days later in a private meeting of the Coronavirus Task Force.

When it came to masks, his private message did not match the public one. In private, Dr. Fauci insisted that they were crucial to handling the spread of the virus. In fact, he said that if we didn't get enough masks to hospitals and healthcare workers all over the country, the effects could be disastrous. At the time, I had no opinion on whether masks were useful in preventing the spread of the virus. Like anything else, I was willing to wait for the evidence and draw conclusions based on data. I eventually asked him if we could avoid a lockdown if we mandated masks at work. His response again contradicted his previous statements: Masks would not protect you enough to go to work. So according to Fauci, masks would work in hospitals, but not in factories.

To Dr. Fauci, however, data was malleable. So was truth. He said whatever sounded good at the time. Often, he would make things up out of thin air. When someone asked him a question, he would give an answer. It mattered little whether that answer was based on evidence. If the cameras were pointing at him, he was happy.

During one early meeting, I had heard him suggest that eventually, everyone in the United States was probably going to come down with the virus. He said that this was inevitable, but that it would provide us something called "herd immunity." Then, just a few minutes later, he was talking about how important it was to make sure everyone stayed inside and off the streets, ensuring that they would *never* get the virus.

These two things did not seem to go together, at least not from my perspective.

But I was not—and still am not—an expert in infectious disease. During my first days on the job, President Trump and I did not know how to determine whether the advice Dr. Fauci was spouting was correct or not. All we knew was that he gave *a lot* of it, and that sometimes he seemed to contradict himself.

But we gave him the benefit of the doubt for a while, chalking those contradictions up to the mercurial nature of pandemics. We assumed that when he said two contradictory things in the same day—or the same *sentence,* as was often the case—he was doing so based on information that we simply didn't have. So, we allowed him to go on television, to speak in the Rose Garden. By his own efforts, he was profiled by every magazine in the country. At first, his presence seemed soothing to people, and what President Trump cared about at the time was keeping the American people safe as well as calm.

But it wouldn't be long before we realized what a destructive force this little guy could be—or how much damage he had already done to the country. Over the next few days, I watched—or, rather, I listened from my home—as Dr. Fauci and a few other "experts" in the room completely dominated the conversation around what steps we needed to take in response to Covid-19. Whenever they spoke, the rest of the people in the room would assume that whatever they were saying was based on hard data or verifiable truth. In most cases, no one even bothered to check their numbers. During a meeting in the Oval Office on Tuesday, March 10, for instance, both Dr. Fauci and Dr. Birx told the president that if we didn't act quickly to shut down the country, more than two million people in the United States would die. Later, we would learn that these numbers were vastly inflated, based on a few faulty assumptions and some wild guesses by crazy government scientists.

But no one, including me from my living room, dared question them during the early days of the crisis. We were too concerned with saving our country to stop and wonder whether our top experts might be misleading us.

From my home, I listened to meetings on speakerphone between President Trump and his advisors, often as a silent observer. While doing so, I was coming up with more questions than I could possibly keep track of. So, I made a list. Whenever Dr. Fauci seemed to contradict himself, or whenever someone from his team put forth numbers that seemed off to me, I would write down my questions on a legal pad, planning to get to the bottom of what was really going on once I entered the West Wing.

By the middle of the week, I had come up with a lengthy list.

Why, I wondered, were we telling people that when they came into contact with a person who might have the virus, they had to quarantine for fourteen days? I had heard this number repeated several times now, mostly by Dr. Robert Redfield and his colleagues at the CDC, but I had no idea where it came from. I had never seen any data to back it up.

Why were we even talking about shutting down schools when every study that had been conducted so far showed that the virus posed virtually no danger to children?

Why were the CDC and the WHO taking the numbers that China was giving us at face value when we knew from our intelligence that those numbers were false?

What was the source for all these numbers that I kept hearing about death rates, infection rates, and the number of people who were probably going to die if we didn't lock down the country immediately? If they were just models based on what was happening in other parts of the world, how were those models being formed, and who was accountable for them? Were there any dissenting voices to be heard?

And perhaps most critically, if we really were going to shut down the economy of the United States, telling people to remain inside and hide from the virus until there was an effective treatment or a vaccine, what plan did we have for opening it back up again? Were we prepared to deal with people who lived in areas where there were virtually no cases of the virus, many of whom owned businesses that were at risk of collapsing if the economy shut down? Moreover, had anyone properly considered the effect that such a shutdown would have on mental health, small businesses, or families who were living on the edge of poverty already?

The answer to that last question—every part of it—was a resounding *no*.

There was no plan for opening the country back up again, at least not in the minds of the scientists and bureaucrats who, much to their own surprise, were making major decisions on behalf of the American people for the first time in their lives. A few weeks later, just after I started in the White House, Dr. Fauci would inadvertently tell me why.

"Mark," he said, seeming exasperated after I had dared to ask him a question about his methods. "You've got to look at the bigger picture. That's your job. I don't. All I have to do is look at someone's physical health."

I remember asking him whether someone's economic well-being, including whether they had food on the table, could broadly be considered their "health" under Dr. Fauci's definition.

"All of that is important," he said, "and I guess you have to balance that. But all I have to do is make recommendations based on someone's *health*."

When President Trump asked about plans for reopening, he was usually given a few vague answers, coupled with dire warnings that if we didn't shut down *right now*, millions of people could die.

When the president was faced with that choice, he made the call that he thought was right. He was acting on the advice of people who were supposed to be the top experts in their field, and they were telling him that there was only one option. During one memorable meeting in the Oval Office, President Trump was shown large, full-color photographs of a hospital in the borough of Queens, New York—one that he was intimately familiar with, having grown up just a few blocks away.

The photographs, which had been printed out before the meeting by members of the Coronavirus Task Force, were gruesome. They showed bodies being packed up in bags and then loaded onto refrigerated trucks in the parking lot. I have no doubt that when President Trump saw those images, he thought of the people he'd known growing up. Any one of those body bags could have contained a friend, a family member, or a person he had known as a child. I'm sure it was instrumental in his decision to allow Team Lockdown to shut the economy down indefinitely.

Still, at the time, President Trump was not focused on the kind of broad mitigation measures that Dr. Fauci and his team were pushing. He was putting all his energy into fixing Covid-19 itself—making sure that people who got the disease would be treated and, eventually, cured. From the early days of the crisis, he was asking about how quickly we could get a vaccine out on the market, and how we should go about inventing treatments for the virus. He asked about drugs like hydroxy-chloroquine, which had hundreds of testimonials from doctors and patients, indicating that it worked. Doctors were reporting that its early use was effective in stopping the harmful effects of Covid. Almost every time, his requests were sidestepped by the federal bureaucracy. They did not seem to want to offer help with anything unless it involved a complete and total shutdown of the United States.

Eventually, he would prevail, as always, despite heavy opposition. He would find allies in the private sector to develop therapeutics and treatments for the virus just as he had done during the disastrous rollout of testing kits. He would continue to campaign for reelection and support those who wanted to reopen the economy when it became clear that the time was right, sending a message to the country—and to the world— that the United States was not going to cower in fear and wait out the virus. He would oversee the production of a vaccine in a time frame that had never before been accomplished, and he would receive scant credit for it from the mainstream media.

When I entered the White House for the first time as chief of staff, I felt like I had been on the job for six months rather than six days. Working for President Trump in those days was like stepping up to the plate during a Major League Baseball game when all I had ever played before was high school softball. Sure, I had been involved in the legislative process before; I had even worked with President Trump on bills, often taking his phone calls all through the night so that we could get certain details right.

But there was nothing like being in the driver's seat, making the calls that were going to affect people around the country. Suddenly, everything on the front page of the newspaper was my problem, and that was an adrenaline-producing experience. On my first day alone, I met with Jared Kushner to develop a plan to make sure that Covid-19 tests would be available at corner drugstores all over the country. I attended a meeting in the Situation Room with President Trump about a possible retaliation for the deaths of two American soldiers who had been killed during rocket attacks at Camp Taji in Iraq. During this meeting, President Trump listened to his military advisors and ordered a retaliatory strike. The next day, the United States launched a rocket attack against Kata'ib Hezbollah, sending a clear message to terrorists all over the globe that American soldiers were untouchable.

It was another instance of President Trump looking out for the brave men and women who served overseas in our armed forces. Often, he had to do this against the advice of his top military advisors. Time and again, I watched as he asked

General Mark Milley why we could not get our armed forces out of the Middle East.

"You always say, General, that we can get any soldiers anywhere in the world in twenty-four hours. So why can't we get those soldiers *out* in twenty-four hours, too?" The president demanded that General Milley and Secretary Esper come up with a definitive plan that protected Americans and brought them, along with our troops and equipment, home. Not in twenty-four hours but certainly not in twenty-four months.

Every time, General Milley would give an excuse. Mark Esper, his secretary of Defense, was the same way. The truth was that in the time President Trump had been in office, the Department of Defense had become extremely political, and not in the right direction. I always found it interesting that while General Milley, Secretary Esper, and others made grand speeches about how the military was supposed to be an apolitical institution, they ignored the fact that many generals got where they were because they had the ability to navigate the halls of Congress and the White House. No matter what anyone said, generals were politicians at heart, and the generals around President Trump were clearly swinging toward the radical left. I had been in several meetings where secret details had leaked to the press, and it was clear that Mark Esper was the culprit. While President Trump was fighting to secure millions of dollars in funding for the military, these people were working against him, even going so far as to cut money for the famous *Stars and Stripes* military magazine.

But there was another battle coming between President Trump and his newly "woke" military advisors, and it had nothing to do with funding.

— FIVE —

Answers

BY THE TIME I stepped into the Oval Office as the White House chief of staff, the place was nearly as familiar to me as my own living room. President Trump and I had spent many hours sitting there over the past three years, and I had become familiar with the rhythms of West Wing life. I knew about the doors in and out of the building. I knew the names of the Marines who stood guard outside the doors of the West Wing, and I had spoken with the maintenance people who kept the place running.

It was generally understood that in President Trump's Washington, the door to the Oval was a little more open than it had been under other presidents. When President Trump had a decision to make, he didn't go only to the people who worked for him for advice. He was much more likely to call on business leaders, old friends, and members of Congress—anyone he could to find out what real people around the country were thinking and feeling. Despite being in the middle of the swamp, President Trump did not want to lose touch with the people who had elected him president in the first place.

I remember one of these meetings clearly. This was in President Trump's first year, just as he and his advisors were putting the final touches on his signature piece of economic legislation, the Tax Cuts and Jobs Act of 2017. President Trump was sitting at the Resolute Desk, a beautiful, massive piece of furniture carved from the hull of a rescued British ship, then given to the United States as a gift from Queen Victoria in 1880. NEC Director Gary Cohn and Secretary of the Treasury Steven Mnuchin, two of his top economic advisors, both of whom had played a major role in writing the legislation, were sitting on the other side of the desk in wooden chairs. When I arrived, I found them flipping through pages, studying the bill line by line to find any potential weaknesses or areas in need of improvement. Every few lines, President Trump would stop and ask questions. On one page, which had to do with an obscure tax credit, he asked Secretary Mnuchin to reread a particular passage.

"Hold on," said President Trump, looking up from the desk at both men. "This doesn't look right. How does this help the coal miners I met with in West Virginia?"

President Trump knew the exact date that he'd spoken with these people. He remembered their names, what they looked like, and the minute details of their predicament, which, he said, should have been addressed in the first draft of the Tax Cuts and Jobs Act. He had promised them personally that it would be. Now that he knew it wasn't, he was growing visibly agitated.

Gary and Steven looked at each other, perplexed.

"We're not sure," they said.

"Well, then find out," President Trump said, not so much saying the words as hurling them. "The reason we're doing this is to help the people I said I was going to help. It's all about the people I campaigned for. We need to know how this is going to benefit them, and I want to be able to tell them the next time I'm in West Virginia and Pennsylvania, too."

Gary and Steve promised that they would find out. I looked on in awe. For years, I had been watching politicians, especially presidential candidates, make ridiculous promises on the campaign trail. I had watched while they "listened" to factory workers, coal miners, and the owners of small businesses, always promising to remedy their problems once they were elected. In 99 percent of cases, those politicians had forgotten all about the people they'd spoken with once they got into office. In Washington, that was just part of the game. You lied to people to get elected, doing whatever the insiders in Washington told you to do, then blamed "the system" when you went back out to campaign for reelection. We referred to this as "Potomac Fever."

I'd had a feeling since the campaign trail that President Trump was not going to follow the Washington playbook, but it wasn't until I sat with him in the Oval Office and watched him in action that I understood just how radically he was going to depart from it. Here was a guy who not only made big promises but kept them—and forced his team to do the same. When people in his administration forgot why they were there in the first place, President Trump was always happy to remind them, often at earsplitting volume if he didn't think the message was getting through the first time.

When he called me into the Oval Office during his first years on the job, it was usually to ask questions about how a certain policy or law was going to affect the people of my district—the families and wage earners of North Carolina with whom he'd spoken, often at great length, during the campaign of 2016. Of course, I was always eager to provide this pertinent information.

Occasionally, our conversations would expand from the specific people we were trying to help to broader political questions. How, for instance, were we supposed to work with a Congress that seemed completely opposed to anything with President Trump's name on it? Were there any allies in either chamber of Congress who were willing to cross the aisle and help us make a difference for the American people? There were days when these conversations would stretch on for hours at a time.

I would sit in front of the Resolute Desk, watching the steady parade of aides and advisors who came in to give the president crucial information—about everything from military strikes and tax cuts, to foreign governments, appropriations bills, and important local elections—and talking with President Trump about the issues of the day. Then, as soon as we were done talking or the president had another engagement, I would head back to my congressional office or my home, still somewhat incredulous that I had spent so much time speaking with the leader of the free world.

Now that I was his chief of staff, those meetings were going to happen regularly. Rather than coming in for conversations a few times a month, I was going to be in and out of the Oval Office multiple times a day. I had heard that in some White Houses, the president and his chief of staff went days at a time without meeting or speaking. Clearly, that was *not* going to be the case with President Trump. From now on, it was my responsibility to give the president guidance on a full-time basis, and not only as it related to the men and women of my district. All those stray comments that I used to hear while sitting in the Oval Office with the president, about meetings and rallies and military raids overseas, were now my responsibility. So was every single headline on the front page of the newspaper.

Hundreds of people were praying for me, and there was no doubt that I needed it. Only God's wisdom would be sufficient for this task.

For a long time, I had been hearing about how quickly things moved in the White House. Every once in a while, during my frequent visits with President Trump, I got a glimpse of the sheer volume of issues that passed through the West Wing on any given day. But I did not fully grasp just how much there was to deal with until the morning of March 13, when I sat down for my first official intelligence briefing as chief of staff.

These briefings, first given by a general from the Pentagon and then by someone from the CIA, are an important part of life in the West Wing. The chief of staff got one every morning. Most of the time, they happened in my office, which was a one-minute walk from the Oval Office. During my first week on the job, Mick Mulvaney was still working out of that office, tying up loose ends before he left the building for good to become the US special envoy to Northern Ireland. Despite that fact, General Howerton and I sat down there and got to work.

Sitting there in the office that would soon be mine, flipping through the government tablet that would become my most critical piece of technology, I was floored by the amount of intelligence that the United States collected every day. It was, and still is, amazing what we know. I learned about the intelligence community's first forays into finding out where the Wuhan Virus had come from, then flipped the screen to find information on the progress of several military operations in the Middle East. A morning briefing might bring news from Russia, Japan, or any number of other countries that rarely made the A-block on the nightly news. Reading through the briefing was like having a secret newspaper that only a few people in the world could access. It was a weighty responsibility, and I tried to treat it as such.

I was, however, always careful to keep the source of this information in mind. While the intelligence community was full of smart, hardworking men and women who wanted the best for their country, several of them had also shown themselves to be no fans of President Trump, especially when he was a candidate. During the campaign, he had made promises to disrupt the established order of things in Washington, and that didn't sit well with certain Washington insiders. I always remembered that it was these agencies, working with a law firm hired by the Clinton campaign, that sought—and were granted—permission to spy on the Trump campaign in 2016. They had taken a dossier full of lies to the Foreign Intelligence Surveillance Court and used it to justify a years-long surveillance campaign against an American citizen, Donald J. Trump.

When the 2016 election did not go the way it was "supposed" to go, the elites of the intelligence community were all too ready to try to get it overturned. Key members of that community, particularly Andrew McCabe, insisted that he had seen "proof of collusion" in private, admitting only under oath—and under penalty of perjury—that they had seen nothing of the sort. James Comey, former director of the FBI, denied knowing that the DNC had paid for the dossier even though there were emails from years earlier proving that he did know.

In other words, I wasn't going to take anything that came out of the intelligence community at face value, especially not when it came to the most politicized issues of the day. I had no doubt that the so-called raw intelligence was accurate—meaning the actual material that was collected every day by our various intelligence agencies—but I did think there was a chance that when it came time to write up the reports for the daily briefing, the people in charge were trying to shape a certain narrative. As a congressman, I had seen this first-hand in my investigations into the Russian hoax. Ric Grenell would see this up close and personal as the head of ODNI; John Ratcliff would as well when he took over for Ric. Leaks, political bias, and agendas have crept into our intelligence communities. So, I got into the habit of requesting raw intelligence whenever I could, to better understand what we knew, apart from an analyst's interpretation.

Every time I sat for the daily briefing, I was reminded again that when it came to our nation's capital, the swamp, President Trump had very few friends.

And he wouldn't have it any other way.

For the rest of the day on March 13, I attended meetings all around the White House. When I took the job, it was generally understood that Mick Mulvaney was going to be involved in the transition, showing me the ropes, and helping me get a sense of how things worked in the West Wing.

That didn't happen.

From the moment I stepped inside the front door, an orientation was out of the question. The pace would not allow for it. I didn't see much of Mick, though his stuff was still in the chief of staff's office. So, I went from meeting to meeting in a building full of people who—with the notable exception of just a few—all worked for me. I tried to figure out exactly what was going on. Outside, the worst part of a global pandemic was gaining steam, and it was becoming more and more important that the president do something about it.

During a meeting in the Oval that afternoon, we worked out the wording for a speech that President Trump would deliver from the Rose Garden. There was a lot of screaming between Steven Mnuchin, who wanted to protect the economy, and Peter Navarro, our resident expert on all things China, who yelled at Steven at the top of his lungs for being "soft on China." The fight went on for nearly fifty minutes, and President Trump watched it all with a calm, though not disinterested, look on his face.

This, I would come to learn, was part of his process. When he was in the middle of making a decision, President Trump would want to hear from all sides, often allowing heated arguments to break out in the Oval Office. He asked questions, encouraged disagreement, and tried to arrive at his own conclusions based on the best evidence available. I called this process "creative chaos." Then, once he reached a decision, he displayed the kind of unflinching determination that you would hope to see in a president. When his mind was made up, there was nothing that could deter him from doing what he believed was right.

I also thought about personnel, which, in every White House, was an issue of vital importance. My first hire was John Fleming, the former congressman who had become one of my closest allies in the Freedom Caucus. John was one of the smartest people in the House of Representatives, and unlike most people who were working on the task force at the time, John was a medical doctor. He knew what the real risks were when it came to Covid-19 (as much as anyone could have known at that time), but he was also a principled conservative who didn't want to crash the economy based on a few bad models and fears. On March 6, he agreed to come be a deputy chief of staff, bringing the vital experience that he had gained during his time at the Department of Health and Human Services to bear on this crisis. Officially, he would be an assistant to President Trump, but he would function as one of my top deputies in the building, going into rooms I couldn't be in and handling the problems I didn't have the bandwidth to handle myself.

I also kept on Chris Lidell, a former Microsoft executive who had served as one of Mick Mulvaney's deputies. I had known Chris for a while, and I thought he would be able to assist me greatly. Chris was one of the best, if not the best, at running process, helping put structure on meetings and decision making.

Finally, I thought about the press—or, more accurately, the person who was going to have to get up in *front* of the press every day, giving them news about this crisis and outlining our administration's response to it. I knew Stephanie Grisham, the president's current press secretary, and I did not think she was up to the job ahead. When she signed up for the press secretary position, the economy was in great shape, unemployment was falling, and Americans were happier than they had been in years.

Now the opposite was happening. The country was falling apart, people were going to die, and the liberal press was going to be hell-bent on blaming the whole thing on President Trump. That room full of reporters, which had been intimidating enough when things were good, was going to turn into a pit of venomous snakes. Stephanie Grisham was actually holding down three full-time jobs at the time, trying to be the communications director *and* the press secretary, as well as senior advisor to the First Lady. As a result, she wasn't performing well.

She hadn't held a single press briefing, which was now going to become absolutely necessary. The person up at the podium was going to have to be tougher than nails and as smart as a whip. I knew only one person who fit the bill.

Before she joined the Trump campaign, Kayleigh McEnany had attended Harvard Law School and served as a Republican strategist. When I first learned about her, she was serving as the National Press Secretary for the Trump campaign. I had been impressed by her headstrong determination to tell the truth as well as her unwillingness to bend in the face of massive opposition from the press. I called and offered her the job of White House press secretary.

She accepted on the spot. During the next crucial months, Kayleigh would prove herself to be a worthy adversary for the press, never willing to let their lies go unchecked, especially on national television. Using her famous binder, which was the product of hours of daily research, she quickly dispensed with journalists who were bent on distorting the facts when reporters attempted to frame the president's criticism of the World Health Organization (which he had pointed out, correctly, was biased toward China) as racist, she enumerated the vast array of lies that the WHO had told during the early days of the pandemic. When the press took the president's words out of context, she immediately reminded them what he had really said. To this day, I consider hiring her one of the best moves I made as chief.

For the rest of March, although I didn't officially have the job, I felt that things were starting to come together.

On Monday, March 16, I walked into the building to find the chief of staff's office empty. Mick Mulvaney seemed to have come in over the weekend, loaded up his things in boxes, and left the building for good. Walking inside, I was amazed by how bare it was. There seemed to be nothing left but a few stray slips of paper and a coaxial cable for my internet. Even the pens were gone.

I called Debbie, who took our car over to the Capitol Building to collect a few things from my old congressional office. Because of my surprise Covid-19 scare, I hadn't been able to go back and clean the place out. By the afternoon, Debbie was parked outside with boxes full of my old things, including some pictures for the walls and briefing material that I had been using when I left the office for the last time in early March. Working throughout the afternoon while I was in meetings, Debbie got the place in shape. By the end of the day, it looked like a real office again.

During the decorating process, Debbie worked with a maintenance man who'd given us some help hanging pictures. When they were done, the man told her that he knew me—not from the news, but from a prior visit when I had been at the White House for a meeting. I had spoken to him about his job, his life, and how he liked working in the West Wing.

"That's unusual," he said. "Around the White House, most people don't talk to the guys in short sleeves."

For me, that was a compliment. Throughout my time in Congress, I had always made a point to treat everyone the same way. This isn't something that I ever had to consciously attempt, but it was important to me nonetheless. I didn't speak any differently to the people who ran a restaurant, for example, than to the people who were back working in the kitchen. Watching President Trump on the campaign trail, I had noticed that he did exactly the same thing. There was virtually no difference between the way he talked to the senators, big donors, and major media figures who'd come out to support him and the way he talked to the people out on the rope lines. To him, they were all the same. Looking back, I think that this is a large part of the reason that we ended up becoming so close in later years.

I happened to know that people noticed. During one campaign stop in 2020, I asked a union worker from Pennsylvania why he found President Trump—a billionaire businessman from Manhattan with his own private plane—so attractive as a candidate.

"It's simple," the man said after a beat. "He is *just like me*."

Once I had an office in the West Wing, the days moved at the speed of light. Every day, many people would come in and out of that office, wanting my attention on dozens of issues. I moved all over the building going to meetings, signing papers, and helping the president make key decisions about how we were going to handle our nation's response to Covid-19, the economic challenges and all the international crises going on simultaneously.

I had also gone looking for answers to all the questions on my list. What I found was not encouraging. During a meeting with Dr. Redfield, I asked why we were forcing people who thought they might have been exposed to the virus to quarantine for fourteen days. All the evidence I had seen so far, I said, suggested that they should need to isolate themselves only for seven days, at the most.

When Dr. Redfield described the study, I grew confused.

Apparently, the CDC had taken eighty-one people who may have come down with the virus and studied how long it had taken them to develop symptoms after exposure. For eighty of these eighty-one people, that was about seven days. For one of them—just *one*—the symptoms had appeared after about twenty-one days. Then the CDC, in their infinite wisdom, had taken the average of all those numbers, added a few days for good measure, and come up with the number fourteen. That's how we ended up with guidance that had gone out to parents, businesses, and schools all over the country.

Now, do I think that it was the worst thing in the world to make people who thought they might have Covid-19 isolate for a few days longer than they really needed to? No. But it does illustrate just how ill-considered and random some of these federal agencies were in the development of their guidance. For months, these people had been using bad data to come up with their rules, and then handing those rules down to the public as if they had come straight from heaven. Eventually, I knew, someone was going to figure out that these rules were based on faulty reasoning, and that was going to lead to an epidemic of mistrust in the government.

I learned that their guidance on shutting down schools was based on . . . well, nothing really. They just assumed that if adults could get the virus, children probably could, too. As long as we didn't *know* whether children could spread it, according to the CDC, we would just act as if they could. It was the perfect example of the playbook that seemed to exist at the NIH, CDC, and other federal agencies during the pandemic. When they knew something for sure—say, that masks weren't necessary outdoors, or that hydroxychloroquine was sometimes effective in mitigating the symptoms of Covid-19—they tried their best to keep it from the public, contradicting anyone who dared say it in the press. On other hand, when they *didn't* know something for sure, they made a guess, then issued compulsory guidance based on those guesses until someone was willing to step up and prove them wrong.

And for a while, this was no easy task. Anyone who even suggested that certain medications worked, for example, was banned from Twitter and Facebook. Anyone who dared talk about the fact that the virus probably leaked from a laboratory in China was treated in a similar fashion.

This, I can now see, was a dark harbinger of things to come.

———————

Although Dr. Fauci failed to find consistent positions on his mask policy, herd immunity, and the origins of Covid-19, there was one thing he was extraordinarily consistent about, and that was his fondness for Governor Andrew Cuomo of New York.

The obvious failure of New York's Covid-19 mitigation efforts would pop up on every statistical chart and yet Dr. Fauci would consistently find ways to speak about New York and its governor in a favorable light. This was puzzling to me because most of us in the West Wing were working double time to find resources for New York as it seemed to be the epicenter for this dreaded disease. One night, working late in the East Wing residence, it became clearer to me why this was. The boss had asked Tony if he wanted to join him in calling the governor to give him a bit of good news. It was common for the president to allow others to be the bearer of good news and Dr. Fauci indicated that he had known Andrew Cuomo for some time. The excitement and giddiness of their interaction from Dr. Fauci's perspective bordered on a man crush. It was hard to ignore the interaction and the only thing that didn't make it uncomfortable was the brevity of the call.

Cuomo was consistent, too, in his request for every federal dollar he could get his hands on, while complaining that President Trump was letting New Yorkers down. The governor would bash the president in his daily press briefings and privately call to thank POTUS for everything he had done.

But it was one strange request from the governor that would stick out from all the others. Before a scheduled visit to the White House, Governor Cuomo called and asked whether Hope Hicks could join his meeting with President Trump. Hope often joined our meetings, and she was one of the few people who interacted at the highest levels on a variety of subjects.

But clearly, that wasn't why Cuomo wanted her in the room.

I don't recall a single question he asked Hope that day, but I do recall him arranging his chair in such a way that allowed him to creepily stare at her for most of the meeting. It wouldn't be the last time Governor Cuomo would visit the White House, but it would be the last time that Hope Hicks joined him for any meeting.

A little after sundown on March 29, my last Sunday as a member of Congress, Debbie and I stepped out our front door in Alexandria and went for a long walk on one of the narrow paths along the river near our home. It would be the last time I would be able to do so without the protection of my Secret Service detail, which would begin early in the week. The next day, I would officially resign from Congress and become the chief of staff. The training wheels were coming off, and I had serious concerns about the magnitude of the job and the fast pace of critical decisions that I would have to make.

But I knew that God was with me every step of the way, and that my family would be there to support me.

For the rest of my time as chief of staff, we would continue to take these walks at night whenever we could. With everything happening, we got to go only a few times a week, usually on Sunday evenings. We felt it was important to disconnect from the world just to be able to talk without anyone listening. Beginning on Tuesday, March 31, we had to walk with a Secret Service agent following closely behind us. This made the whole "privacy" aspect of the walks a little difficult, but it was good to have someone around with a phone in case President Trump needed to get in touch with me.

As we walked, we could see the Capitol Dome. Beyond that horizon lay the White House. Inside that building, there was a man who had the uncanny ability at times to see "beyond the horizon."

"Beyond the Horizon" capability is a term we have come to use for military attacks, being able to see beyond the current terrain to attack a target. In ice hockey, they would call this skating to where the puck will be. One of the most interesting examples of this came during the dramatic oil fluctuations of 2020. Because of the Covid lockdown and a dispute between Saudi Arabia and Russia, oil plummeted by almost $30 a barrel. If this was not addressed immediately, there would be long-term harm to the economy. President Trump quickly got Vladimir Putin and the King of Saudi Arabia on the phone to broker an economic ceasefire. In a conversation—one that could only be described as one for the ages between these three leaders—the boss negotiated, encouraged, and promised his way to a solution.

During the three-way back and forth, President Trump stressed that their three countries needed to lead the way on a deal. During one impasse, President Trump said, "If you don't find a way to address this over production issue, oil will go to zero, I am telling you that oil will go to zero." The boss had a way of cutting to the chase, even with an interpreter communicating on his behalf. His business acumen was well known. But oil going to zero? The Russian Leader pushed back: "Donald, oil will not go to zero, perhaps dip lower but not zero." At the end of the call, President Trump made sure the United States started buying oil in an effort to provide stability to the market and save jobs. A few weeks later, oil futures approached zero and for the first time that I could remember actually went into negative territory.

Seeing this as a buying opportunity for the US taxpayer, the president had me call the Secretary of Energy and tell him to buy as much as he could. The boss said "fill up the strategic oil reserve, fill up tankers, there are caverns in Louisiana, get them and fill them up. Fill up government bathtubs if we have to. But make sure the American Taxpayer gets the benefit. Oil will stabilize, and we need to save jobs." So, it was this unconventional Beyond the Horizon vision that I now credit in part for an oil market that has rebounded, jobs that were saved and an American taxpayer that wasn't left footing this bill.

SIX

Lafayette Square

WHEN I AGREED to be President Trump's chief of staff, I took the job with just a few conditions. In my mind, it was an honor to serve, and I didn't think it would be appropriate to ask the president of the United States to accommodate me. This was a time when America needed its leader to be working twenty-four hours a day, seven days a week, and to do that, that leader would need someone by his side. I was prepared to forego meals, sleep, and valuable time with my family to make sure that happened.

There were only two exceptions.

The first was a long-planned vacation in August with my family, a gift from our grown children, which would take us to Yellowstone National Park for five days. I would still have cell phone service, but I wouldn't be in my office. I figured that in these unprecedented "work from home" times, it wouldn't be all that big of a deal.

But the most pressing event—the one that nothing short of a nuclear war or an attack on the White House was going to keep me from attending—was going to happen in Atlanta on May 31.

That was the day that our daughter, Haley, was going to get married.

When I told the president about the wedding in March, he was thrilled for me. As the father of two daughters himself, he knew what a special day it was. He told me that for a few days, the White House could run without a chief of staff.

"We should be fine," he said.

But President Trump didn't know what was coming.

No one did.

In the final days of May, just after Debbie and Haley had completed the final, Covid-19-adjusted guest list for the wedding, we began getting reports of civil unrest in Minneapolis. In the beginning—meaning the minutes and hours following the horrible events of May 25—the gatherings were small, and the protestors remained largely peaceful. There was nothing that we believed warranted federal attention, though we did resolve to keep an eye on the situation as it developed. At the time, we had been working on Covid-19 issues more or less around the clock, and I was perplexed as to what could be sending so many people out into the streets during a pandemic.

Then I saw the footage. So did President Trump, who reacted with absolute disgust and sorrow.

I didn't know what to say. Obviously, the killing of George Floyd was a monstrous act, committed by someone who never should have been wearing a badge that day. I couldn't imagine the pain that was being suffered by members of the African American community who felt that Floyd's death was sign a that American police officers viewed them as expendable or criminal. I wished there was some way to get the truth out to the American people.

I wished we could tell them, for instance, that in reality, the vast majority of interactions between African Americans and police in any given year were peaceful and civil. According to an analysis by *The Wall Street Journal,* nine unarmed blacks were killed by police in 2019, compared to nineteen whites. That was down from thirty-eight and thirty-two in 2015, when Barack Obama was president. If it hadn't been for the riots that occurred as a result of George Floyd's death, that number would almost certainly have continued its downward trend.

But with the mainstream media being what it was, I knew that getting the facts out wasn't likely—impossible, even. Nearly without exception, just about every major news outlet in the United States had committed itself to a narrative about race and policing, and about race in general, that was needlessly inflammatory.

Inspired by certain strands of a discipline known as Critical Race Theory (though we didn't quite know to call it that at the time), these media activists printed stories based on the belief that the United States of America had been founded on explicitly racist ideals, meant to secure the subjugation of black people forever. Their evidence for these extraordinary claims, by the way, came straight out of their imaginations, but that didn't stop them from spouting this nonsense to anyone who would listen. These "activists" (soon to be looters and rioters) believed that you could divide the citizens of this country up into two groups: those who were racist, and those who had committed themselves to fighting racism at all costs, sometimes using violence and vandalism if they believed it was called for.

In their world, there was no middle ground, and there was no way of being neutral.

In other words, if you weren't out there in the streets with them, burning down buildings and flipping vehicles over in the street, you were against them, and that meant that soon they would be coming for you.

These protesters, many of whom were members of the organization Black Lives Matter, reserved special scorn for the men and women of law enforcement. They claimed that most modern American police forces had evolved from the southern "slave patrols" of the nineteenth century, even though this pseudohistorical analysis had been debunked repeatedly.

But the liberal media ate it up anyway. Whenever a young black person was killed during an altercation with police, nightly news anchors and newspaper reporters gave the case wall-to-wall coverage for days on end, bolstering the illusion that police officers were nothing more than angry, violent racists out for blood.

So, it should not have been a surprise when some people, who had been trapped inside watching these biased news networks with their false narratives, began taking to the streets en masse to protest what they now viewed as the culmination of centuries of racial injustice. In Minneapolis on May 26, small groups of protestors that had begun gathering after George Floyd's death grew into larger and larger crowds. Eventually, these crowds became far too big for local law enforcement to control, and all hell broke loose. Windows were smashed. Buildings were burned. Cars were flipped, and millions of dollars in merchandise was looted from local businesses, many of them black-owned.

On May 28, President Trump and I watched from the White House as the third police precinct in Minneapolis was nearly burned to the ground. Officers who had been trapped inside by rioters were stuck on the roof. On the ground below, the protestors had set fire to an AutoZone, which had largely been left empty after a few rounds of looting. Several other small businesses had been forced to shut their doors completely.

For a city already teetering on the edge, thanks to the pandemic lockdowns, this was catastrophic.

A few hours earlier, President Trump and I had organized a call with Governor Tim Walz, a staunch liberal who had said several disparaging things about President Trump in the past. Nevertheless, President Trump offered him help. He said that he would like to send in the National Guard to stop the violence. Local police didn't have the resources to handle this on their own. True to form, Governor Walz pushed back, saying he didn't need the help. But a few hours later, when it became clear that the violence was going to be twice as bad if he didn't act, the governor agreed to accept the president's offer.

It got only worse as the protests spread to other cities. Over the next few days, we got reports about similar riots breaking out in Portland, Chicago, and New York City—all of them liberal strongholds, run by mayors who had campaigned against law enforcement and in favor of some of the half-baked ideas contained in Critical Race Theory. We followed their progress closely.

In the middle of the week, the protests began in Washington, DC. Fearing for the safety of people in the city, we attempted several times to call the office of Mayor Muriel Bowser, another liberal who had been in charge of our nation's capital for about five years. For days, she ducked our calls. After this happened three or four times, I seriously wondered whether she had abandoned city hall altogether and headed for Joe Biden's basement bunker to wait out the protests while the city burned.

Back at the White House, President Trump was fuming. He had seen protests from several major cities on television, and he had gotten a sense of how they mutated. First, he said, you had a bunch of nice people, all wanting to protest something that they thought was terrible. Then, you mixed in radical elements of Antifa, Black Lives Matter, and other outside (sometimes paid) agitators, and the whole thing devolved into violence. If we didn't act quickly, he knew, more of the country was going to look like Minneapolis did on those two horrible nights at the end of May.

Around one o'clock in the morning, he tweeted out a message to anyone who believed they could break windows, burn cars, and loot with impunity.

"These THUGS are dishonoring the memory of George Floyd," the tweet read. "When the looting starts, the shooting starts. Thank you!"

Now, this message was not quite as polished as a chief of staff might have liked. But it was direct. And it did carry an important sentiment. People in the streets needed to know that despite the unwillingness of some local officials to do anything about their rampant lawlessness, the federal government was not going to condone crime in the name of so-called racial justice. President Trump knew that if he didn't come out strongly against crimes like looting, it would be only a matter of time before these lunatics began to believe they could get away with murder.

Literally, *murder.*

Within a few days, they would take the life of Sergeant David Dorn, a retired Black police officer who was killed by looters while protecting a pawnshop in St. Louis. They would also murder Dave Patrick Underwood, an officer who was guarding a federal courthouse in Oakland, California, as well as several more officers who were doing nothing more than trying to keep the peace.

Clearly, something needed to be done. President Trump's tweet had been nothing more than an acknowledgment of this simple fact.

Executives at Twitter, however, disagreed.

Almost as soon as President Trump's tweet went up, it was censored for "glorifying violence," which constituted a violation—their words, not mine—of Twitter's terms of service. President Trump's followers could see it if they went looking for it on his Twitter feed, but they couldn't interact with it at all. "Censored" meant that they couldn't share it, like it, or comment on it. Here we were, in the middle of a terrifying period in our country's history, with constant riots in the streets, people being killed, and no end in sight, and Twitter was more worried that President Trump was going to hurt the delicate feelings of liberals than they were about stopping the violence.

I almost had to rub my eyes to see if I was dreaming.

If these Twitter executives really cared about people "glorifying violence," for instance, they might have spent their energy trying to stop these riots from occurring in the first place. Many of them had been organized via Twitter and Facebook. Big Tech also might have taken down messages that encouraged people to loot and steal and cause damage to cities.

But they didn't.

Obviously, this had nothing to do with preventing violence or keeping people safe. The tech companies like Twitter thought that these riots made President Trump look bad, and so they wanted them to go on for as long as humanly possible.

That they could also use this civil unrest as an excuse to censor President Trump—effectively building their case for when the moment came to ban him for good—was just a bonus.

By Friday morning, the White House was effectively surrounded. I could see crowds beginning to form in Lafayette Square, the seven-acre park that sits just north of the White House. Among other things, the park is home to a massive statue of President Andrew Jackson on horseback, notable for being the first bronze figure ever cast in the United States.

But the most important feature adjacent to the park is a small yellow building known as St. John's Church. Officially opened in 1806, this church is the place where every president since James Madison has gone to worship. It's where Abraham Lincoln mourned his son, and where Lyndon Johnson held a service after the death of John F. Kennedy. For Americans, this is one of the treasured historical sites in our nation's capital.

On my way into the White House, I noticed that the crowds were getting a little too close to the small church for my liking. I knew that these protestors had done massive amounts of damage to buildings over the past few nights, and I shuddered at the thought of the same thing happening to a sacred place like St. John's. In the Oval Office, President Trump expressed similar concerns. He had been working all night on plans to take back control of the country, conferring with his advisors to draw up a draft of the Insurrection Act, should it become necessary to send out the United States military to control the protests. Still, it was something he hoped that he wouldn't have to do. We both held out hope that the worst of the violence would soon recede.

That afternoon, President Trump called George Floyd's brother to express his deepest condolences. It didn't mean much to Philonise Floyd, which was understandable. President Trump knew that the man was in pain, so he brushed it off when he criticized their phone call later in the day.

As much as the Fake News tried to portray President Trump as insensitive or mean, he never expressed anything other than compassion for the Floyd family, often saying that anyone who committed violence in his name was dishonoring his memory.

Before I knew it, the day was over, and it was time for me to leave for the wedding in Atlanta. I thought of asking President Trump one more time if he needed me to stick around the White House, but I thought better of it. In the days following this outbreak of violence, President Trump, had repeatedly told me, "Go. We'll be just fine here."

The only hitch, if you can call it that, had come a few days earlier during a ride on Air Force One. We were coming back from an event, and it would be another ten minutes or so before we arrived back at the White House. I was sitting across from President Trump, and First Lady Melania Trump was by his side. Melania had just asked about my daughter's wedding. We were talking about the location, the ceremony, and some other general plans.

"So," President Trump said, poking fun at me, as he often did. "You're going to leave me for a wedding? You care about your *only daughter* more than me? Your favorite president?"

Melania patted him on the arm.

"Donald!" she said, "Of course he's going. His daughter is getting married, and that is a once-in-a-lifetime event."

We all sat silently for a moment. Melania smiled.

"You know," she said. "Not everyone does it three times like you did."

The president smiled and shrugged his shoulders, and that was that.

So, after a quick check-in with President Trump, I left the White House for the airport and boarded a commercial flight for Atlanta. Watching the lights of Washington, DC disappear as the plane ascended, I said a prayer for the president and for the country.

Whatever was coming for us, I was glad that President Trump was in charge.

A few hours later, the White House entered Code Red. Protestors had jumped the fence on the Treasury side of the compound, and they were running toward the Oval Office. I'm sure that if President Trump had the choice, he would have headed out to the lawn and knocked their heads in one by one.

But he didn't have a choice. When it comes to the United States Secret Service, no one does. Either you do what they say, or they pick you up and make you do it. So, when the Secret Service asked President Trump to head downstairs to the White House bunker, he complied. He knew that he could go to the bunker with a few agents by his side, or he could go on their shoulders kicking and screaming. For everyone's sake, the first option was better.

Almost immediately, news of the president's trip to the bunker found its way to Peter Baker and Maggie Haberman of *The New York Times*, and they began spinning a story about it.

To this day, I do not know how this information got out, but I have my suspicions and it's a short list. I have no doubt that it was leaked by someone who had every intention of hurting the president.

It was not the first time that this had happened, and it certainly wouldn't be the last.

I touched down in Atlanta around ten o'clock and got in a car with the head of my Secret Service detail. We drove slowly into the city from the airport, careful to take routes that would avoid any potential riots.

When I got to the hotel, I turned on the local news to see the global headquarters of CNN, which was only a few minutes away from where I was staying. Earlier that evening, the building had been savagely attacked by the mob. The massive plate-glass window that once adorned the building's front had been shattered.

I shook my head in disgust. I'm not above mocking CNN when they deserve it—and given that their on-air talent had been encouraging these riots from day one, particularly Governor Andrew Cuomo's brother, Chris, this would have been a perfect time. But the sight of their headquarters smoldering this way filled me with a profound sadness.

Upstairs, I made a few calls to the office to make sure everything was under control. The protests were still happening, and the president was frustrated. I spoke with him later that night, and he wondered aloud why the mayor of Washington, DC was allowing this to continue. We still hadn't been able to get her on the phone, so I had my staff call one more time.

Again, no answer.

Later that weekend, I turned on the news, which showed an aerial view of the protests in Lafayette Square. The crowds were growing, encouraged by the presence of news cameras.

They were spreading toward the edges of the park.

On the north side, relatively unprotected against the encroaching mob, was St. John's Church. With every second that passed, the crowd inched closer to it.

Arriving at the wedding venue, I exited my car to find a strange-looking man in a Bernie Sanders T-shirt filming me with his iPhone. I have no idea how he knew where I was going to be, but it was clear that he knew my name. I could tell because he screamed it four or five times before I could get from the car into the Biltmore Ballrooms. He yelled a few things in my direction. Other than my name, I didn't understand all that much of it.

For a moment, though, I was concerned—although, considering that I had a Secret Service agent with me, I probably shouldn't have been. Still, it was hard not to remember a previous time when a deranged Bernie supporter decided he wanted to go after Republican lawmakers and my colleague Steve Scalise ended up with a bullet in his side. But it was clear that this nut wasn't armed or dangerous, just trying to make a statement. He filmed me with his camera phone on my way into the lobby and posted it on Twitter, unsuccessfully trying to disrupt our daughter's wedding.

My daughter was married at four o'clock on Sunday, May 31. I walked her down the aisle, gave her away, and watched as she and her new husband took their vows. It was a rare bubble of peace during an immensely difficult time. During my early years in Congress, a newspaper article once described me as "walking around Washington like a father of the bride," meaning, I suppose, that I was in a great mood all the time. Finally, I understood what they meant by that.

Despite a small protest that occurred outside—made up mostly of people who had seen Mr. Bernie Bro's video on social media—the whole wedding went off without a hitch.

But the calm didn't last.

A few hours later, the story about President Trump going to the bunker hit the web version of *The New York Times,* and the president was furious. He demanded to know who leaked the story, and it was up to me to figure it out. I said I would deal with it once I got back into town, but I could already tell, based on the way the story was reported, that the leaker was probably not someone with firsthand knowledge of Secret Service protocols. To this day, everyone has a theory about where the leak came from. If I had to bet, I would say that it was probably Stephanie Grisham, Emma Doyle, or someone from the VP's team.

But it doesn't matter much now, and in truth, it didn't matter then either. For the moment, we had much bigger problems to deal with.

That night, a mob of rioters smashed a window on the basement level of St. John's Church. They piled into the building in small groups, attempting to set a fire in the nursery, likely in the hope that it would spread and bring the whole thing crumbling down. It didn't surprise me that of all the historic buildings standing around Lafayette Square, these rioters would go after a scared house of worship.

It all seemed terribly on brand for them.

But I wasn't going to stand for it. And neither, apparently, were conservatives anywhere in the country. Since I had been gone, my phone had been ringing constantly with calls from Republican members of Congress. They were getting phone calls and emails from their upset constituents, all of whom were watching the same footage that I was. To them, the sight of a church being burned in the United States of America— just a few hundreds yards from the White House, no less—was simply too much to take.

That night, we sent an email out to the staff of the White House, letting them know that if they were going to come into the building for work—which we strongly encouraged them to do—they should not wear their ID badges as they moved through the crowds. We had received intelligence that anyone working in the Trump White House—or anyone believed to be *supporting* those who worked in the Trump White House—would be viewed as a direct threat by the mob and treated accordingly.

Every night, these people showed us exactly who they were. And it was only going to get worse. For what felt like the thousandth time that day, I prayed for the safety of everyone who was serving in the White House with me, then marveled briefly at the fact that I even needed to.

At 10:30 p.m., May 31, after the wedding, I was on the phone with AG Barr and Secretary Esper. I ordered National Guard to protect our nation's capital city. The next morning, I boarded a predawn mil-air flight back to Washington, DC, which got me to the White House by around eight o'clock.

Almost as soon as I got into the building, I found myself in an emergency meeting in the Oval Office. President Trump was behind his desk, along with a small group of his top advisors. Attorney General Bill Barr, who'd been our point person so far, was present. So was Mark Milley, President Trump's chairman of the Joint Chiefs of Staff, and Defense secretary Mark Esper. A former chief of staff of the United States Army, Chairman Milley had been seemingly supportive of the president's agenda during his first three years in the job. President Trump had chosen him for the position largely because his previous generals, who had disappointed him greatly, did not support him. But it would turn out that General Milley was just as bad, if not worse, though for different reasons.

Together, Milley and Esper formed a two-man obstacle to just about everything President Trump wanted to get done. They were perfect representations of the establishment rot that had taken over the Pentagon. If something was going to make President Trump look good, they were dead set against it. At the beginning of the pandemic, Mark Esper had opposed sending the USS Comfort to New York, to help treat Covid patients. Yet he showed up for the photo op anyway. Then we had General Mark Milley, who seemed to be more concerned with speaking to the press, checking his Twitter feed and reading the latest politically correct textbook than worrying about the rigorous demands of his job. There were several rogue actors who tried to destroy the Trump agenda, but I don't think there were many who made quite so many covert attempts as Milley and Esper.

In the months to come, General Milley and Secretary Esper would begin a negative PR campaign against President Trump that rivaled even the most disgruntled former staffers. But the truth is that when they were in the West Wing, Milley and Esper went right along with everything the president said to them. Not only was Milley in agreement when President Trump suggested doing something to show the nation that we would not stand for the desecration of St. John's church, he was, in fact, just as outraged as anyone else, even suggesting himself that something had to be done.

In a previous meeting that had occurred on Friday, General Milley had convinced people in the room that sending the United States military into the streets would be the wrong move. He was not the tiger he portrayed himself to be. He downplayed the severity of what was going on, telling the president that a few small skirmishes in our major cities did not mean that we were in the midst of a national crisis. I could have pointed him to a few dozen burned-out buildings in Atlanta and Minneapolis that suggested otherwise. I might also have pointed out the fact that in Washington, DC alone, more than sixty law enforcement officers had sustained serious injuries, having endured bricks, rocks, frozen water bottles, and other projectiles thrown by the mob.

But I didn't. We had to fix this problem, and I didn't think more infighting was going to do that.

At the time, we all agreed that it would not be proper to send the United States military out. But we did agree that a strong show of force was necessary. We decided that Mark Esper would go to the Pentagon and get enough National Guard troops from neighboring cities to secure our nation's capital. Those National Guard troops would work with other law enforcement officers—many of whom were from agencies as varied as the US Park Police and the Federal Bureau of Prisons, the latter group being well trained in handling violent riots—and the whole thing would be under the supervision of Attorney General Bill Barr. Together, they would expand the security perimeter of the White House to the north in an attempt to secure Lafayette Square, something that the Park Police had been planning for days.

For the moment, though, we wanted to make arrests. We wanted to show that when you broke the law in the United States, especially when you did it at the front door of the commander in chief, you weren't going to get away with it. All day, rioters had been climbing on statues and vandalizing the park. One person had spray-painted F**K TRUMP on a wall in Lafayette Square. They knew that law enforcement officers had been told not to engage, so their tactics were growing more sinister by the hour.

Later that afternoon, President Trump got on the phone with all the governors who would make the time to listen. Speaking to them, he stressed that they needed to "dominate" their cities, making it clear to the rioters that their behavior was no longer going to be tolerated. Sensing that this was a moment that would probably be recorded for posterity, Governor J. B. Pritzker of Illinois took the opportunity to say that he was "extraordinarily concerned" with President Trump's "rhetoric." He suggested that President Trump call for calm instead of trying to impose order, saying that we needed to give people space to peacefully protest, and that if we did that, things would die down on their own.

In the previous three nights alone, two people had died as a result of riots in Chicago, a city with one of the highest murder rates in the nation. During one recent weekend, eighty-five people were shot there in the span of forty-eight hours. So, in a sense, taking advice from the governor of Illinois on how to keep things "peaceful" was a little like getting a marriage counseling session from Bill Clinton. It wasn't going to happen.

"Well," President Trump said. "Thank you very much, Jay. I don't like your rhetoric, either."

And that was the end of it.

From there, President Trump went back to the Oval Office and prepared for an address in the Rose Garden. Bill Barr, who was officially in charge of the White House's response, went to the FBI's Strategic Information and Operations Center to monitor protests from all around the country. He remained there for a few hours before moving to the FBI's field office across town.

Earlier that day, Ivanka Trump had stood in the Oval Office and made a suggestion. Hope Hicks and I were also in the room, along with a few other members of President Trump's staff. Apparently, Ivanka had been getting the same messages of disgust from people all over the country who were outraged at what had happened to St. John's Church. She believed that it was important for President Trump not only to show that he was in charge and that law and order would prevail, but also to send a message to people of faith. As I watched President Trump listening to his daughter, I could tell he loved the idea. Having just come back from my own daughter's wedding, I knew that they enjoyed a unique bond that went far beyond words.

Ivanka's idea was simple. President Trump would give his address in the Rose Garden as planned, and then lead a group of his closest aides and advisors over to St. John's Church, where he would deliver a short message to the American people. We would not announce this to the press until it was absolutely necessary, and we would keep it as secret as possible, even within the West Wing.

All we needed was a Bible.

For a moment, we all looked at one another in silence. Was it really possible, I thought, that we didn't have one somewhere on the shelves that sat all over the walls of the Oval Office?

Somehow, word got out to the whole West Wing that we were looking for a copy of the Good Book. I got a few from my own office, and the rest of the staff managed to track down one or two as well. In about two minutes flat, we had a big stack of Bibles on the desk of Molly Michaels, who sat in the Outer Oval and assisted President Trump. During my entire time in the White House, I don't think I ever saw Molly away from that desk; nothing got into the Oval without her signing off on it first. Still, choosing a Bible for President Trump was not her prerogative.

In the end, President Trump picked the one he wanted. He was less focused on the look of the Bible than the way it felt in his hands. He, along with everyone else who walked with him that day, was under the impression that we would be going *inside* the church when we arrived to inspect the damage and possibly to say a prayer. Later, on the walk over, President Trump handed the Bible to Ivanka, who kept it in her purse until we arrived.

But first, President Trump addressed the nation from the Rose Garden. After making sure to note that he stands with all peaceful protestors, he said:

In recent days, our nation has been gripped by profes-sional anarchists, violent mobs, arsonists, looters, crim-inals, rioters, Antifa, and others. A number of state and local officials have failed to take necessary action to safeguard their residents. Innocent people have been savagely beaten like the young man in Dallas, Texas, who was left dying on the street. Where the woman in upstate New York, viciously attacked by dangerous thugs. Small business owners have seen their dreams utterly destroyed. New York's finest have been hit in the face with bricks. Brave nurses who have battled the virus are afraid to leave their homes. A police precinct has been overrun here in the nation's capital; the Lincoln Memorial and the World War II Memorial have been vandalized. One of our most historic churches was set ablaze. A federal officer in California, an African American law enforcement hero, was shot and killed.

These are not acts of peaceful protest. These are acts of domestic terror. The destruction of innocent life and the spilling of innocent blood is offensive to humanity and a crime against God. America needs creation, not destruction. Cooperation, not contempt. Security, not anarchy. Healing the hatred. Justice, not chaos.

The mood in the Rose Garden was solemn. From there, he walked through the recently cleared streets of our nation's capital toward St. John's Church, surprising the reporters who had watched his Rose Garden speech. There were a few lingering wisps from the smoke bombs that law enforcement had set off just minutes earlier, which were deployed more as a diversionary tactic than anything else. In the days to come, the liberal media would write stories claiming that the park had been cleared specifically so that President Trump could walk to the church to give his address. But this, as even the *Washington Post* would be forced to admit nearly a year later, was not true. A report carried out by the inspector general's office would later find that the law enforcement officials who cleared the park were carrying out a plan that had been in place for days; only the delayed shipment of some equipment, readiness of backup personnel and a stroke of bad timing made it so that the two events happened so close together. In fact, these law enforcement officials didn't even *know* that President Trump was planning to walk over to Lafayette Park until they saw him out in the street with a small team behind him, preparing to address the nation.

As I walked behind him, I thought that our walk from the White House was a perfect metaphor for President Trump's career in politics thus far. He knew that there were millions of people in the United States who wanted something from him. He knew this because, unlike any other person who had ever held the office, he was willing to *listen* to them. Americans had seen horrible things happening in our nation's capital, and they wanted to see President Trump address their concerns—not only with words, as he had done a few minutes earlier in the Rose Garden, but with action. No matter how ill-advised or politically unwise fulfilling that need might have seemed to the outside world, he was going to do it.

He was going to leave the White House, walk among the people, and show them that law and order was restored to DC. Walking over to that church was yet another signal to the world that President Trump would not bow down to pressure from the outside world. I doubt that we could have stopped him from walking to the church that afternoon with ten military tanks. I was never prouder to be serving under President Trump than I was walking with him across Pennsylvania Avenue to declare once and for all that in the United States of America, we would not stand for the degradation of our heritage or the burning of churches. I thought of the millions of people watching from home, who could finally take some comfort that there was *someone* who wasn't going to stand by while our cities burned to the ground, while the mob came for everything that we held dear.

When we arrived at St. John's we couldn't enter because it was boarded up. President Trump said little. He knew that the image of the president of the United States standing in front of a church that was attacked the night before was powerful enough.

When a reporter asked President Trump if he was holding a family Bible, he said that he was holding *a* Bible. Then he said that we were living in the greatest country in the world.

"It's not going to take long," he said. "It's coming back strong. It'll be greater than it's ever been before."

There were more shouted questions, but President Trump ignored them. He called me over to stand with him, and he also motioned to Robert O'Brien, Kayleigh McEnany, Bill Barr, and Mark Esper. We all stepped over while photographers snapped pictures. Looking at those pictures, I realize that I was the only one of us who wasn't facing the cameras. Instead, I was turned around, looking at the boarded-up façade of St. John's. I found it disturbing that of all the things that could have been attacked, these rioters chose a house of worship. I prayed, once again, that we would finally see an end to the violence and chaos.

But that was not the end—far from it, in fact.

———————————

Back in my office on June 22, I was watching rioters climbing on Lafayette Park's famous statue of Andrew Jackson, tearing at the legs and throwing ropes around the head in an apparent attempt to bring the whole thing down. It had been less than three weeks since they had tried to burn down St. John's

Church, and the violence, although it never reached the White House again, was still raging outside. I remember hearing a story from Ivanka Trump, who, one day, was standing beside Molly Michaels's desk in the Outer Oval. They were having a routine conversation. During the middle of it, a message came over the radio letting everyone in the building know that we were officially at "Code Orange," a designation of danger that sat right below Code Red.

"Don't worry," Molly said. "That happens every day now."

Upstairs in the Residence, President Trump was growing anxious. He had given an order for the park to be cleared, and it was not being followed. The various law enforcement agencies that were supposed to be under the command of Bill Barr were clearly not communicating with one another, and it did not seem that a single arrest had yet been made.

Fed up, I called President Trump.

"It looks like we have a situation out here," I said. "They're trying to tear down statues and vandalizing the park. I assume that we have the authority to deploy whatever law enforcement is necessary to fix this?"

President Trump had had enough. "Not only do you have the authority," he said. "I want you to go out there and bust some heads and make some arrests. We need to restore order."

Now, *I* was not quite prepared to crack anything. But I went to the front door of the White House and spoke with the head of the Secret Service. I pointed out that we had orders from President Trump to open up Pennsylvania Avenue. The leaders of these forces were resisting, but it was clear that the officers on the ground felt the same way President Trump did.

Then I walked out to Lafayette Park, just shy of the Andrew Jackson statue, where rioters were loosening bolts so that they could topple it. I ordered law enforcement surrounding the statue to go in.

"Now?" they said.

"Yes, now!" I said. "Go in. Stop them from taking down that statue."

A few minutes later, we had officers clearing protestors from the tops of the statue. It was a way of signaling to the mob—which was growing by the minute—that violence would not be tolerated that evening, or ever again—not in our nation's capital.

This was a message that President Trump kept up for the rest of the summer, and it was especially poignant on July 13, when he held a roundtable with several members of the law enforcement community. Standing in the room that day, watching President Trump express support for these police officers, I was reminded once again how important it was to have a president who was willing to go against the "politically correct" current.

It had been a rough few months for police officers all over the country, and the hard times weren't going to end anytime soon. It was important then—and it is important now—that President Trump let them know that he stood by them.

"Things are happening that we have never seen before," President Trump said. He added that cities like Chicago were worse than the Middle East. He said that law enforcement all over the country had the full support of the White House, and I could tell that it made a difference. Finally, someone was listening. If nothing else, I left that room knowing that the law enforcement community was going to turn up in huge numbers to support the president in November, because he was willing to support them every day.

— SEVEN —

Audience of One

IN THE FIRST days of July, President Trump was beginning to feel disheartened. He didn't show it, especially not to the American public, but I could sense a certain slackness in his shoulders, a sense that the pain of 2020 might finally be getting to him. Considering the events of the past few weeks, this was understandable.

First off, the campaign was in disarray. Brad Parscale, our six-foot-eight-inch digital guru who dressed like a lumberjack and spoke like a young tech billionaire, had proven that he was not quite up to the job of campaign manager. He'd been given this job in 2018, when the pundits were still aghast at President Trump's victory, asking every day just *how* they had managed to pull off such a landslide. They certainly weren't willing to give President Trump the credit. Most of these news outlets had written their stories with Brad as the hero, pretending that his gadgets and digital innovations were what made 62 million people turn out to vote for President Trump that year.

So, Brad was hired to run the campaign. He had been there since the beginning, and he had a good handle on the technology, some of which he had designed himself. For a while, things worked just fine. Brad built a great campaign team, and he designed several strategies to boost voter turnout in key states. But soon, it became clear that something was wrong. Brad had become the focus rather than President Trump, which was a deadly sin in the any campaign. Brad had spent too much money on areas that weren't making an impact. He let the media's adulation go to his head. He also seemed to be making far too much money from his job as campaign manager, as was frequently rumored, and this rankled President Trump greatly. I know that they had several confrontations about it in the Oval Office.

But the final swan song came near the middle of June, when Brad was in charge of organizing the president's first major postpandemic rally, which was set to occur in Tulsa, Oklahoma, on June 19. In the weeks leading up to the rally, several African American staffers in the White House approached the president to let him know that this day was also Juneteenth, the day that the Black community celebrates the end of slavery in the United States. They said that it would be deeply offensive to them to hold the rally on the same day as this holiday. One of them was a Secret Service agent who had been with President Trump for years. In a show of support for the Black community, President Trump immediately agreed to push the rally back a day to Saturday, June 20, though he was miffed at the campaign staff for making this mistake in the first place.

But that was only the beginning of our troubles.

In preparation for the rally, Brad sent out an email to several of the campaign's mailing lists asking for RSVPs. Within a few days, he had hundreds of thousands, which, as several people pointed out, was more than the population of the entire city of Tulsa. Clearly, something was up. But the campaign team didn't bother to look into it.

In the days following the rally, reports would claim that teams of hackers, using the Chinese app TikTok, encouraged one another to spam the RSVP site with messages, giving the impression that hundreds of thousands more people were attending the rally than was physically possible. Rather than investigate this, Brad had arranged for an overflow space to hold the extra attendees. He had painted a picture of himself as a brilliant campaign manager who could make impossible things happen, so when *this* seemingly impossible thing happened, it was all too easy for him to believe that it was real.

When the night of the rally arrived, the results were terrible. President Trump spoke to a half-empty crowd for the first time in his political life, and the blame, fairly or not, went straight to Brad and the campaign team. The liberal media had a field day with it, celebrating the misfortune of the Trump White House like it was Christmas Day, Thanksgiving, and Karl Marx's birthday all rolled into one. They dedicated absolutely no time to the reports that this misfortune was likely made possible by a shady group of hackers using an app that was heavily controlled by the Chinese Communist Party. That would have been a real story, but the Fake News stopped reporting on real stories some time ago. Once again, anything that was bad for the Trump Team was good for the media, and vice versa.

In the weeks after the rally, President Trump would lash out at Brad in the Oval Office, making sure to impress upon him the importance that nothing like Tulsa would ever happen again. There are things that President Trump can forgive— anyone who's seen the list of pardons he issued knows that for sure—but for Brad, the unholy trinity of grandstanding, profiting off the campaign, *and* making the president speak to a half-empty arena was too much. Eventually, Brad would be demoted, and Bill Stepien would step up to run the campaign. Looking back, each of these men did a good job during an extremely difficult point in history; if it hadn't been for the pandemic, we wouldn't even be talking about these problems.

But the pandemic was with us, and so were its terrible side effects.

Beyond the debacle of the Tulsa rally, there was the general feeling that the country was spinning out of control. The rioters and looters seemed to be running our cities, and the media was all too willing to defend their worst actions. News coverage of the president's walk to St. John's church, which was meant to be a show of defiance against these anarchists, was being touted as nothing more than a failed publicity stunt. President Trump, who generally didn't let the bad press get to him, was upset about it.

At the time, morale in the White House was about as low as I had ever seen it.

Then, just when it seemed that things were at their worst, President Trump came up with an idea. He'd been listening with disgust to the rhetoric of the anti-American protestors who'd taken over the streets. Many of them had said that America was useless and racist and needed to be burned from the inside out. Others said that anyone who stood up and expressed pride in their country was only "perpetuating a culture of white supremacy," whatever *that* means.

He wanted to push back.

In the Oval Office, President Trump laid out a vision for a spectacular rally that would take place on the Fourth of July. It was going to be held right at the foot of Mount Rushmore, one of our nation's great monuments. The president had already approved fireworks for Mount Rushmore. Now he wanted to write a speech that reminded the American people of our Founding Fathers and what they stood for, sending a clear message to the haters and anarchists that the patriots of this country would not sink quietly into the night while their country was overrun. For weeks, he worked on the precise wording of that speech, going back and forth with Ross Worthington, Stephen Miller, and Vince Haley, his speechwriters. When the moment came to deliver it, he looked as ready for action as I had ever seen him. The fire had returned to his eyes, and it was clear that the frustrations of Tulsa were behind him.

He was back and stronger than ever.

On July 3, we boarded Air Force One and flew out to South Dakota, where Governor Kristi Noem had arranged to meet us on the tarmac. After a fiery introduction by the governor, President Trump took to the podium, and the place erupted with cheers. It was as if all the things that these patriots had been afraid to say for so many months—all the pride in their country and excitement at being an American that the liberal mob wanted to eradicate—were finally being released, and the effects were joyous.

"There could be no better place," he said, "to celebrate America's independence than beneath this magnificent, incredible, majestic mountain and monument to the greatest Americans who have ever lived. Today, we pay tribute to the exceptional lives and extraordinary legacies of George Washington, Thomas Jefferson, Abraham Lincoln, and Teddy Roosevelt. I am here as your president to proclaim before the country and before the world: This monument will never be desecrated, these heroes will never be defaced, their legacy will never ever be destroyed, their achievements will never be forgotten, and Mount Rushmore will stand forever as an eternal tribute to our forefathers and to our freedom."

The applause came loudly and often. Later, there were fireworks. Military jets flew overhead, making for an impressive sight in the night sky. Debbie and I watched from the stage and thought about how fortunate we were, even in the midst of this challenging moment in our nation's history, to have a leader who understood the importance of our heritage, our founding ideals, and the bonds that unite us all as Americans. Along with President Trump's State of the Union addresses, this speech at Mount Rushmore was one of his best performances. In fact, it was one of the finest in American history

On its face, it was a speech. But it was more. It was a reminder to all that American history would remain, and that destroying statues and rewriting history would not be tolerated in the United States of America. This reminder showed a great deal of bravery on President Trump's part, and it was one of the most inspiring things that I ever had the privilege of witnessing during my time in the White House.

It was the same bravery that he had shown just over a month ago during his historic walk to Lafayette Park. I could not have imagined the sheer carnage, or the abject surrender to the mob, that might have occurred under a Biden or an Obama presidency. I prayed that I would never have to find out.

When we returned to the White House, we did so with a renewed sense of purpose. We had just a few months to go before the election, and a few more important promises to keep before that day. We needed to get another relief bill done for the American people who were still suffering as a result of

Covid-19, and we needed to make sure that vaccines would be available to all "at-risk" Americans by the fall.

These two issues alone would have been enough to occupy our every waking hour. Any normal president would have put all other initiatives on hold to get them done. But President Trump, ever mindful that a second term might be denied him, did not want to waste any time. He had made a promise to the American people on the campaign trail—one that he was roundly mocked for at the time by the elite political class—and he was intent on showing them all up by keeping it.

"Where are we," he asked during a meeting in the Oval Office that summer, "with peace in the Middle East?"

For months, Jared Kushner had been working day and night with Avi Berkowitz, the White House Special Representative for International Negotiations, to secure a historic peace agreement between Israel and its neighbors in the Arab world. Steven Mnuchin was also a major player in the talks, as was Mike Pompeo, President Trump's Secretary of State. To many outside the West Wing, this was a fool's errand. Every presidential administration for the last fifty years or more had attempted to make some kind of lasting peace in that region, and they had all come up short. The liberal media, and even some conservatives, believed that if professional politicians— many of whom had made it their life's work to achieve peace— couldn't get it done, then how were a businessman from New York and his son-in-law going to do it?

Yet by the time President Trump traveled to Mount Rushmore to deliver his address on patriotism and pride in the United

States, we were on the verge of breakthrough peace treaties for the first time in decades. Avi and Jared had arranged high-level meetings between emissaries of several Arab countries and Israel, and we were planning on holding the signing ceremony sometime in the fall.

During the negotiations to make this plan a reality, I looked on with wonder. This was an issue of great importance, I knew, both to the United States and to the world. But it was also a deeply personal one for me.

———————

In 2012, just after I was elected to Congress, Debbie and I took a trip to Israel. While I was in the Holy Land, I saw some of the places that I had been reading about in the Bible since I was a young man, including Mount Carmel where Elijah called on the Lord to answer by fire and the empty tomb after Christ's resurrection.

One day, near the beginning of the trip, I had an experience that still resonates with me today. Standing in the middle of Israel, looking out over the ancient land, I felt that God was speaking directly to me: *Hidden in Christ, you are free from condemnation, performance, and fear. You are accepted in the Beloved. Live your life from that foundation. No other will uphold you.*

As a new congressman, I found the message poignant and timely. When I explained my revelation to Debbie, I remembered a mantra that has been with me ever since.

"I took it to mean that you can't please everyone, especially not in Washington," I said. "It means that I have an Audience of One, and that audience is God. No one else matters."

When I went to Washington, I worked to represent the interests of the American people. And I always tried to keep my

Audience of One in mind. The way I saw it, I had made several promises to my constituents when I asked for their votes during the campaign, and if I didn't do absolutely everything in my power to keep those promises, I wouldn't hear the "well done" I was hoping for from my Audience of One. I was also mindful of another quote, this one from someone who has significantly less standing in my book than God: President Ronald Reagan. "There's no limit to what you can accomplish," Reagan once said, "if you don't care who gets the credit."

Using those principles, and working with the Freedom Caucus, we managed to do great things. We ousted Speaker John Boehner, although a little more slowly than we had hoped. We stripped key provisions of Obamacare. We passed historic tax cuts, and changed the dynamic of the Republican conference. Thanks to our efforts, the American people finally had a seat at the table. Later, we helped successfully defend President Trump from the bogus Russia collusion attacks, and certainly from impeachment.

But there was one thing that I was especially proud of President Trump for.

Almost twenty years earlier, in October 1995, Congress had passed a law called the Jerusalem Embassy Act, which was supposed to move the US embassy from Tel Aviv to Jerusalem and recognize Jerusalem as the capitol of Israel. But despite the celebrations that occurred after the bill's passage, it didn't happen. Due to some fine print in the original law, the president of the United States was allowed to delay taking action on the bill for six months at a time, issuing a waiver to stop the embassy from moving. There was no limit to the number of six-month delays a president could issue, meaning that the law could languish in obscurity forever, never amounting to more than a legislative footnote.

To me, this law was a perfect example of the way things seemed to work in Washington—all symbolism and fanfare, yet no hope of actual change. During my time in Israel, I had been struck not only by the beauty of the country and its innumerable holy sites, but also by Israel's commitment to being a bastion of peace and democracy in the war-ravaged Middle East. It wasn't right that we weren't holding up our end of the relationship by recognizing the validity of their capital city. I had pushed for the issue with the previous administration, trying to make it happen via various back channels and negotiations.

Still, we got nowhere.

Then, in what seemed like the blink of an eye, President Trump came on the scene. During a few speeches on the campaign trail, he promised to do what no president had done before and make the move happen. This, of course, wasn't new. Every president before him, including Bill Clinton, George W. Bush, and Barack Obama, had all promised exactly the same thing.

Even with all the moves President Trump was making to shake up the established order of things, I wasn't certain that this was going to happen.

———

Then one day in 2017, just as I was leaving the new Trump White House after a meeting, I got a call on my cell phone from Reince Priebus, who was then chief of staff to President Trump. At the time, I was sitting in traffic, heading home for the night.

"Mark," he said. "I need you to come back here. You need to tell the President what you just told me."

What I had just told Reince and Steve Bannon in my
earlier meeting was that we needed to move our United States
embassy to Jerusalem.

I shared that my constituents were adamant about this. But
I was unsure of the impact my words would have. I had passed
along similar messages to people in the White House before,
and gotten nowhere.

Still, this was President Trump. If the first few months of
his presidency had taught me anything, it was that things were
different now—much different.

I looked left, swung my car around across the double yellow
line, and headed back for the White House. Debbie, who had
been in the car with me, hopped out and caught a taxi back to
our apartment.

When I arrived, I was ushered straight into the empty
Oval Office, where I had never been. President Trump called
me into his side working office. There were newspapers and
briefing memos spread out on the desk in front of him, and he
seemed to be studying them with special intensity.

"Mark," he said. "My favorite congressman! Come on in."

It was just the two of us.

I took my seat and launched right into the reasons why
President Trump needed to fulfill this campaign promise right
away. If he wanted to keep delaying the process, he would
need to sign a waiver that would stop the move for another six
months. If he wanted to make it happen, all he needed to do
was not sign that waiver.

As I spoke, President Trump noticed that I kept looking
down at a twelve-inch wooden box with a red button on it in
the corner of his desk. At first glance, this button seemed like
something you might use to launch a nuclear missile, or maybe

to order SEAL Team Six into action. Given that we were sitting in the office of the most powerful man in the world, I figured my imagination wasn't far off the mark.

"Makes you nervous, doesn't it?" the President said.

"Oh no," I equivocated, and kept on with my advocacy plea.

Still, I was surprised, and a little nervous, when President Trump reached out and pressed the button.

I braced for whatever sonic boom, breaking glass, or cloud of smoke I assumed was coming.

I sat there with my eyes wide.

A few seconds later, a naval steward emerged from a hidden door with a glass of Diet Coke on ice.

"That's impressive," I said.

He asked if I wanted to see it again, smiling. He pushed the red button again, and out came a Diet Coke for me.

Before I could say anything about the button, President Trump was asking rapid-fire questions about moving our embassy from Tel Aviv to Jerusalem. How long was it going to take? What kind of blowback could we expect in the region? Which of his constituents believed it was the right thing to do? Was there any downside?

I answered these questions as best as I could, knowing that there were dozens, probably hundreds of other, more qualified people he would also be speaking to.

As I left the White House that afternoon, President Trump assured me there would not be another waiver.

True to his word, President Trump announced that the United States was officially going to recognize Jerusalem as the capital of Israel.

The pundit class all predicted that disaster was on its way, making outrageous predictions about terrible repercussions in the region that never came to pass—at least not while President Trump, who made it clear that he would be tough on terrorism all over the world, was in office.

The story of the Jerusalem embassy is one that would recur, in some form or another, dozens of times during the presidency of Donald Trump. He would come across something that had been lodged in the slow, rusty gears of our federal bureaucracy for years, sometimes decades, and yank it out, against the advice of every establishment politician in the country. He would ask around, develop a plan, and then execute that plan with military precision.

And now it was about to happen again.

All throughout the spring and summer of 2020, I listened in on meetings between Jared and his team, giving reports to President Trump about the progress we were making. When it was clear that we were on the verge of a real agreement, we decided to call them the Abraham Accords, a name chosen to honor the biblical figure Abraham, whom Christians, Jews, and Muslims regard as their common ancestor. It was yet another stroke of marketing genius from Donald J. Trump, the best brander in the business.

Jared, Avi, Pompeo, and Mnuchin took several trips abroad to get these agreements done. Brian Hook, another expert on the subject, would also go along. Thanks to his experience in the private sector, Jared could look at the agreements from an economic standpoint as well as a political one, which was a perspective that the negotiations had been missing in the past. By the end of the summer, we had reached agreements with Israel, the United Arab Emirates, and Bahrain. There was a formal signing of the historic agreement on the South Lawn of the White House, and we celebrated in the building.

Once again, President Trump and his team had done the impossible.

EIGHT

A Quick Confirmation

ON SEPTEMBER 18, 2020, President Trump boarded a flight for the small city of Bemidji, Minnesota. We were less than two months out from the election at the time, and we believed that a campaign speech in this bustling college town—which, thankfully, is much easier to get to than it is to pronounce—might give us a shot at winning the whole state. Four years earlier, President Trump had come within 40,000 votes of turning the state red for the first time in decades, a feat that went largely unnoticed under the shadow of his historic landslide victory. This time around, we hoped that if we could get a few more Republicans to show up in places like Minneapolis and Bemidji in November, we would be able to win not only Minnesota, but the whole election—assuming, of course, that everyone *else* who voted was alive, a real person, and an actual resident of the state they were voting in.

That last part turned out to be a little harder than we thought.

But in the middle of September, President Trump and the campaign team were hopeful about our chances. He knew, for instance, that the people of Minnesota were some of the biggest beneficiaries of his administration's decision to remove President Obama's ban on copper-nickel mining, a move that created thousands of jobs in the state. The president had also passed a stunning array of agricultural subsidies in 2018, a move that put hundreds of thousands of dollars back into the pockets of Minnesota farmers during the worst of our tough (and very necessary) trade war with China. And all of that came on top of the historic tax cuts, the enormous stock market gains, and the unprecedented support for small businesses that had been hallmarks of President Trump's first term. You might think that with a record that good, the president would have been able to hang back in Washington, get a few extra hours of sleep every night, and do the bulk of his campaigning Biden-style, hopping on a Zoom call from the White House basement every now and then while minor surrogates like me made the speeches for him.

But that wasn't his style, and it never had been.

Of all the Fake News I encountered working in Washington, there was no single lie that irritated me more than the one about President Trump's lackluster work ethic. Every time I saw another story in *The New York Times* or on CNN about how the president would show up late, get distracted, or leave the office early, I couldn't help but roll my eyes. I consider myself a pretty hard worker, and even *I* was exhausted working for this man. A few months into the job, I found myself having to arrive at the office before seven o'clock in the morning if I was going to have even some chance of catching up with the fifteen things he had already gotten started up in the Residence. Every day, there was a new policy initiative, a new strategy for fighting Covid-19, a new way to put pressure on some senator who wasn't voting the way we wanted him to on a particular bill. It was an honor to do that work with him, even if it did almost kill me.

Fortunately for us—and rather *unfortunately* for our poor advance team—President Trump brought the same mile-a-minute energy he used to govern out on the campaign trail with him. No matter how tight our schedule was or what kind of horrible weather we were dealing with, he would always insist on giving the crowd every ounce of what they had come for. I still have vivid memories from the campaign of younger staffers asking, practically *begging*, the president to settle down, maybe keep this rally a little shorter tonight because we were running behind schedule and the windchill was dragging the temperature down nearly to zero. Every time, he would cut them off before they could even finish speaking. *They came here for us,* he'd say. *You can handle it. The staff can handle it. I can handle it. We're going out there.*

He knew that the past few months had been hard—nearly impossible—for a lot of people, and he knew that they needed to hear from their commander in chief. If there was even one person in a crowd whose vote President Trump thought he could secure by showing up and giving a speech, we all knew he would walk to wherever they were straight from Washington to do it. Fortunately, given the fact that he had always owned a private plane (even before he became president) that could get him just about anywhere in the United States in a matter of hours, we never had to test that theory.

For the people of Minnesota, a strong show of support from the White House was more important than ever. For nearly four months, their state had been the site of unspeakable violence and governor-endorsed domestic terrorism. What had begun near the end of May as a series of peaceful protests over the death of George Floyd had become a national emergency, and the president had said as much from the White House. Nearly every night, small businesses in Minneapolis and other major cities were looted. Police officers were attacked with startling frequency. Radical leftists clad in black athletic gear roamed the streets, causing violence to anyone who stood in their way. Fires had been burning in major sections of those cities all summer. I wouldn't be surprised if President Trump, who began his initial descent toward the regional airport in Bemidji around five o'clock, could see the lingering smoke from those fires in the sky.

I know that when he got close enough, the president and the small team he was traveling with saw thousands of people waiting for him on the tarmac. During President Trump's first term, this happened whenever Air Force One appeared in the sky over a city. Crowds would follow this man the way crickets and tumbleweed seemed to follow his opponent, Joe Biden. Every time President Trump showed up to a place, whether it was for a small address or a massive, packed-to-the-rafters rally, people would begin lining up in the early hours of the morning. They would spend the day crafting signs, making new friends, and anxiously awaiting an address from their president, Donald J. Trump.

I'm sure that when the plane landed, the roar from that crowd was enough to shake the roof of the airplane hangar he'd be speaking in. It might have even been enough to shake the advance team out of their midcampaign exhaustion.

If my experience on the campaign trail is any indication, I'm sure that noise only grew as it came time for the president to speak, culminating in uproarious applause and cheers when he strode out onto the stage toward the podium. I said it already, but it bears repeating: I have never seen *anything* like the crowd at a Trump rally. The energy of these patriots, all united for a common cause, celebrating their prosperity and patriotism in a shared space, is something you can't describe until you're in the middle of the crowd with them. If you're reading this, there's a high probability you've experienced it at least once.

If not, I hope you get the chance someday.

———————————

To be honest, I can't be sure what the crowd sounded like that night. Back in Alexandria, Virginia, my house was quieter than the crowd at a Joe Biden rally. I had made the decision a few days earlier to stay behind, assuming that my time would be better spent back in the swamp, where, as always, there was a mountain of work to be done. In my absence, I had sent along one of my deputies, Dan Scavino, who could handle just about anything that got thrown at him. If there was anyone I trusted during my time in the White House to be my eyes and ears—and, by extension, the *president's* eyes and ears—it was Dan.

I was in dire need of some time alone to work. All day, I had been working with several experts in the White House to find a way to reduce prescription drug prices across the board and to aid us in the development of a vaccine. President Trump had ordered us to find a plan that would allow us to make 100 million doses of the vaccine available as soon as possible. His intent, as he explained it to me, was not to force anyone to get the vaccine, but only to make sure that anyone who wanted the shot would be able to get one. But due to the continued unwillingness of Nancy Pelosi and her team to pass another round of Covid-19 relief in the House, finding the money to do that was going to be very challenging.

A few days earlier, Secretary Alex Azar had come to my office asking if we could find some money from one of the *first* Covid-19 relief packages—the one we had passed in April, nearly six months ago by this point—and reappropriate it to purchase doses of the vaccine. He knew as well as I did that if Nancy Pelosi had her way, she would hold up the money we so desperately needed until long after the election, making sure it was her preferred candidate who would be able to take credit for the vaccines. That wasn't sitting well with me, so Secretary Azar and I got to work. By that evening, we had reallocated somewhere around $32 billion for the vaccine effort, making Operation Warp Speed the largest federal expenditure I ever personally signed off on as chief of staff (or as anything else). Still, the bulk of President Trump's focus remained on making sure that therapeutic treatments like convalescent plasma and Regeneron would be available to Americans who were infected with the virus; he never wanted to place his hope fully in the vaccine, knowing that some Americans might not want to take it.

We also had to work twice as hard to distribute money to hospitals all over the country that were already teetering on the edge of bankruptcy. This was the greatest medical crisis in the history of our nation, and the allocated funds had to get where they were most needed.

Meanwhile, due to Secretary Mnuchin's around-the-clock diligence, he and his team had provided relief for businesses in record time, focusing on economic recovery.

While HHS and I were working to get billions of dollars out the door for hospitals and healthcare providers, Mnuchin was working to save our economy. Because of his extraordinary work ethic, Steven became my favorite cabinet member.

As always, Trump Time was in full effect. *Faster, quicker, better* was the refrain that came from the Oval.

That evening, I was also working out the finer points of an executive order that would ban government contractors from pushing the radical ideology known as Critical Race Theory. Supposedly this set of ideas was to help educate white Americans about racism and help the country move beyond its legacy of racial oppression. But in reality, it did exactly the opposite. It held, for instance, that all white people were inherently racist by virtue of being born white; it didn't matter what these people actually believed or what they had done. It said that there were inherent differences among the races, and that people should be treated differently according to the color of their skin. To me—and to anyone else with a working brain—that sounded like a precise reversal of Dr. Martin Luther King Jr.'s dream for the United States. It made me livid.

When President Trump began learning about this stuff, he reacted with horror. "If that isn't racism," he said. "I don't know what is. Teaching our military—let alone our kids—that the color of your skin is somehow responsible for your actions is political correctness *bullshit*."

I wholeheartedly agreed. In fact, I thought, if you made some small cosmetic changes and swapped a few terms around, the books upon which this twisted ideology was based would make the most depraved member of the Ku Klux Klan snort with evil delight.

Although there was a time when this sort of thing was popular only among the nuttiest radical left fringe groups (*The New York Times*, for instance), that time was clearly over. CRT was here, and it was spreading quickly. On September 2, sitting in his private office off the Oval around nine thirty p.m.,

President Trump saw an interview on *Tucker Carlson Tonight* with a journalist named Christopher Rufo. Over the course of a few months, Rufo had obtained slides from a so-called diversity training seminar held by the city government in Seattle, and the information was shocking.

During the training, white people and black people had been divided up into groups based on their race—something we used to call *segregation*—and ushered into different rooms. The white people were given a presentation called "Internalized Racial Superiority for White People" and told that they would be "working through emotions that often come up for white people like sadness, shame, paralysis, confusion, denial." It said that traits like perfectionism, objectivity, and showing up to work on time were not things to strive for, but expressions of "internalized racial superiority." Again, I wasn't seeing anything in these slides that wouldn't have seemed perfectly situated on the home page of a white supremacist website. Whatever it was, it needed to stop.

Rufo ended his segment on *Tucker Carlson Tonight* with a direct address to the president of the United States. "I'd like to make it explicit," he said. "The president and the White House—it's within their authority to immediately issue an executive order to abolish Critical Race Theory training from the federal government. And I call on the president to immediately issue this executive order—to stamp out this destructive, divisive, pseudoscientific ideology."

And that's what we did.

The morning after that segment, I gave Christopher Rufo a call, and we got to work on an executive order. In a few days, he would be flying out to Washington to help us fine-tune the wording, along with a few other respected scholars and journalists. It would be done and ready to sign by the end of September.

In most White Houses, this kind of thing would have taken months, if not years, to draft and enact. There would have been a few dozen meetings, drafts, and opinion polls to determine when the best time was. But President Trump was at the helm.

This wasn't the first time we had been tipped off by a good report on Tucker Carlson Tonight. In April, Tucker shocked many of us as he reported "Fauci-directed" taxpayer dollars were still flowing to the Wuhan Virology Lab. I called Secretary Azar immediately to order him to stop this lunacy. President Trump, watching the show an hour later by virtue of what the Boss calls the greatest invention known to man, TiVo, made a similar call.

Alex said, "I know, I know, the Chief has already called me, we will terminate the funding tomorrow."

A somewhat puzzled President called me as he hung up from Alex. "Mark, I didn't tell you to stop the funding for the Wuhan Lab."

"No," I said. "But you would have."

"Finally," President Trump said. "A Chief of Staff who thinks for himself! Good Night."

In the West Wing, we used to tell jokes about Trump Time. When the president yelled at you to get something done, that didn't mean you should set up some exploratory meetings, make a few phone calls, and write him a memo. It meant that the next time he saw you, that thing had better be *done*, as in complete, buttoned up, and ready to print in the papers. I can name a few young staffers who found that out the hard way.

If there was something we believed the American people needed, we did it.

Delays would not be tolerated by the boss.

Around seven o'clock, just as the final rays of light were fading from my kitchen, I got a notification on my iPhone. It was a text from Tony Ornato, the man who was in charge of monitoring all events in the world. Often, he would know long before our communications did that some major event—a protest, a coup, or a lunch between two foreign dignitaries that we wanted to keep our eye on—had occurred. This was how I learned that Ruth Bader Ginsburg, a dedicated public servant had died at the age of eighty-seven.

"RBG has passed," he said.

That was all I needed to read. I had known this day would come eventually, but the news came as more of a shock than I had expected.

Justice Ginsburg had been dealing with health issues of one sort or another for almost as long as she had been on the court. Every time, she managed to win the fight and rule another day. She'd beaten colon cancer in 1999, then early-stage pancreatic cancer in 2009. In 2014, she received a coronary stent to clear a blocked artery, and in 2018, during a scan conducted after a fall that broke three of her ribs, doctors had found two tumors in her lungs. People in Washington—especially those, like myself, who had to be prepared to fill a Supreme Court vacancy at any second—had learned never to underestimate Justice Ginsburg's staying power and obstinate nature, particularly when it came to retaining her seat on the Supreme Court.

As much as I might have disagreed with Justice Ginsburg on . . . well, just about everything that it's possible for two people to disagree on, I had developed a deep admiration for her strength and resolve. I also knew that she was the last of a rare breed in Washington: someone who could be kind, even friendly, to people who didn't share her political beliefs. Her close friendship with Justice Antonin Scalia, a hero in the conservative movement, was legendary, built on warmth, kindness, and mutual respect. But she never wavered when she believed she was right.

It was an open secret in Washington, for instance, that when Barack Obama tried to pressure Justice Ginsburg into retirement during a lunch in July 2013—likely viewing her exit as his one chance to nominate an ultraliberal justice to the bench—she politely refused, telling an interviewer one year later that it was a question "for her own good judgment." Now that I've been in the Oval Office and seen the way that room, not to mention the office of the presidency itself, seems to intimidate people into acquiescence, I know that it must have taken an iron will to refuse such a request.

On that night in September, however, I wasn't thinking about any of that. The only thing on my mind was that newly vacant seat on the Supreme Court, and how it was my job—my *only* job, at least for the next few weeks—to make sure President Trump was allowed to fill it, as was his duty according to the United States Constitution. I thought about the vehement opposition we would likely get from Democrats in the House and Senate, all of whom seemed dead set on stopping the gears of government from moving for as long as President Trump was in charge. I also considered the smaller, but not unimportant opposition we would get from members of our own party, many of whom believed that it was time to nominate a moderate or liberal justice in order to gain votes from the other side of the aisle.

My first call was to Dan Scavino. I knew it was unlikely that the team in Minnesota hadn't already learned of Justice Ginsburg's death, but I thought it was important to call and make sure we were all on the same page. Dan delivered the news to Johnny McEntee, then informed me that it was too late to inform the boss; the president had already begun his speech.

From my kitchen, I could imagine the two of them sitting there, watching the president speak in front of several thousand people, desperately wanting to give him a piece of information. For Johnny, it must have been particularly frustrating. A thirty-year-old former quarterback at the University of Connecticut, Johnny had been with the Trump campaign from the very beginning, working his way up from a low-level staffer to the unique position of "body man." During that time, he was hardly ever more than a few feet from President Trump. As a body man, it was his job to follow the president everywhere—and I mean *everywhere*. When President Trump needed anything, from a crucial bit of intelligence to a Diet Coke or a cell phone, it fell to Johnny to track that thing down, get his hands on it, and get it to the president.

As soon as Johnny heard the news, his first impulse was to run out onstage and tell the president. Dan agreed with me to wait until he was done. Through the phone, I was surprised to hear the president approaching a section of his speech about the Supreme Court—an odd development, given that he was probably one of very few people in the country who *wasn't* aware that another vacancy had just opened up. Then again, the president always did have an uncanny ability to know what was coming around the corner. At one point, he even suggested Senator Ted Cruz, a principled conservative who'd been a good friend to me over the years, as a potential nominee.

"Ted's the only man I know who could get one hundred votes from the Senate," the president said while the crowd cheered. "He's a great guy, a brilliant guy."

Thinking about this now, I have to laugh. Ted is indeed a great guy, and one of the finest legal minds in the country, but I seriously doubted—and I doubt now—that he'd be able to get one hundred votes in the Senate. That's largely because for as long as I've known him, Ted Cruz has stood up for conservative principles—and I mean *real* conservative principles—against unbelievable opposition. He had fought hard for the president during the battle over the Tax Cuts and Jobs Act of 2017, and always went to bat for him against the Fake News. Often, the opposition would come from within the Republican Party itself, which is something I could relate to. But Ted never wavered in his commitment to what he believed was right. In the Senate—and in the House, as I know all too well—that'll usually make you more enemies than friends.

Up on the podium, President Trump showed no signs of slowing down. "Many presidents have had none," he said, referring to open seats on the Supreme Court. "They've had none because they're there for a long time . . . Think of that. That will totally change when you talk about life, when you talk about the Second Amendment, when you talk about things that are *so* important to you."

If only he knew how pertinent his words would turn out to be. We'd find out later that as he was speaking, someone from the crowd had actually tried to get him the news, shouting "Ginsburg is dead" while holding up a smartphone. But the president couldn't hear him. Having been under those lights one or two times myself, I know that the podium can completely cut you off from the outside world.

Because of the energy of the crowd, and the general tendency of people in large groups to act unpredictably, I decided to direct Dan and Johnny to withhold the news about Ginsburg from the president until he had finished speaking. To be blunt, I believed that if he announced the news from the podium, the crowd would likely erupt in cheers over the new vacancy on the court. There were three thousand people watching the president speak inside that airplane hangar and another three thousand or so watching it on massive screens outside in the parking lot. The sound of all of them cheering at once would have been deafening. Leaving the optics of the situation aside, I know it would have been very upsetting to the president to hear so many people cheering after the passing of someone I know he respected.

But this wasn't my first rodeo. I knew how the media worked. Cheering at this time was the kind of thing that would have given CNN and MSNBC B-roll for the next three months, right up to election night. I figured we were going to get enough heat in the coming weeks when we nominated someone to replace Justice Ginsburg—which, again, was our duty according to the Constitution. I didn't think we had anything to gain by making the whole country think we were cheering while we did it.

Although the president was not finished speaking, I did tweet out a message of support. I felt that it was important that the world know that I and the White House were saddened by the news of Ginsburg's death.

"Joining the whole nation tonight in mourning the loss of Justice Ruth Bader Ginsburg—a trailblazer, a dedicated public servant, and an inspiration to so many," I wrote. "My prayers are with her family and friends."

Beyond that, all I could do was sit in my kitchen and wait. It was nearly eight thirty. I wasn't sure how the next few weeks were going to go, but I knew one thing for sure.

This was the last quiet moment I would get for a long, long time.

———————

During his first three years in the White House, President Trump had appointed two justices to the Supreme Court. That was an impressive feat, especially given the opposition he'd endured, but it wasn't unprecedented. In fact, every president dating back to George H. W. Bush had managed to appoint two justices each. This had created a kind of back-and-forth game in Washington. For every two justices appointed by a Republican president, there were another two appointed by a Democrat. Bill Clinton put Stephen Breyer and Ruth Bader Ginsburg on the court, then George W. Bush countered with Samuel Alito and John Roberts. The next year, Barack Obama appointed Sonia Sotomayor and Elena Kagan to the bench, hitting the proverbial volleyball back over the net just like everyone expected him to.

As soon as President Trump took office, he was able to keep the game going—largely thanks to Senator Mitch McConnell and a few of his headstrong colleagues in the Senate, who gave Obama no quarter when he sought to replace Antonin Scalia with Merrick Garland. As one of his first acts in office, President Trump nominated Neil Gorsuch, a principled conservative who had displayed a razor-sharp legal mind during his time as a circuit court judge. Despite strident opposition from Democrats, this confirmation went off largely without a hitch. Justice Gorsuch displayed a great mind during the hearings, and he never allowed grandstanding from senators to deter him.

The same, unfortunately, cannot be said of the president's next choice. Brett Kavanaugh was part of the Republican establishment, having served major roles in the White House under President George W. Bush and then moving on to a federal judgeship. He seemed a perfectly fine choice to President Trump, who nominated him at the suggestion of several influential Republicans. During the interview process, Judge Kavanaugh had shown himself to be calm, capable, and sharp when it came to the details of his prior cases. We thought that his nomination would be a slam dunk. But when the heat started, that calm façade melted.

Anyone who wanted a seat on the highest court, the president once told me, needed nerves of steel. Such a person needed to be ready for anything—meaning *anything*, up to and including ridiculous lies about a youthful indiscretion—that the other side could throw at them. President Trump knew better than anyone that when the other side came at you, the only logical response was to remain calm, take the hits, and then fire back twice as hard. He was *so* good at it, in fact, that he often forgot that other people could not operate at this level. When President Trump saw Judge Kavanaugh declare that he "liked beer" several times in front of Congress, he was extremely put off. He was also disappointed by Judge Kavanaugh's almost apologetic testimony during the Senate confirmation hearings, which he viewed as being weak. If there is one thing for which President Trump has absolutely no tolerance or patience, it's weakness.

Above: Unlike some of his predecessors, President Trump would always have his guests sit around the Resolute Desk during meetings in the Oval Office. Below: Getting orders from the boss before a rally. (All photos, including White House photos, courtesy of the author.)

ABOVE: White House chief of staff is a big job, and it comes with a big office. Sitting on my couch making calls. BELOW: Walking with President Trump along the colonnade, which connects the West Wing to the East Wing, where the president's private residence is located.

Despite what you've read, everyone in these photos was just fine with walking over to inspect the damage that had been done to St. John's Church after several nights of rioting in Washington, DC.

The speech that President Trump gave at Mount Rushmore on July 3, 2020, will go down as one of the finest addresses ever given by an American president.

ABOVE: The nomination of Amy Coney Barrett to the Supreme Court was quick, easy, and effective because we adhered to the "Trump rule." BELOW: Even after he had Covid-19, President Trump was always willing to get up and deliver his message. It didn't matter if the temperatures were below freezing.

Top: A meeting of Republican congressmen in the chief of staff's office. Above: Even with all that was going on, we managed to have a great White House Christmas party. Left: Debbie and I traveling on Air Force One.

Before he boarded Air Force One for the last time, President Trump turned to me and delivered a few parting words.

Standing with President Trump and First Lady Melania Trump in the Oval Office, where I hope President Trump will be sitting again after the 2024 election. (All photos, including White House photos, courtesy of the author.)

For a short time, he strongly considered dropping Kavanaugh in favor of another, stronger candidate.

President Trump proposed this idea to me during a trip we took together on Air Force One in the middle of the hearings. In doing so, the president was following his usual habit of asking around to a few dozen people before making a firm decision. Still, as a member of Congress, I'm sure I was just one of many people whose opinion he asked for during this period. In any event, I let the president know that if he dropped Kavanaugh as a candidate, the blowback could be severe. It would be viewed by the press as a failure and as a victory by his enemies on the left. The lunatics in Congress who had picked up the accusations against Kavanaugh and run with them would come up with something only wilder and crazier when the next nominee was sitting before them; it wouldn't matter if they had to go interview people who said that the new candidate had bullied them on the playground in the fourth grade.

In the end, President Trump's combative spirit won the day. He stuck by Kavanaugh in public, speaking out in support of him whenever he was given the chance, and Kavanaugh, largely *because* of that presidential support, was confirmed. It was yet another example of a maxim that President Trump held dear for his entire time in the White House, which can be expressed, roughly, like this: *Fight until it's over. Then get up and keep fighting.*

That is how, after a rough and tumble confirmation fight that will probably not be remembered much by historians outside of the odd footnote, President Trump ended up with his second appointment to the Supreme Court.

For the most part, the team had adhered to a pretty standard playbook to make appointments to the Supreme Court, one that was all but set in stone by the time President Trump arrived in the White House. The routine went something like this: When a vacancy came up on the court, advisors close to President Trump would confer with various experts and scholars of the court, most notably Leonard Leo, who had been an early member of the Federalist Society in the 1980s. Together, these groups would come up with a short list of names for the president, ultimately selecting a few for interviews at the White House. A graduate of Cornell University and a self-appointed expert on the court, Leonard had been a fixture in Republican politics for decades, aiding in the nominations of everyone from Clarence Thomas to John Roberts to Samuel Alito. According to Jeffrey Toobin, a journalist who's covered the American judicial system for a few decades (in addition to partaking in a few, shall we say, less reputable activities), Leonard Leo was "responsible, to a considerable extent, for one third of the justices on the Supreme Court."

For a while, this system worked fine. You can't argue with the results. After all, it gave President Trump two appointments to the court. However, President Trump would quickly learn that when you rely on the establishment to pick your justices, you're going to get justices who serve the establishment, and not necessarily the voters. In the years since Brett Kavanaugh had been confirmed, he and Justice Gorsuch had both ruled in ways that were deeply disappointing to the MAGA movement that had made their appointments possible. When the verdict came down in *Washington State Department of Licensing v. Cougar Den* in March 2019, for instance, conservatives were surprised to find that Justice Gorsuch had sided with his more liberal colleagues, showing a willingness to "interpret" laws rather than adhere to them. During Justice Kavanaugh's first term, things were even worse. He voted with liberals like Elena

Kagan more often than he voted with conservatives, and when he *did* side with conservatives in a ruling, his opinions were usually weaker than a can of his light beer. In July, he had voted to allow Cyrus Vance Jr., the district attorney in Manhattan, access to President Trump's tax records for another witch hunt. Clearly, it was time for a new strategy.

By the time I joined the White House as chief of staff in March, it seemed increasingly likely that the rest of our chances to appoint justices—thereby *actually* changing the balance of the court for the better—would come after President Trump was reelected in 2020. That's why I, and White House counsel Pat Cipollone, had already drafted a new list of potential Supreme Court nominees. These were judges who had displayed a commitment to conservative causes throughout their careers, brilliant jurists I knew we could rely on to uphold the Constitution rather than interpret it. One of the candidates, as I mentioned, was Senator Ted Cruz. Another was Senator Josh Hawley of Missouri, who's as strong a conservative voice as you could hope for. I also knew that there were several qualified judges from around the country, including Alison Jones Rushing, Barbara LaGoa, and James Ho, whom President Trump should add to the list. But there was only one person I felt conservatives could rally around, the one that President Trump wanted and had considered strongly before Kavanaugh.

Amy Coney Barrett was a brilliant jurist who had worked as a lawyer, federal judge, and a renowned professor at Notre Dame Law School. She was an expert in constitutional law and statutory interpretation. Outside of the court, she had raised a wonderful family with her husband, Jesse Barrett, a respected lawyer in his own right. Together, they had seven children, two of whom were adopted from Haiti. I knew from reading some of her rulings that her Catholic faith was immensely important to her, both inside the courtroom and out of it. In 2017, President Trump had nominated her to the US Court of Appeals for the 7th Circuit, and, as the president would later point out in his address, every law clerk from her time at the Supreme Court endorsed her and endorsed her nomination.

But the Supreme Court was a whole different ballgame.

She would not be the easiest candidate to get confirmed, especially given her convictions on issues like abortion and the right to possess firearms. But it was her commitment to her faith and to conservative ideals that bothered the Left the most. Because of that, she was the jurist that the Supreme Court—and the country—needed at the time, and she was the perfect pick for Donald Trump. Like everything else that occurred in the year 2020, I knew that one false move could knock us off course and affect the direction of the United States for decades to come. But if we pulled it off, we would be able to change the country for the better.

And if we couldn't do that from the White House, the most powerful seat in American government, I figured we might as well just pack up and go home.

———————————

After a speech that lasted close to two hours, President Trump began his customary walk away from the podium around eight forty-five, posing for pictures and tossing out MAGA hats as he went. While he walked, the song "YMCA" by the Village People blared from the speakers. We had chosen that song carefully for the ends of President Trump's rallies; he'd choreographed every step of it himself.

I watched from the television in my kitchen, waiting for the Trump Twist.

This was a slight dance move that President Trump would always perform near the end of the first chorus of "YMCA." He would stick his hands in the air, rock his hips, and then point out at the crowd with a triumphant expression on his face. Backstage at most rallies, the staff would play a game to see if they could guess exactly when he was going to deploy this signature move, which always sent the crowd into rounds of uproarious applause. It was yet another thing that you could see only if you were at a rally in person; the cameras that filmed the rallies for the news networks' live feeds never quite captured it.

After they saw the Trump Twist that night, the crowd cheered for a long time; many remained standing near their seats long after the president had left the building.

By the time he reached the steps of Air Force One, Dan Scavino had whispered a few phrases into the president's ear: *There's been some news; let's get on the plane, call the chief, and figure out a plan*. At my request, Dan had also asked that the president avoid talking to the reporters who'd gathered under the wing of the plane. We were hoping to get the news to him before the press could ask about it, and I wanted President Trump to make an official statement rather than give off-the-cuff remarks. I knew that this was a sensitive topic and that even a few wrong words could significantly decrease our chances of filling the vacancy left by Justice Ginsburg. But as any of President Trump's staff can tell you—particularly the long line of prematurely gray-haired people who've served on his communications staff—telling Donald Trump to avoid the press is like telling a lion to walk through a field of wounded gazelles without stopping for a quick snack.

For as long as I was the chief of staff, President Trump *always* stopped to chat with reporters. It didn't matter what was going on that day or what else we were late for. We called it "chopper talk," so named because it usually happened as he was boarding Marine One on the White House lawn. In my opinion, the chopper talk was the president's unique way of making sure he was always sharp and on high alert, ready to debate or deploy facts at a moment's notice. Whatever my personal feelings about this little habit were, I can't deny that it kept him on his game. Neither can any of the debate partners he had demolished over the years.

This time, thankfully, the president adopted a less combative tone. Faced with a reporter who informed him of Justice Ginsburg's death he spoke softly. "This is the first I'm hearing of it," he said. "She led an amazing life. What else can you say? Whether you agree or not, she led an amazing life." In the time it took him to leave the hangar and arrive at the wing of the plane, YMCA had given over to Elton John's "Tiny Dancer," which, accidentally or not, provided a light, contemplative backdrop to his words which were spontaneous and perfect.

When the president had boarded the plane, he called me to discuss our next steps. I told him that it was important for us to put a nominee forward immediately, meaning within the next twenty-four hours. When I mentioned that Pat and I believed Amy Coney Barrett to be the perfect nominee, the president agreed wholeheartedly. In fact, it was President Trump who had wanted to go to Justice Barrett before he nominated Brett Kavanaugh in 2018. We had passed over her then in favor of a more establishment-friendly nominee, and that decision had come back to bite us.

The president was determined not to make the same mistake twice.

Of course, that didn't go over well with everyone. Before Air Force One landed back in Washington, President Trump had taken dozens of calls from prominent Republicans, most of whom were pushing less conservative, more centrist nominees. Among them was Senate Majority Leader Mitch McConnell—a man whose support we would desperately need if we were going to get this nomination done in the Senate. Leader McConnell suggested we go with Thomas Hardiman, a respected judge on the Third Circuit, instead. President Trump pushed back, likely knowing that his legacy was at stake, and McConnell agreed to get behind Justice Barrett 100 percent by the next morning. We also heard from Leonard Leo, who, I would imagine, was a little miffed that some nobody from nowhere—aka *me*—who just so happened to be chief of staff, was muscling in on his hard-earned turf. I had been expecting this, especially given the fact that Leo had gone on the record the previous year saying that if a vacancy *did* open up before the 2020 election, President Trump should wait until after the election to fill it.

Eventually, they would all come around.

They knew that the fate of the United States was at stake.

The next day, I walked up to Pat Cipollone's office so that we could call Judge Barrett on the phone to ask if she'd even be interested in the position. When I got there, I was surprised to find that we didn't have her phone number on file. (It's amazing, even in the White House, the things you can overlook.)

Thankfully, Pat did have the cell phone number of Judge Barrett's husband, Jesse Barrett. A few months earlier, President Trump had been considering Jesse, who had served as an assistant US attorney in Indiana for thirteen years, for a potential federal judgeship. Somebody had had the good sense to keep *his* phone number around in case we needed it. Together, Pat and I called Jesse and got Judge Barrett's phone number. A few hours later, we learned that she would be happy to come in for an interview.

This was a delicate meeting to arrange. There was speculation that Judge Barrett would be the nominee, but we hadn't announced it yet. We wanted her to be able to come to the White House without the reporters from Pebble Beach—our name for the place on the White House lawn where reporters gather to take photographs and do their news reports—finding out about it. Judging by the distance, you might think you're safe from the prying eyes on Pebble Beach when you enter the White House, but you're not. Some of these high-quality lenses used by reporters are strong enough to pick up ten-point font on a piece of paper you're carrying, so identifying a possible Supreme Court nominee when she was right there in front of them would be easy.

In September, we arranged for Judge Barrett to come to the White House in secret, making sure that no one in the building would know that she was coming in other than a select few who would be present for our initial in-person meeting with her. During that meeting, we learned what Amy would soon reveal to the country during her confirmation hearings—that she had a brilliant legal mind and a sharp wit and could discuss even the most minute details of jurisprudence without recourse to notes. In all the time we spoke with her, the pad we had provided remained empty, as it would during her hearings in the Senate a month later.

That same day, we arranged for a meeting in the Oval Office between Judge Barrett and President Trump, who always insisted on a thorough interview with his nominees to the Supreme Court. Somehow, we managed to keep this meeting completely hidden from the press—and, to my genuine surprise, from virtually everyone in the West Wing who might share it with the press (which included more people than you might think). By the time the day of the meeting arrived, the only people who knew about it (other than Pat and I, who'd been coordinating the process) were Michael Haidt, who kept the president's schedule, and Molly Michael, his executive assistant, and a few people who worked with Pat and me.

In the Oval Office that morning, the mood was extremely serious. President Trump was laser focused on Judge Barrett from over the Resolute Desk, choosing to mostly listen when the meeting began. He had learned a hard lesson from the Kavanaugh nomination, and he was determined not to repeat it.

"If we nominate you," he asked, finally, "will you be true to the Constitution? You're not going to try to do all this legislating from the bench that the liberals do?"

She said that she would be true to the Constitution. From that point, there wasn't much else he could say. He knew as well as anyone in the building that the president was not supposed to ask questions about any specific rulings that a nominee might make, lest that candidate be asked about them during the confirmation hearings. After about twenty minutes, President Trump asked the real question.

"Are you prepared for the attacks?" he asked. "They are going to come at you with everything they've got. And you need to be ready. *Are* you?"

Judge Barrett didn't miss a beat.

"Yes," she said. "I am."

President Trump smiled—a more common occurrence in the Oval Office than you might imagine—and clapped his hands together. He said that barring any issues with the background checks and vetting process, she had his full support. And after the Kavanaugh nomination, there was no question about what President Trump's full support was worth. The other rumored interviews and outreach, never occurred.

All we had to do was make sure she sailed through the Senate.

For the next two weeks, Pat and I, along with an attorney from the White House counsel's office named Kate Todd, worked like mad from the White House to make the confirmation happen. Together, we made a promise to the president that Justice Barrett's confirmation would be the quickest and cleanest that had ever occurred under a Republican president. Given the partisan rancor that was sure to come with any nomination, it wasn't going to be easy. But I had a few ideas. First of all, we would do it without a "Sherpa," which is the name given to the former senator who usually walks the candidate around to the offices of sitting senators, helping to introduce them and making sure everyone gets off on the right foot. If we *did* want to use a Sherpa, the job probably would have fallen to me. But Leader McConnell had expressed reservations about me going door-to-door with the nominee, and I tended to share those reservations. I wanted to foster a sense of trust and do away with the impression that I, some schlub from the House of Representatives, was trying to strong-arm any senators into voting for my preferred nominee.

Luckily, there had never been a candidate for the Supreme Court less in need of help than Amy Coney Barrett. By all accounts, her initial interviews with senators went as well as her interview with President Trump. She impressed every-one in the room that was worth impressing, and she avoided further alienating the ones who were going to hate her anyway.

In going about this nomination in the way that we did, we followed something that I have taken to calling the Trump Rule: We didn't use a Sherpa; we didn't delay; and we allowed every senator to have each and every one of their questions answered, not waiting for the Left to fabricate evidence against our candidate. President Trump's headstrong desire to get this nomination done is what powered the whole thing, and we couldn't have done it without him. I hope that in the years to come, when President Trump—or, in the distant future, another conservative Republican—is in the White House, we'll always adhere to the Trump Rule for judicial nominations.

It all culminated on a bright, sunny Saturday at the end of September, when we arranged for a small ceremony in the Rose Garden to announce Judge Barrett's nomination. Just about every prominent conservative in the country—even some who had vehemently opposed our choice—was there to watch Presi-dent Trump announce the pick. (Sadly, when her future confir-mation ceremony arrived, Chief Justice Roberts found every excuse not to attend. This was a poor but expected commen-tary on the chief justice, who had betrayed the conservative movement as he attempted to appease elitists. Justice Clarence Thomas, fittingly, did the honors on the South Lawn.)

When President Trump spoke, he highlighted Judge Barrett's lifetime commitment to her country and the rule of law, paying special attention to her focus on family and her faith.

"Amy Coney Barrett will decide cases based on the text of the Constitution as written," he said. "As Amy has said, being a judge takes courage. You are not there to decide cases as you may prefer, you are there to do your duty and to follow the law wherever it may take you. That is exactly what Judge Barrett will do on the US Supreme Court."

In the months to come, President Trump would thank Mitch McConnell for his efforts, which allowed him to appoint not only Amy Coney Barrett, but also close to three hundred other federal judges. Leader McConnell rarely received praise for speed on anything else, especially the confirmation of other judicial nominees that seemed to be held up for no good reason other than the possibility that some senators might have their naps interrupted by the proceedings. But in this case, Leader McConnell came through with flying colors.

According to the media, Justice Barrett's nomination ceremony was the event that triggered a massive outbreak of Covid-19 in the United States government. Conveniently for them, the confirmation ceremony of a justice they hated seemed to coincide perfectly with a viral outbreak that would give them a story to run with for weeks, if not months. It was a story so perfect for them that it seemed to have been scripted by the staffs of CNN and MSNBC combined.

As always, the truth is a little more complicated.

— NINE —

Positive

BY THE MIDDLE of September, the fight against Covid-19 was raging, and no one was battling harder for the American people than President Trump. Every day, he inquired about different ways we could help the people who'd been affected by the virus.

"I know we have to wait for a vaccine," he said to me one morning after watching Dr. Fauci drone on and on about the importance of hunkering down until there was a vaccine. "I know that. But we need to give people hope, too. People need to know that if they get this thing, they're not going to die."

Whenever Dr. Fauci heard these words, he'd usually hang his head in frustration. In his opinion—which, as I'm sure you know, he never tired of sharing with the president, his staff, or just about any reporter who got within ten feet of him—the only solution for people who got sick with Covid-19 was . . . well, nothing, really. Every day, he would tell us that all we could really do was wait. We had people working on the vaccine, and now it was our job to hand out money, give vague and conflicting guidance on how to behave, and keep the economy locked down until we were sure we could get shots into the arms of a vast majority of Americans.

Needless to say, President Trump didn't take kindly to this idea. Unlike some people in the White House, he hadn't forgotten Dr. Fauci's early pronouncements about "herd immunity." President Trump knew that eventually, the virus was probably going to come for us all; it didn't matter how many masks we wore or how many hours we spent sitting inside on our couches. It was only through "herd immunity," as Dr. Fauci and his colleagues had reminded us several times, that pandemics die out.

So, we got to work. One afternoon, in the middle of the fight to get Judge Amy Coney Barrett confirmed to the Supreme Court, the president called me into the Oval Office with an idea. There was a company called Regeneron, he said, and they had just released a promising study on a therapeutic treatment. According to this study—which, amazingly, the president seemed to understand about as well as any of the so-called experts we'd been dealing with—if the Regeneron treatment was given in the very early stages of Covid-19 infection, the monoclonal antibodies contained in the drug could effectively fight off the disease. But if it was given too late, even a few *days* too late, the positive effects would not occur, and the infection would spread like normal. Now, I wasn't going to pretend I understood every word of that particular study. Neither was the president, although he knew more than I did.

But President Trump knew a guy who probably understood it *extremely* well. It turns out that Leonard Schleifer, the CEO of Regeneron, was an old golfing buddy of the president's; they used to play together all the time at Bedminster, his private club in New Jersey.

"Lenny came to me twenty years ago when we were playing golf, asking for an investment when he was starting the company," said President Trump. "I turned him down! Can you believe that? Anyway, check on the progress of this. I want an update."

With that, I had someone get me the phone number for Leonard and I gave him a call later that afternoon. I had learned during my few months as chief that when the boss said he wanted an "update," that meant that you had better have a detailed dissertation on whatever he asked you about by the next time you saw him.

If not, you were in trouble.

When I connected with Lenny, the voice on the other end couldn't have been kinder. We spoke about the study that had just come out, the progress his company had been making on therapeutics in general, and a timeline for making Regeneron's monoclonal treatment available to the American people. Before long, I was talking a mile a minute, excited by the possibility that we might be able to help some people who were in need. After all the proverbial storms we'd been dealing with for the past few months, it felt wonderful to see a little light beginning to creep in through the clouds.

A few minutes into the call, though, the president's old friend asked me to slow down. Then he went quiet for a second. I thought he might be about to address a few problems with his company's treatment, maybe tell me that it'd be another five years before we could get it out to the public.

Whatever it was, it didn't sound good.

"I'm sorry," he said. "But I couldn't help but notice that you're calling me Lenny. Nobody calls me Lenny but the president of the United States."

I laughed out loud. "I'll call you whatever you want," I said. "As long as you can help us get some aid to the American people."

When I hung up with . . . well, let's just call him Mr. Schleifer, it felt like things were beginning to look up. Considering how low we had been, it was bound to happen sooner or later. We were on the verge of nominating a third justice to the Supreme Court, and we were going to help some patients deal with serious Covid-19 symptoms. In some areas of the country, we were well on our way to opening the economy again. All of this, we believed, was going to help President Trump win the presidency in a landslide.

———————————

By the evening of September 26, when the president was scheduled to fly to a rally in Middletown, Pennsylvania, I was starting to feel secure again for the first time in a while. We had just wrapped up Amy Coney Barrett's nomination ceremony in the Rose Garden, and we knew that there would be enthusiasm at the rally for our new Supreme Court nominee. Plus, I was staying back at the office, which was going to give me an opportunity to get some work done.

Around six o'clock, the president left the White House with Dan Scavino and made his way out to Marine One. Before the Boss headed out, I pulled him aside for a few minutes to go over the progress we had made on reducing the prices of certain prescription drugs. He asked again about therapeutic treatments for Covid-19, and I promised to get another update for him by the time he returned to the White House.

I noticed that he looked a little tired, which was unusual, and said as much. I mentioned that his eyes looked slightly red around the edges, then asked if he was feeling up for the rally that night—which, I knew as soon as it left my mouth, was a pointless question. This man was getting on that helicopter if he had to take a run out of the White House, jump ten feet into the air, and then grab the chopper's metal runner like Sylvester Stallone in *Rambo*.

The president shrugged. He said he hadn't slept well, that he might be coming down with a slight cold. I was content to leave it at that. To be honest, I was a little surprised that he didn't get sick more frequently given the punishing hours he had been putting in.

When he left, I headed home, planning to work on a few lingering issues. Then my phone rang, and the number for Dr. Sean Conley, the White House physician, flashed across my screen. Before I even said hello, I sensed that the news wasn't good.

"Stop the president from leaving," he said. "He just tested positive for Covid."

In the ten months that I served as President Trump's chief of staff, I don't think I was ever out of touch with him for longer than a few minutes at a time. When your boss is the leader of the free world, a few minutes can be the end of the world, and I am not speaking figuratively when I say that. Each one of those minutes has the potential to hold what might constitute a whole year's worth of catastrophes and calamities at any other job. Markets could tumble, foreign governments could collapse, and military operations could go horribly wrong, all in the time it takes to read the newspaper or eat a sandwich.

So, I tried to be available every second of every day, which was a good thing. When I spoke with the president by phone on my way home from the office, for example, I would always have the Secret Service detail stop a few feet in front of my house until the conversation was over, knowing that I would lose the call once I drove under the thick roof of my garage. (Anyone who doesn't believe me, by the way, can ask Debbie, who used to prepare dinner for me when I told her I was leaving the office, then look out the window and see me sitting there, sometimes an hour or two later, while the food sat cooling on the counter.)

For eleven months, whenever I wasn't in the office, I kept my phone as close to full power as possible. And if I didn't have my phone, I always made sure there was someone around me with a direct line to the president. Even when Debbie and I would take long walks at night without our phones we would always have a Secret Service agent trailing a few feet behind us, just in case the world began to end and I needed to take a phone call.

There was, however, one situation that put me completely out of touch with the president, and I hated it every time. It happened whenever he would leave the White House without me, usually to attend a rally or a meeting in another state. For a short period, while President Trump was traveling on Marine One—usually heading toward Joint Base Andrews, where he would board Air Force One—I would occasionally have trouble reaching him.

It seemed only fitting, given the way our year had been going so far, that he was up in the air when I found out about his Covid-19 diagnosis.

Dr. Conley was still speaking when I cut the line and started dialing Dan Scavino. There would be plenty of time to freak out later, I figured, but right now it was time to deal with the crisis. To my shock, Dan answered the phone, and he could hear about every other word I was saying to him.

What he heard probably went something like: *"Dan . . . President. . . . positive. . . . Covid. . . . keep. . . . six feet. . . . don't let anyone near—"*

And the line went dead.

In the four minutes I had remaining until the chopper touched down, I went through my plan of action. First, I knew we had to get the president another test. Fortunately, we had stocked Air Force One with a bunch of new Binax tests by the private company Abbott. These were supposed to be quicker and far more accurate than the standard Abbott test that had given this positive reading at the White House. The preceding Friday, we had completely overhauled our testing regime so that it would use mostly these newer, more accurate tests. The test President Trump had been given before he left the White House was one of the last of the old model that we would use. I figured that if we could get him a negative reading on the Binax test, we could be reasonably sure that the White House test was a false positive.

Whatever happened, though, I wanted us to *act* as if the president was positive. That meant no handshakes at the rally, no pictures in the wings before we left, and no one—absolutely *no one*—within six feet of the president. Whatever else we had to do, I wanted him back in the White House that night for another round of testing and, heaven forbid, treatment.

With that all firmed up, I sank back in my chair and went over the schedule for the next few days. They were mostly events at the White House, so there was nothing to worry about there. But on Tuesday, President Trump was supposed to be flying to Cleveland, Ohio, for his first debate with Joe Biden. I knew that the debate commission would require each candidate to test negative for the virus within seventy-two hours of the start time, which meant he'd be able to get onstage as long as we got him tested within the next day or two. I shuddered at the thought of having to tell President Trump, a man who does *not* like to shy away from a fight, that we were going to have to cancel the debate with Joe Biden all because of an illness. For months, the president had been watching Biden on the campaign trail—or, rather, watching him cower in his basement while friendly reporters lobbed softball questions at him from their studios—and he had been itching to get onstage and fight it out on the issues.

Nothing was going to stop him from going out there.

Beyond the debate, though, lurking in a dark corner of my brain, there was another possibility to consider, though I prayed I would never have to. Any good chief of staff knows that if the president becomes incapacitated, there were a few options for us to consider. He could sign over control of the country to the vice president voluntarily, which I did *not* think was going to happen. President Trump would not willingly admit weakness, especially with the whole world watching. He knew better than anyone that giving up control of the White House during this difficult time would be the ultimate sign of weakness.

Or . . .

Before I could even imagine the other scenarios, my phone rang again. This time, it was President Trump himself. The chopper had landed, and he was calling from a secure line on Air Force One. He knew something was up, and that this particular something had to do with Covid-19, but Dan hadn't been able to give him the whole story.

"Mr. President," I said. "I've got some bad news. You've tested positive for Covid-19."

His reply—which, let's just say, rhymes with *oh spit, you've gotta be trucking lidding me*—came quickly. He seemed concerned, but more for his campaign than for his health.

This surprised me.

As most people know, President Trump is a massive germophobe. Always has been. In fact, of all the fake, exaggerated stories the press has put out about the man over the years, this is probably the only one that they've actually managed to *downplay*. I've been in meetings with President Trump where if one person coughs, even if it's into the crook of their elbow or a handkerchief, that person is made to leave the room immediately, no questions asked. During a meeting in the Oval Office, he had famously kicked Mick Mulvaney out in full view of the press for letting out an uncovered cough.

Every time we went on a trip, even in the days before anyone had even heard of Covid-19, he would go through buckets of hand sanitizer. He wouldn't use anyone else's phone, touch anyone else's food, or shake anyone else's hand without a thorough before-and-after wipe-down of his own.

Yet even *that* wasn't enough. Somehow, the most protected man in the world—a man who works a few hundred feet from his bedroom, applies hand sanitizer several times a day, and hardly sees anyone who hasn't been rigorously tested for Covid-19—had come down with a virus that we were all trying to avoid.

If that hadn't worked for the president, who'd taken sensible precautions while trying to do his job, what hope did everyone else have?

When the president had gotten his initial reaction out of the way, I told him we were going to test him again with the Binax system, and that we were hoping the first test was a false positive. He agreed and hung up the phone. After a brief but tense wait, we got the results, and the news was good. *Negative*. I could almost hear the collective *Thank God* that echoed through Air Force One's cabin from my office.

President Trump called me as soon as he got the news, which he'd taken as full permission to press on as if nothing had happened. He wasn't going to go kissing anyone (unlike Joe Biden, who was perhaps a little too fond of physical contact), but he was *definitely* going to press on with the rally. Still, I instructed everyone in his immediate circle to treat him as if he was positive. I didn't want to take any unnecessary risks, but I also didn't want to alarm the public if there was nothing to worry about—which, according to the new, much more accurate test, there was not.

The rally that night went off without a hitch. If you'd been watching the president from the crowd, you'd never have known that anything was amiss.

By Tuesday, September 29, the morning of the first debate with Joe Biden, the president was looking slightly better than he had a few days earlier, emphasis on the word *slightly*. His face, for the most part at least, had regained its usual light bronze hue, and the gravel in his voice was gone. But the dark circles under his eyes had deepened. As we walked into the venue around five o'clock in the evening, I could tell that he was moving more slowly than usual. He walked like he was carrying a little extra weight on his back.

For the past few days, we had been sticking to the schedule we'd set out earlier, mostly staying within the campus of the White House. This wasn't because we were afraid the president had Covid-19 or anything; it just so happened that there'd hardly any outside events planned. In fact, the only time the president left the grounds of the White House during those few days was Sunday morning, when he visited his golf club in Sterling, Virginia. After a quick round of golf, he went straight back to the White House, where he had organized a reception for Gold Star families in the East Room. President Trump greeted the families warmly, then sat with First Lady Melania Trump, while Steven G. Xiarhos, who lost his son Nicholas in the war in Afghanistan, gave a moving speech. The president then spoke about the value of sacrifice and the nature of grief, which brought tears to the eyes of several people in attendance.

On Monday, September 28, President Trump had met with the heads of an automotive start-up called Lordstown Motors, which had recently unveiled an electric pickup truck. He had stood with the leaders of the company, discussed the future of electronic vehicles, and took a look inside the cab of the new truck. Later that afternoon, he'd appeared for another press conference in the Rose Garden on the work we had all been doing to combat Covid-19. He spoke about declining rates of hospitalization, the rebounding economy, and—somewhat ironically, considering his circumstances—a new testing strategy we'd been working on, one that was supposed to give quicker, more accurate readings about whether someone was positive or not.

On the day of the debate, in a small room at Case West-ern Reserve University in Cleveland, we'd set up tables and chairs for a few last-minute debate prep sessions. During these sessions, Hope Hicks and Jason Miller would pepper the president with questions, and he'd give a test answer or two off the top of his head to see how they played in the room. From the early days of his first campaign, President Trump had never done debate prep in the traditional way—certainly not the way I had learned to do it when I was first running for office. He didn't plot out his answers in paragraph form, memorize figures, or choreograph cool moves that he thought the audience would like. He approached debates the way he approached most things in his life: with energy, spontaneity, and a steady determination to win. It was always a sight to behold.

These prep sessions before the debates usually served to warm up his voice and let him test a few answers to see how they came out. Usually, they didn't bear much resemblance to the answers he ended up giving onstage. This time, that would be particularly true.

A few minutes into the final prep session, around eight o'clock, I left the room to see my son, Blake, who'd just arrived at the venue with his wife, Phoebe. They were about to take their seats. When I had taken the job six months earlier, my children had one request: If they could attend one or two major events to see me, they would deal with my being more or less MIA for months at a time. When I invited them to the first debate, Blake had been honored to attend.

They remarked how different it was to be there watching the debate in person, and how many cameras there were point-ing in all directions.

"Be careful," I said to Blake. "These cameras love to catch family members making poor expressions. So, no expressions. *None.*"

He nodded.

"They're going to be trying to catch anyone affiliated with President Trump doing something bad. So be very careful about the way your face looks. You, too, Phoebe. Don't even blink."

They nodded again and wished me luck.

"Other than that, relax and enjoy yourself."

With that, I headed back inside and spoke briefly with President Trump. He seemed ready for anything, almost vibrating with energy. I braced myself.

Around eight thirty, Blake and Phoebe took their seats, along with the rest of the crowd. They were right next to each other, but most people were not. Because of the lingering threat of Covid-19 infection, the producers of the event had decided to have an audience of only about one hundred, placing all of the seats six feet apart. For President Trump, this was a little strange. It meant that he'd have to go without the usual cheers and hollers that accompanied some of his best lines during a normal debate. For Joe Biden, who'd gotten used to the sound of crickets during his campaign, I don't imagine it was all that different. When Chris Wallace of Fox News, who'd be our moderator for the evening, introduced the candidates, I found the relative silence from the audience slightly unnerving.

Of course, that would be the least of my problems that evening.

For the most part, the debate was a poor performance by both candidates, especially Joe Biden. He flip-flopped on positions,

fumbled for words, and trotted out the same boring policy positions he'd been pushing for years. But President Trump did not
put his best foot forward, either. Rather than allowing Biden to
stumble his way through the debate in front of a live audience,
displaying his shocking inability to form a thought or finish a
sentence, the president interrupted him constantly. Every time
Sleepy Joe was on the verge of embarrassing himself or trailing off like a confused old man, the president came at him with
everything he had. It was like watching Muhammad Ali step
into the ring with an eighty-year-old man.

Of course, some people didn't mind the combative approach.
In the aftermath of the debate, we got a few great reviews. Sean
Hannity got on television and congratulated President Trump
for "steamrolling" Joe Biden. The response from conservatives on
Twitter—back in the days when Twitter at least tried to hide their
open contempt for pro-Trump content—was similarly positive.

Opinions aside, when you're dealing with Joe Biden, as I
would later tell the president, the right course of action isn't
to always attack and try to make him look stupid; that'll only
make people feel sorry for him. The right way to handle him is
to sit back, contradict him, and let him do the work for you. If
you've caught any of his press conferences recently, you'll know
exactly what I'm talking about.

After the debate, I spoke with President Trump about how
horribly Chris Wallace had performed as a moderator. We
believed that this, and not either candidate's performance, would
be the story of the night. Other than that, he didn't seem to want
to talk much about what he had said or how he'd said it.

Looking back, I knew something was off about the president that evening. Perhaps his overly combative approach to
Joe Biden was a result of how sluggish and off his game he

was feeling. Of course, it's also possible that he was releasing a whole lot of pent-up aggression at the thought of what Biden might someday do to the country if he ever managed to cheat his way into the office. Given the events of the last few months, I think he was probably way ahead of the curve on that.

Either way, we'll probably never know whether President Trump was positive that evening. We do know, however, that the virus eventually caught up to him, hitting us hard and making my worst fears—the ones I had managed to push away when the president's first positive test had come in—come shockingly, terribly alive.

———————————

Hope Hicks was first.

It was the following Thursday morning in the White House, and I had received yet another positive test result, this one for Hope. Once again, I was virtually alone in the West Wing. President Trump, who'd held a rally the night before in Duluth, Minnesota, was on his way to a fundraiser in Bedminster, New Jersey, which would be held at his private golf club. Hope was quarantining. I had gotten reports that others had tested positive for the virus. Out of precaution, Ivanka and Jared had canceled their trip to Bedminster. So had Dan Scavino, Nick Luna, assistant to the president, and Kayleigh McEnany. All of these people had come into contact with Hope and a few other people, and we wanted to behave out of an abundance of caution. We were arranging for planes and cars to get them all home safely.

My thoughts, as usual, turned to the president. The night before, he had spoken for just over forty-five minutes. For him, that's a short span of time. As anyone who's ever attended a

Trump rally knows, it's not uncommon for his off-the-cuff, freewheeling speeches to go well beyond the ninety-minute mark. Personally, I had never seen one of his rally addresses conclude before the one-hour mark. Watching from the wings, I was concerned that the president's cold might be something worse. He was still moving slowly, and his eyes were bloodshot. Even during his choreographed walk off the stage, he didn't look his best.

Earlier that afternoon, during a private fundraiser at the home of a local CEO, Hope had let me know that she wasn't feeling very well, either. She had a sore throat, and she'd begun feeling fatigued. This was extremely out of the ordinary. Typically, Hope was willing to keep up with the president's crazy pace and then some. She had followed him step for step, rally for rally, and flight for flight during the 2016 campaign. That persistence is how she'd become such a valued asset to the Trump team. The fact that she was feeling tired enough to say something was deeply concerning to me.

She remained on Air Force One during the rally, then isolated herself in the back of the plane on the way back to Washington. We soon learned that she was positive. As I sat with that information, I could feel my head spinning with questions. Who, for instance, had infected Hope, and where was that person now? How many other staffers in the West Wing were going to come down with the virus? Was I one of them? And how likely was it that President Trump, who'd shown an uncharacteristic level of fatigue over the past few days, traveled all over the country, and already registered what we believed to be a false positive on Sunday, had managed once again to evade infection?

The answer to the last question, I decided, was *not very likely*. Beyond the feeling in my gut that something was wrong with President Trump, I considered all the people he'd come into contact with and decided that he would probably come down with Covid-19. Even the debate prep sessions alone—where Hope, Chris Christie, and Jared Kushner had all come within a few feet of him—would have been enough to infect him. I decided that we should act from now on as if he was positive, allowing him to finish the event only if everyone in the room stayed far away from him. I conveyed these instructions to Tony Ornato, and the president finished the event after a short speech to donors.

Later, some of these donors would remark that he did not look like he was feeling his best during that speech. But thankfully, we have not been able to trace a single positive case of Covid-19 to that fundraiser, other than that of the president himself. The same goes for the reception he held for Gold Star families in the East Room earlier that week.

Back in the White House, however, we weren't in the clear. Later that afternoon, I learned that Melania Trump had tested positive for the virus, and that she was isolating in the Residence. Surely, I thought, if the First Lady had come down with Covid-19, President Trump couldn't have escaped it. I wondered for a moment how the virus could have broken our bubble, given the strict testing protocols and tight security we had set up to protect against it. Whenever someone was going to meet with the president, they reported to the Eisenhower Building thirty minutes prior to their appointment for a test from the Navy medical team, which had a permanent location in the building. Staff members did the same thing. Anyone who came down with a positive test had to report it to the White House physician, and anyone who was scheduled to meet with the president needed to test negative before they did so. Anyone who saw the president on a regular basis, myself included, got a test every morning.

The media would blame it all on an Amy Coney Barrett "super spreader" event, but our contact tracing, that was conducted later, would indicate that the virus entered the White House from three different sources.

But I didn't have much time to wonder. If the president was coming down with Covid-19—and by this point, I was all but certain that he was—we had to make sure that he could recover quickly and fully.

I found it interesting that what President Trump had been saying all along really was true. No matter what we did or how many precautions we took, we were all at risk for the virus. Even the most guarded man in the world had managed to come down with it. What mattered was that we gave people a fighting chance to get better when they got it. What mattered, according to President Trump, was that we gave people hope.

With that, I thought of my old friend Lenny from Regeneron and began dialing the phone.

— TEN —

Emergency Use

"I NEED YOUR HELP," I said.

It was late in the afternoon, and President Trump was still about ninety minutes from the White House. I had managed to get Leonard Schleifer on the phone after a few rings, which tends to happen when you're calling from a West Wing phone number. I wanted to keep my suspicions about the president's health quiet, so I told him we were looking for a few doses of Regeneron to use as a prophylactic measure, but I didn't say for whom. I did tell him that Hope Hicks and the First Lady had tested positive for the virus, and that others in the West Wing were at risk. At the moment, though, I said we needed four doses, and we needed them *now*. I also asked him to speak candidly with me for a moment about the real efficacy of his drug; if there was something better out there—no matter what it was or where it came from—I wanted to know.

"What would you do," I asked him, pleading, "if it was your family?"

For a moment, Len stopped being the head of a cutting-edge biotechnology company and became a friend, both to me and to the president. He explained why his drug, which was supposed to have the same effects as a similar drug introduced by Eli Lilly earlier in the year, was superior. He said that if it were him and his family who were at risk, he would administer the drug without thinking twice. The Regeneron treatment, according to Len, looked at the monoclonal treatment from two different aspects, while the Eli Lilly drug used only one. He predicted that eventually Eli Lilly would have to change their treatment so that it was more like Regeneron's. A few months later, he would turn out to be correct.

Again, I wasn't going to pretend that I had any real idea what he was talking about at the time. For all I knew, Len could have been describing the inside of my blender. What I did know was that we were in trouble, and the word of a trusted friend of the president—who, as it happened, was also one of the sharpest biotech CEOs in the country—was good enough for me.

I asked Len if we could have four doses sent by plane, and in secret, to the White House. I impressed upon him once more that secrecy was of the utmost importance, and he agreed. He said he would arrange for a jet to fly the doses from an airport near their manufacturing plant in New York to Reagan National Airport in Washington, DC. The Regeneron would arrive in a matter of hours. When it did, the cowboy pilot got out in his boots and jeans, with a fresh coffee stain on his shirt. But he had our precious cargo.

Now all I had to do was get permission from the FDA to use it.

———————

Now, that might not sound like the hardest thing in the world. You might assume that when multiple people around the leader of the free world have come down with a virus, the White House chief of staff won't have too much trouble getting an emergency use treatment for that virus—a treatment, by the way, that had been scientifically proven to work in multiple clinical trials. Anyone who thinks that, though, probably hasn't spent much time around the men and women who work in the federal agencies of the United States government.

Around town, there's an old joke about the two speeds at which things get done in government: "slow" and "never." I thought that was fairly humorous when I worked in the House of Representatives, but I didn't realize quite how true it was until I came to work in the West Wing during a pandemic. Time and time again, I would see people drop the ball on direct orders that President Trump had given. I watched government bureaucrats slow-roll things they didn't want to see enacted. I was forced repeatedly to check the status of different potential treatments for Covid-19. The same problems that had plagued the rollout of Covid-19 tests in January and February were now plaguing the development of key therapeutics for the same virus. If it hadn't been for the president's constant insistence that we monitor our progress on therapeutics, I don't know that we would have nearly as many today as we do.

Every time a company wants to bypass the normal approval process, it needs to go through what we call emergency use authorization, which is granted by the Food and Drug Administration. Typically, this takes months, and it happens in stages. First, the company submits details about its treatment and data about how its trials were run. Then, they wait for that paperwork to move around the FDA, which can take a long time. On Thursday, October 1, 2020, the Regeneron treatment that I had requested for President Trump had not yet been granted emergency use authorization.

As soon as I got off the phone with Len, he began getting the paperwork together that would allow us to expedite the FDA's process. Some of it had already been submitted. He assured me that the clinical trials had been conducted to the satisfaction of everyone at the company, and that the drug was about as safe as you could hope for. There was only a sliver of red tape left to cut. I wasn't exactly thrilled at the prospect of having the first patient for the drug, beyond the trials, be the president of the United States, but at this point, I didn't think we had much choice.

That evening, with President Trump just a few minutes away from the White House lawn in Marine One, I called Tony Ornato into my office. I needed him to get special authorization to land a small jet at Reagan National Airport a few miles from the White House, making sure to mention the importance of being confidential. I had been working with Tony for seven months now, and I trusted him implicitly. I was confident that he could carry out the operation, along with Beau Harrison, without having details of it leak out. If word got out too early that the president was being treated with an emergency drug, the effects on the economy could be disastrous.

"This is extremely important," I said. "No one can know."

Tony left the office and began working to get clearance. From there, I asked Pat Philbin, a White House attorney, and Pat Cipollone to meet me in the office that they shared upstairs, which was a SCIF, short for "sensitive compartmented information facility." Inside the SCIF we could be reasonably sure—or, as sure as it's possible to be in this age of mass global surveillance—that our conversations couldn't be tapped, recorded, or listened to by bad actors. There were only a few staffers remaining in the building at that hour. For all they knew, we could have been engaged in an operation to take down a foreign terrorist rather than trying to get the president some medication.

The first call we made was to Stephen Hahn, the commissioner of the FDA. During the early months of the Covid-19 crisis, Stephen had been quite accommodating. Then the National Institutes of Health, led by Dr. Fauci, had begun speaking with the press about how the FDA was moving "too fast" on getting Covid-19 drugs approved. The NIH said that the FDA should not have approved certain treatments such as convalescent plasma due to a minuscule amount of risk. After that, fear set in and Stephen Hahn had transitioned into a full-blown bureaucrat, determined to slow things down rather than to help people, which should have been his top priority.

He certainly had fallen off Trump Time, which, in this White House, was deadly.

With Pat and Pat listening in, I told Stephen the same thing I had told Len: Someone close to President Trump and the First Lady has come down with Covid-19, and we need to authorize the emergency or compassionate use of four doses of Regeneron. This was of national importance, I said, and it needed to happen tonight.

Stephen said he would see what he could do. This request, I could tell, was beginning to move at the speed of "slow."

That wasn't good, but it was better than nothing. I was intent on making sure that we made it move much faster than that.

Marine One touched down on the White House lawn, and President Trump disembarked without saying a word to the press.

If there was ever a sign that he wasn't feeling well, *that* was it.

We administered a rapid test as soon as he entered the building, which is meant to give a quick though not necessarily accurate result within about fifteen minutes. Almost immediately, we received the news that he was positive. He wondered whether it might be another false positive. He was eager to keep up the campaign schedule and afraid of what would happen with the election if it was revealed that he was sick.

Looking at the president, I could tell that wasn't likely. Even compared to the run-down way he'd been looking for the past few days, he was in rough shape. He was pale, exhausted, and nearly asleep on his feet. Even he was willing to admit that he wasn't feeling great, which was unusual, given that he didn't like to talk very much about his own condition.

"I've lost so much strength," he said, shaking his arm. "The muscles are just not responding."

As soon as we got the initial positive result from the rapid test, the White House doctors did another, more extensive exam on the president—what I like to call the "Q-tips-to-the-brain" test, known formally as the PCR test. They stuck a long swab up his nose and into his sinus cavity to collect a sample, put that sample in a small bag, and sent it via medical courier to Walter Reed Medical Center for a close evaluation. In about one hour, we would know for sure that test was Covid-19 positive.

But I didn't want to waste a second.

Around nine o'clock, I went back upstairs to their office, where Pat and Pat were waiting with bad news. They had heard from several people at the FDA that the agency was not willing to grant emergency use authorization for Regeneron—at least not if it was for "people close to the president," as I had said it was. Although it was on the "fast track" to being approved for emergency use, the FDA was still asking for more paperwork, more details, and more time, none of which we had. If this drug was going to be of any use to us, it was going to need to happen tonight.

I got on the phone.

"Stephen," I said. "This is of national importance. You are going to issue the emergency use authorization *now*." I took a deep breath before speaking again: "It's for the president of the United States."

There was a pause on the other end of the line.

Finally, Stephen said they could make it happen.

Upstairs in the residence, President Trump was doing a phone interview with Sean Hannity. For years, Hannity had been a personal friend to the president. He was an early supporter when he announced his run. All throughout the Russia hoax, the impeachment, and the thousands of daily attacks from the press, Hannity had continued to support the president, trying to bring the American people the truth and cut through the spin narrative of the mainstream media. I was glad (relatively speaking) that if the news had to break, it would happen during an interview with someone who had the best interests of the president, and the people of the United States, at heart.

"You know, it's very hard," he said, addressing an audience of somewhere between 3 and 5 million people. "When you're with soldiers, when you're with airmen, when you're with the Marines, and the police officers—I'm with them so much. And when they come over to you, it's very hard to say, 'Stay back, stay back.' It's a tough kind of situation. It's a terrible thing. So, I just went for a test, and we will see what happens."

It didn't take long for Twitter to light up with expressions of joy from the left. As I had expected, people were saying that the president had gotten just what he deserved for not wearing a mask, that he was going to die, that the world was going to be a better place without him. If you ever need proof that there is evil in this world look at the Twitter feed of a Trump-hating liberal.

At 10:35 p.m., shortly after President Trump had finished his interview with Hannity, our approval from the FDA arrived—which was good news, considering that the four doses we'd ordered had just been brought into the Residence from Reagan Airport, and we were going to use them no matter what.

Then, like clockwork, the news we had all been dreading came back from Walter Reed: They had finished the long test, analyzed the sample, and declared that President Trump was, beyond a shadow of a doubt, positive for Covid-19. Before Dr. Conley could even finish reading the results, we were working with him to set up an IV system to administer Regeneron to the president. We'd rigged the four-poster bed in the president's room so that he could recline and take the drug while he was still alert and giving orders.

By this point, Dr. Conley was working with a team of medical experts. While some of them were setting up the makeshift hospital bed in the Residence, Dr. Conley told me something that he found strange. He said that although the virus was definitely inside the president's body, there were no natural antibodies fighting the disease. Typically, he said, when a person has a case of Covid-19 that's advanced enough to result in a positive PCR test, you would expect a certain level of antibodies for the disease present. For President Trump, that number was zero. This meant one of two things, he said: Either we had caught this case of Covid-19 almost *immediately* after infection, or something was off with the president's immune system, and this dose of Regeneron—which takes over for the immune system and fights the drug with artificial antibodies—was going to save the president's life.

I was downstairs in my office when the doctors began administering the Regeneron treatment. It was around eleven o'clock, and news of the president's health had spread all over the world. I was getting calls from hundreds of people in government, the media, and corporate America. They were worried about the global economy, worried about what the markets were going to do in the morning, and—it shocks me now even to write it—worried that the president of the United States might go to sleep tonight and not wake up.

For a moment, I considered the same thing. But I shook it off. I could not imagine, even given the president's age and relative health risk, that this virus was going to take him down. There was something about his personality, his tenacity, and his general strength of character that made it seem incredibly unlikely.

I stayed there until around three o'clock in the morning, making the long walk from the West Wing to the Residence probably twenty times to check on the president's progress.

Most of the time, I walked down the colonnade that connects the Oval Office to the Residence—the same one President Trump took when he had come to work that morning.

Walking back from the president's bedroom around two a.m., I saw the lights of the Oval Office shining. Not for the first time, I thought of the awesome privilege of working here. I had joined government to change people's lives, and I was working for a president who was willing to fight every day to do that—at the expense of his wealth, his time, and, as we had just found out, his own health. I thought it was fitting, too, that the drug that ended up saving President Trump's life was the exact one that he had asked me to make available for the American people a few days earlier. The same drug he had been fighting to get authorized for the American people, people who didn't have a chief of staff who could call and put pressure on the FDA to get a drug approved for them. That, I thought, was who this man was in a nutshell. If he thought there was even a small chance of curing someone of this disease, which had separated hundreds of thousands of people from their loved ones and ravaged the economy he had worked so hard to build, he was going to do it. It didn't matter what Dr. Fauci, Dr. Birx, or anyone else said to him.

That night, the hours dragged on like days. I got briefings from the White House doctors every few minutes, but nothing much changed. The president was stable, sleeping, and getting the drug cocktail we'd secured for him.

By the next morning, there was a small crowd of reporters at the sticks—our name for the area outside the White House where the press hangs out, not far from "Pebble Beach"— waiting for an update. I spoke with Dr. Conley, who assured me that the president's prognosis was good, and then walked outside to brief the press. They began yelling questions at me before I could even say hello—none of which were about how the president was feeling. I started by telling them that unemployment was once again down below 8 percent, and that the economy was continuing its V-shaped recovery (not that I actually thought that was going to make it into the stories they were writing that morning). From there, I let them know everything that I knew: The president was in good spirits, giving orders, and under the close watch of some of the best doctors in the country.

Then the questions about who else might have the virus started coming, and they wouldn't stop for another few months. When CNN's Jim Acosta asked if we would be taking any additional protocols in the White House, I let him know that we were going to try to find a cure for this disease, not run from it.

"What you have" I said, "is a virus that is contagious, that certainly continues to be, regardless of whatever protocol we have, that it has the ability to affect everybody. As you know, the president, we keep a pretty wide circle. All of you that have interacted with him know that and so even with that wide circle around the president, we find that he's having to deal with this, like so many millions of other Americans and people around the world have had to do. I can tell you that what we're doing is focusing on the therapeutics, the vaccines, and that doesn't change."

———————————

That morning, Dr. Conley pulled me aside and delivered some bad news. Although the president's condition had improved slightly overnight, his oxygen levels had now dipped down to about 86 percent and could be trending lower, a dangerously low level for someone his age. By this point, Dr. Conley was working with doctors from Walter Reed and Johns Hopkins, not wanting to manage the situation alone. They had decided to put the president on oxygen in the Residence and hope for the best.

"That'll be fine for now," he said. "But we need to get him to Walter Reed soon, in case he takes a turn for the worse. We don't have the resources to do it here."

As soon as I heard the words, I knew that President Trump wasn't going to like it. From the start of the Covid-19 pandemic, when the scientists and public health officials in the White House were talking about the coronavirus like some kind of new Black Plague, telling us that we needed to lock down and cower in fear from it, President Trump had taken a different approach. From his first speeches on the topic, he sought to project an air of strength. He wanted people to know that although this virus might be bad, it was nothing that the American people couldn't handle. I worried that the notion of him going to the hospital, in his mind, would seem like an act of capitulation to an invisible enemy, more a sign of weakness than a necessary precaution.

I was right.

When I walked into the Residence a few hours later, president Trump was sitting up in bed in his T-shirt, and it didn't look like he was going anywhere. He wasn't moving around or wearing a suit, of course, but other than that, he acted like it was just any other day. He made phone calls, read intelligence reports, and inquired after the status of several Covid-19 initiatives. It was the first time I had seen him in anything other than a golf shirt or a suit jacket.

If it hadn't been for the oxygen tank by his side, I might have forgotten he was sick at all.

But I remembered what Dr. Conley had said. We were in trouble, and the president needed to get to the hospital. All I had to do was look at the man to know Dr. Conley was correct. The red streaks in the president's eyes hadn't gone away, and his hair was a mess from the hours he'd spent getting Regeneron in bed. Looking at him in those few minutes, I realized that the day before was the first time I had ever seen the president in bed. In fact, until then, I wasn't 100 percent sure that the president even went to bed. I wouldn't have been surprised to learn that he slept for a few minutes a night behind his desk, suited up and ready for action. That certainly would have explained how he managed to get so much done before I even walked through the door in the morning.

After I answered a few general questions about operations and national security, I broached the subject of going to Walter Reed. I tried to be as delicate as possible.

"Mr. President," I said. "I've spoken with your doctors, and we need to get you to Walter Reed, where you can get better care."

"I'm going to be fine."

"I know you're going to be fine. But we need you to be in an environment where you can get the best care possible."

A moment of silence passed between us.

"Mr. President," I said, "it's better that you walk out of here today under your own strength, your own power, than for me to have to carry you out on a gurney in two days. The message that it would send to the American people would not be good. You can walk out today, and we'll call it a precautionary measure, and—"

"Fine," he said.

"I think it's just better that you—"

"I said fine."

And that was that.

———————————

We waited downstairs for the president in the Diplomatic Room of the East Wing. If he was going to the hospital, I was going with him. Marine One sat out on the lawn, motors running, ready for the flight to Walter Reed.

He emerged wearing a suit and a blue tie. He'd showered and put himself together for the press, who'd already begun gathering a few feet from the helicopter. He wore a black overcoat, which looked strangely heavy on him, and carried a briefcase in his right hand. Planning to work, he had stuffed it full of newspaper clippings, briefing memos, and files of reports from various agencies. I would imagine it weighed about ten pounds given all the material inside. Today, though, the weight was too much for him.

Just before he stepped out the door, President Trump paused for a moment, closed his eyes, and placed the briefcase on the floor. He looked at me, almost surprised that he'd had to put it down.

"I'm sorry," he said. "I-I just can't carry that out there."

Then he walked to the door and started across the lawn toward Marine One, waving for the few dozen photographers who'd gathered along the path. Back inside, we stood in a half circle around the briefcase. I looked at Dan Scavino, then at the briefcase, then back at Dan.

We stared at each other in silence for a moment, wondering who was going to pick up the possibly contaminated briefcase. Although I'm sure Dan would have if I had hesitated for a second longer, I ended up being the one to squirt on some hand sanitizer, bend down, and grab it. As I walked with President Trump toward Marine One, he looked down at the briefcase in my hand, seemingly impressed.

"I *knew* you were my guy," he said.

ELEVEN

Walter Reed

IT WAS NEARLY dusk when Marine One landed on a small field beside Walter Reed Hospital in Bethesda, Maryland. We were about six miles from the White House, and the ride had taken us only ten minutes. I sat near the back of the helicopter, ignoring the few dozen phone calls that came in during the short ride to the hospital complex. From my window, I could see a small group of photographers who'd gathered across the street from where we were going to land. They carried video cameras, microphones, and wide-angle lenses, obviously hoping that they'd be able to get President Trump to stop for a few minutes of his usual chopper talk.

But it wasn't going to happen that day.

As soon as we touched the grass, we were followed by five modified Chevy Suburbans, all traveling in a line. They parked in a tight formation around Marine One to block out prying eyes and potential danger. If President Trump had been feeling well that day—even if he had been feeling only slightly under the weather—he might have taken a few moments on his way to the car to speak with reporters, or maybe to give a quick wave to show that he was in good spirits. Today, however, he walked straight into the back of one of the cars and got inside.

Not that it would have been bad to have him talk to the press that day. During the short trip to Walter Reed, President Trump had managed to project an air of strength, and he kept it up as he walked slowly down the steps of the chopper. Considering all that had transpired over the past few days, I found this impressive—inspiring, even. I had seen him before he left the White House. I knew how weak he must have been feeling. But he never let it show. During those harrowing hours, he was aware more than ever that every move he made would serve as an indication of strength—not only the strength of a president, but the strength of a nation. He was determined, as always, to send a message to the world that the United States of America would not back down, give up, or cower in fear. If that meant walking over broken glass with a straight face, that's what he was going to do.

Before we left, he had vowed that no matter what he did during the next few days, he was going to do it on his feet with his head up. The nation, and the world, had come to expect nothing less from him.

As soon as Bobby, the president's lead Secret Service agent, got him safely into the car, they took off for a small building on Walter Reed's campus known as Ward 71, speeding past the gathering crowd of photographers and newscasters. I followed in one of the other cars, still carrying his briefcase and the few files that I had been able to grab from my office before we took off. From the window of the car, I could see another crowd beginning to gather near the gates of the hospital, but this one wasn't carrying cameras or AV equipment. A few of them had signs to show their support; others had brought flowers from local grocery stores. For the most part, they carried nothing. They seemed comforted just to be around one another, not unlike the dozens of crowds I had seen over the years at Trump rallies and campaign events. They spoke to one another, prayed together, and offered one another solace in what I'm sure was a trying time for all of them.

I remembered that not all of them had gotten to see what I had seen over the past few days. They didn't know—none of us could know—that the president was going to recover. The sight of this crowd, which was growing by the minute, filled me with gratitude. For a moment, I wished I could go out and join them.

We arrived at the back door of Ward 71 around seven o'clock, just as the sun was beginning to set. The stock market had closed low that day, and questions about the president's condition were flooding the White House switchboard. For now, someone else would handle them. We were focused on getting the president healthy.

Upstairs in the hospital's presidential suite, the tests began before we even got through the door. Doctors took the president's pulse, drew his blood, and arranged for chest X-rays to check the status of his lungs. We had learned during the past year that when Covid-19 gets serious, it's usually the lungs that were in danger first; their condition is what determines whether patients will or will not need to be intubated. Doctors then led the president to a large bedroom at the end of a hall-way, which didn't look all that different from his room at the White House. There was a bed, a writing desk, and a private bathroom. This is where President Trump, ever mindful of not seeming "too sick," would end up spending the majority of his stay. Across the hall, there was another bedroom, outfitted with more traditional intensive care equipment. This one was a conglomeration of monitors, wires, and blinking lights, more like something from a state-of-the-art spaceship than a hospital room. President Trump went into this room for routine tests, but he never spent any extended periods of time there. Doing so, in his mind, would constitute an act of capitulation to the virus, and he wasn't going to do that.

The rest of the six-room suite was taken up by sitting rooms, a few offices for the president's doctors, and a conference room with secure video capabilities that the president would use to talk with his national security advisors. When we arrived, I put my papers and the president's briefcase in one of these offices, then made some calls to the White House to make sure everything was still functioning. I also asked for an update from one of the president's doctors. The Regeneron treatment we'd given him was working, they said, but his oxygen levels were still dangerously low. Judging by the details he gave me, it was clear that the staff at Walter Reed was prepared for a long stay—weeks, maybe longer. I wasn't happy to hear that, but I also knew it probably wasn't going to happen. If the president had his way, we would be up and out the door in a day or so.

When I left President Trump, he was sitting in a chair following the orders of his doctors. I told him that he should focus only on getting well and keeping his strength up; the routine business was in my hands for the night. With that, I walked back to my new hospital office and got to work.

I took a moment to marvel at the team around me—the technology, the staff, and the military precision of the whole operation. Technically, this six-room suite was part of the White House, or at least it was run by the same team as the White House. Around 360 days of the year, it sits completely empty, and the staff of Walter Reed hopes they'll never have to turn the lights on. When they *do* have to, it's all hands on deck. This is the same facility where Ronald Reagan had cancer surgery in 1985, where Betty Ford underwent a double mastectomy (a rare procedure at that time) in 1974, and where Lyndon Johnson had gall bladder surgery in 1965. Interestingly enough, after Johnson's surgery was complete and reporters started printing baseless conspiracy theories about why the president had *actually* gone to the hospital—saying, for instance, that he actually had some rare cancer and that he was trying to hide it—he invited them into the room so he could show off his scar. I had a short laugh thinking about President Trump doing the same thing, which I didn't think was likely. I also realized just how long Fake News had been plaguing the American government. But only President Trump had had the good sense to give it a nickname that we still use today.

We'd certainly had our share of experience with the press and their penchant for plucking fake stories out of thin air. Almost exactly one year earlier, in November 2019, when President Trump had gone to Walter Reed for a routine check-up, the press had put their tinfoil hats on extra tight, trying to guess what the president was *really* doing in there, just like they'd done with Lyndon Johnson so many years earlier. This time, their guesses had ranged from the pedestrian to the patently absurd. Some of these reporters, without the slightest bit of evidence, suggested that he was being taken in for a heart condition; others said it was an emergency surgery to repair something that was wrong with his brain. But it simply wasn't true. None of it was. Each of these theories, I am happy to report, is 100 percent certified nonsense. He went in to have a routine checkup, just as you or I would do, and he was back within a few hours.

I did wonder, though: If reporters could spin those ridiculous stories out of a routine checkup, what were they going to do with this, a genuine medical crisis? When it came to President Trump, there seemed to be no end to the lies and distortions that the Fake News could cook up. Every time we released the results of a physical, for instance, there seemed to be three or four days of back-and-forth about whether he did, in fact, weigh what the doctors said he did. The same reporters who used to work on real Woodward-and-Bernstein-style stories about theft, corruption, and electoral misconduct were now more likely to sit on Twitter, make up stories, and allow the Trump-hating online community to spread those stories far and wide. It might not have been a bad business model for them, but it was detrimental for the country.

Whatever happened, I knew that the group of reporters outside would someday want to document every moment that the president spent in Walter Reed; they would inquire about every test he took, every phone call he made, and every second he spent unable to make decisions (which, I am happy to report, didn't happen unless he was asleep). So, we were extremely careful not to have any discussions about the presidential line of succession or who would take over if President Trump were incapacitated. In fact, I kept my contact with the White House to a minimum, wanting to focus most of my energy on making sure that we got the president healthy and back to work. The fewer phone calls we made, the fewer opportunities there would be for reporters to infer wacky and wildly untrue things about them.

Still, I could almost see the conspiracy-theory headlines before they were printed. Would *The New York Times* suggest that President Trump was in a coma and someone else—Jared Kushner, Mike Pence, maybe even *I*—was running the country? Would someone report that he'd been replaced by a body double? That he was faking Covid-19 so he could finally have a secret place to meet with Vladimir Putin and collude to conquer the world? I had no idea. What I *did* know was that President Trump wasn't going to leave Walter Reed until he could do so on his own strength, fully cured of Covid-19 and ready to keep fighting for the American people.

I was the only one who stayed with the President those first nights. Doctors and Secret Service agents were in the long halls outside of his room. Around nine o'clock, when the tests were done and the President was settled, he called me into his room. I had turned the staff doctor's office into a makeshift office of my own. At the President's request, I had been working all evening on getting funding to hospitals that were running out of money, and he had been checking in on my progress from his bedroom. When I walked in, I found him sitting up watching Sean Hannity's show on Fox News.

For a few minutes, Hannity had been broadcasting a livestream of the crowd outside Walter Reed. It was ten times the size of the one I had seen on the way in. I could see people who looked like they had come from all over the region to show their support for the president. Again, it was not unlike a Trump rally, all these different people suddenly united by their love for the president and their country. There were burly bikers and groups of tough-looking guys standing right next to little old ladies and children, all facing the direction of the president's window. If he could have, I knew that President Trump would have walked right out there and thanked each one of them personally. But he couldn't.

Still, President Trump couldn't stand to do nothing.

"This is amazing," he said. "All these people who came out to show their support. They left their homes. We need to do something for them."

I remembered that earlier in the afternoon, just after we'd arrived, Cassidy Hutchinson, my White House assistant, had dropped off a few boxes of candies and gifts with the presidential seal on them. These weren't much, just cardboard boxes that said "President Donald Trump" with an eagle and a presidential seal, but they were valued by supporters. It was the best we could do on short notice. Most of the time, we kept these gifts in a small room off the Oval Office—what we jokingly referred to as the "Monica Lewinsky Room," for reasons we probably don't need to go into here—and handed them out to people who visited the White House. We had brought them to Walter Reed so we could give them to the doctors and nurses, who were working around the clock to make sure President Trump was well cared for.

It was always important to President Trump that when people visited the White House, whether they were in the building for a tense meeting on budget reconciliation or a quick tour with their families, they had the best experience possible. He made sure that no one ever left the Oval Office without being offered some small token to remember their time in the White House. I should also note, for all the corruption-sniffing reporters out there, that the taxpayers didn't fund these little gifts at all. The Republican National Committee did, and the

DNC is likely doing something similar (though probably not as nice) for the Biden White House.

I let President Trump know about the gifts, then told him I'd be happy to take them out to the crowd with a message from him.

He told me exactly what to say.

On the brief drive out to the front gates of Walter Reed, which took me past the wide lawns and old redbrick buildings of the hospital's campus, I leaned back in my seat and thought again about the recent twists and turns of my life. In a million years, I couldn't have imagined that I would be here, riding out to express a message on behalf of the president of the United States. But here I was, getting ready to do it. Looking around the car, at the Secret Service agent who was driving and the black leather seats, I couldn't help but think of the first time I had ever been invited to take a ride with President Trump.

It was March 2017, and I had just finished a speech at the Omni Shoreham Hotel in Washington, DC, to introduce President Trump, who'd been in office for only three months at the time. I was a congressman from North Carolina, and I had gotten to know the president the year before on the campaign trail with him. To be honest, he had always been a little fonder of my wife, Debbie. Between the bus tour she'd organized on his behalf during the campaign and the unwavering support she'd shown for him, he knew he could always count on her.

That day I spoke in front of a crowd in the thousands. They weren't there for me, but for the man I was going to introduce. It was my job to warm up the audience for President

Trump—not that he needed it—and welcome him to FRC's Values Voter Summit. I planned on telling a few stories that I had used on the stump before, introducing the president, and then stepping offstage before the applause for him made me go deaf. It was supposed to take about ten minutes in total. Before the speech began, they had warned me that if the president was late, I might have to stretch the stories out to fill more time. They also let me know that if he was early, I would have to wrap the stories up pretty quickly and skip right to the introduction portion. I had been around the block a time or two when it came to speaking on the fly, so I figured I would be able to handle a ten minute speech, plus or minus ten minutes.

About eight minutes into my speech, though, just as the little red clock on the stage in front of me was heading for zero, it suddenly flashed back up to 8:00. I had just come to the end of my last story, and I was running out of gas. But I figured the president was tied up with some official business and couldn't get out onstage. So, I "wound 'er back up" and filled out the story I had been telling. I felt like a student trying to write a ten-page research paper when I only had two pages of good material planned. I kept scrambling, kept talking, and kept the crowd busy for another eight minutes.

This time, when the clock hit zero, it stayed there.

I introduced President Trump, and he came out to uproarious applause.

As I stood backstage with Debbie, listening to the president speak, I told her how long I'd had to keep my own speech going. "He must have been busy with something *pretty* important," I said. "Maybe a missile launch or a life-or-death military operation."

"Oh," she smiled. "Just now? He was chatting to *me* that whole time!"

After his speech, the president bounded offstage, saying, "How was that?" while the crowd shouted *Trump. Trump. Trump.* When it was time to leave, he began walking toward the Beast, and motioned for us to follow.

"Come for a ride," he said. "We're going back to the White House."

"Mr. President," I said. "We would love to. But we brought the car, and I don't know how we'd get it back to my office."

He seemed confused. "Just have your driver take your car."

"Mr. President, you're *looking* at the driver!"

He couldn't believe it.

In the end, we got into the Beast ahead of the president. After all, I thought, when would I would ever get a chance to ride with the president of the United States in the Beast? Inside the car, we snapped pictures of the presidential seal on the backs of the seats, then heard from the driver that photography was *not* permitted inside the vehicle. We were in the car alone because President Trump was doing what he always did backstage. He was taking photos with veterans, law enforcement, and first responders. The unique experience was surreal for us. When we took off, President Trump was telling us all about the limousine, which seemed to bring him great joy in sharing. In all the time I would spend working and traveling with the man, I can honestly say that he never lost that enthusiasm. Every time a new person came into the Oval Office or stepped aboard Air Force One, he showed them around with the same sense of wonder and excitement that he had during that first ride that I took with him. He was proud of everything American, especially the American presidency.

It made for wonderful days, even when times were challenging.

"I've had some expensive cars," he said. "But this one is different."

President Trump told us how much the vehicle cost, how much damage it could take from attackers if necessary, and listed a few other details about the mechanics. This information, of course, is not all public, and I can't share most of it here. But in the privacy of his car, President Trump was fine with letting me, a sitting congressman, in on a few inside details.

The rest of the ride went on like that as we traveled from the hotel toward the White House, passing the great Washington, DC landmarks. When we arrived at the front door of the White House, President Trump jumped out.

"Alright," he said. "I have to go inside and rip up the Iran nuclear deal. It's been a pleasure."

We fully expected this to be a once-in-a-lifetime ride. Reality set in as Debbie and I walked to the street and hailed a taxi.

Even if that had been the last time I ever saw President Trump, I would have remembered it forever. The same goes for Debbie. We could have gone the rest of our lives knowing that in March of 2017, when he was dealing with everything from the Russia hoax to a trade war with China, the president of the United States took the time to give us a ride in his limousine. We would have remembered the joy on his face, as if he wanted to share his enthusiasm for his job with the whole world, and he was doing it one person at a time.

I'm sure there are hundreds of people around the country who have similar stories. I know that I've heard a few dozen since we left the White House.

When my car pulled up to the gates of Walter Reed, I was able to get out pretty much unnoticed. I had been the chief of staff for about six months by this point, but I didn't think these people had any reason to know who I was. (Fortunately, that's still the case in most places I go.) Still, a guy pulling up in a large unmarked black car tends to attract eyeballs no matter where you are. And when you're in front of a building where the president of the United States happens to be staying, people put two and two together. By the time I heard the first inquiry as to whether I was, in fact, Mark Meadows, I had already begun delivering the president's message.

"I am here," I said, "to express a heartfelt message from the president of the United States. Thank you for your encouragement, thank you for being here and showing the president how much you care."

There was a smattering of applause. A few people came up to me to say what a difference President Trump had made in their lives. I was careful not to let them get too close. I was, after all, the only person who had come into contact with a genuinely sick president in the past few hours. I didn't want to infect anyone else by shaking their hands or breathing on them, even with the mask I was wearing. I do remember one person who spoke to me from among the crowd. She was a younger woman who had come from her home nearby.

"You mean the president of the United States saw us on TV and sent you out here just to say thank you?" she said.

I told her that yes, that was exactly what had happened.

"*That*," she said, "is why we love him."

When I got back to the room, President Trump was still watching the crowd on television via the livestream on Laura Ingraham's show. This was a few months before Fox would become more like CNN, so they were still covering the president fairly and with some degree of accuracy. Fox was already pulling to the left, but during the next few days, they would cover the president with no negative commentary.

Standing there watching the wall-mounted television in his room, I could see that some members of the crowd were beginning to go home. But they were being replaced with new people just as quickly. Clearly, this was going to be a twenty-four-hour vigil for the president. It was an amazing thing to see, and I got the sense that President Trump was deeply touched.

After a few questions about news coverage and the economy, the president moved over to the desk in his bedroom and sat down to work. He looked at the television once more, where the crowd was still growing, then back at me. It was almost eleven o'clock at night. Other than two members of the Secret Service, who were on duty in the next room, we were the only two people left in the suite.

"Alright Mark," he said. "I think we're all set here. You can go home. I'll see you tomorrow."

I thought again about the people I had just met outside. I thought about all that President Trump had been able to do for the country since he had been in office, all the long hours and sleepless nights he had put in to make sure he kept his promises to the American people. I thought about how, for the most part, he had done that work alone, grinding on when the rest of the world and the other members of his administration were at home asleep. I decided that tonight, he shouldn't be alone.

"No sir," I told him. "I'm not leaving."

President Trump seemed surprised. "What are you talking about," he said.

"Well, sir," I said, "I am not going to leave the hospital until *you* leave the hospital. America is with you, I'm with you, and I'm going to be here until you walk out of Walter Reed to the applause of a praying nation."

He didn't say much after that. Our work for the evening was mostly done, or at least as done as it *can* be for the president of the United States. My staff would begin tying up any of the day's loose ends in the morning back at the White House.

As I went to my room, the president said good night, then turned his attention back to the crowd on television. There were candles, balloons, and homemade signs with get-well messages written on them in tape. One woman carried a cardboard cutout of President Trump himself and waved it around at the metal barricade. The president was moved by all of it. I said good night to him, then walked down the hall in search of a bed for the night.

I prayed that the worst of this was behind us. At the same time, I knew it probably wasn't.

TWELVE

On the Record

I AWOKE THE next morning in an ICU bed down the hall from the president's room. One of the doctors at Walter Reed had located it for me the night before, along with a small tooth-brush and a towel from another wing of the hospital. After a quick check to make sure nobody had hooked me up to any wires or IV needles during the night, I rolled over on the ergo-nomic mattress, which had shifted electronically a few dozen times to prevent bedsores, and checked the time on my iPhone.

Six o'clock, just after sunrise.

Covid-19 or no Covid-19, I knew President Trump would be up.

I rinsed myself off in a shower off the hospital room, then put on the same suit I'd worn the day before and headed to the president's room. Sure enough, President Trump was up and moving, asking questions like it was any other day. But he was still sluggish, and I could tell that every movement was diffi-cult for him. Every few minutes, he would need to sit back down and rest. There was a group of doctors around him, and they were discussing what to tell the press, who were waiting outside. We decided that it would be best for the doctors to head out and brief the press as a unit; that way, if any medical questions came up, they would be able to answer better than any press secretary could. There wasn't much discussion about messaging that morning. For the most part, the doctors were concerned with who would cover what area of the president's health. I observed their conversations and noticed that they were each stepping forward to speak about their respective areas of expertise. Doctor Connelly was leading the way.

The doctors didn't say a word to me before they marched outside, all lined up like a small army. I figured it was best to let them handle this one. Aside from the fact that I was bleary-eyed from not getting much sleep the night before, I was not a doctor and didn't think that I would have much to offer in the way of medical updates. I followed closely behind them and walked toward the crowd of reporters, who'd been waiting outside since around sunrise. I took my seat on a bench off to the side and listened to them speak.

At first, Dr. Conley spoke in general terms about the president's illness. Things seemed to be going well.

"As reported yesterday," he said, "in consultation with this group, I recommended we bring the president up to Walter Reed as a precautionary measure to provide state-of-the-art monitoring and any care that he may need. Just seventy-two hours into the diagnosis now, the first week of Covid, and in particular days seven to ten, are the most critical in determining the likely course of this illness."

Then, as things got more specific, I grew more concerned. It was clear that these doctors, as good as they may have been at saving lives and looking after the ailments of the body, had absolutely no idea how to handle a hostile group of reporters. They didn't realize that the patient they were looking after was, in the opinion of these people who were currently barking questions at them, public enemy number one. The reporters didn't care at all about his health, which is what the doctors had come out to talk about. They only cared about finding holes in their stories, sniffing out lies and inconsistencies. Even if you've spent your whole life as a professional political operative, this can be impossible to deal with. These doctors hadn't, and they were already getting tripped up.

I could also tell that Dr. Conley was trying a little too hard to paint a rosy picture of the president's health, and he was coming dangerously close to jading the truth. I'm sure that wasn't intentional—in fact, I *know* it was not his intention. But that was what seemed to be happening.

When a reporter asked about the president's oxygen saturation level, things went off the rails. A transcript of that exchange is below:

REPORTER: Can you tell us the president's oxygen saturation level please?

CONLEY: Yeah. So the last saturation that we had up walking around, he was about 96 percent.

REPORTER: And he is receiving no, he has not received any supplemental oxygen?

CONLEY: He's not on oxygen right now. That's right.

REPORTER: He's not received any at all?

CONLEY: He's-he's not needed any, uh, this morning, today at all. That's right. No he's . . .

REPORTER: Do you have an estimated date when he might be discharged?

CONLEY: Well, I don't want to put a hard date on that. He's doing so well. But with a known course of the illness, day seven to ten, we get really concerned about the inflammatory phase, phase two. Given that we provided some of these advanced therapies so early on the course a little bit earlier than most of the patients we know and follow, it's hard to tell where he is on that course. And so every day we're evaluating does he need to be here? What does he need and where is he going?

REPORTER: What is the probability that he will need supplemental oxygen going forward?

CONLEY: I don't want to put a percentage on that. But, but right now, all indicators are that that he'll remain off of oxygen going forward.

The president *had* been on supplemental oxygen. That was misleading. I would have stepped in at this point, but I didn't want to give the reporters any further reason to doubt us or believe that we were trying to hide something from the American people. Behind the scenes, everything was progressing well. The president was recovering, and the doctors were doing what they knew how to do, which was take care of him. If the media would let them do that, we wouldn't have a problem. But they wouldn't.

When the doctors had finished, I walked over to a few of the reporters I knew and asked them to huddle around me. To this day, I'm not sure what made me tell them that I wanted my comments to be anonymous. Anyone who'd been around the White House press corps longer than five minutes would have been able to tell you that this kind of comment never stays unattributed for long. Looking back, I can only attribute it to sleep deprivation and an unbelievable amount of worry about my friend, who I knew was watching me live on television from his suite, just a few hundred feet from where the makeshift news conference occurred. I also wanted to keep the public informed, trying to make sure that no one accused us of lying about President Trump's health.

In the months to come, books and news articles would say that I was "consumed with fear" that the president would die. But I wasn't consumed with anything other than getting him the best care possible and making sure every need was met. I certainly prayed for his recovery, and asked others to pray for him as well.

"Off the record," I said. "The president's vitals over the last twenty-four hours were very concerning, and the next forty-eight hours will be critical in terms of his care," I said. "We're still not on a clear path to a full recovery."

Then I left and went back inside. I could tell before I walked through the glass doors of Ward 71 that I had made an enormous mistake.

In the first round of stories, my comments were attributed to "a person familiar with the president's condition," which is exactly what I wanted. I didn't see any reason to put myself in the story or draw attention to anything other than the president's health. A few minutes later, though, I learned that a reporter in the pool had filmed the whole interaction. It didn't take long for that video to spread all over the web and for most news organizations to identify me as the source. President Trump was not happy when he read the original anonymous quote, and he was even less happy when he found out that it was me, his chief of staff, who had let the press know what rough shape he was in.

He called me into his hospital room. Although he didn't have much to say about the incident, he pointed out that the stories were all about my comments, and let me know that I had made a "rookie mistake," pointing out that I was no rookie when it came to dealing with the press. He did not argue with the fact that he was in rough shape, and, contrary to several fabricated reports, he never had to "blow off any steam." He knew that I would be tougher on myself than he ever could be. I didn't try to explain myself. Then, as is often the case with President Trump, it was over. He was asking questions about how we could get therapeutics to people sooner rather than later, and he wanted an update on the funding that was supposed to be going to American hospitals.

This was one of the key issues that he had been asking about for months, and the irony of his situation was not lost on him. Here he was, sitting in one of the finest hospital rooms in the country, being cared for by the nation's best doctors (although, as we had just found out, they weren't the best PR people). All the while, hospitals around the country had been forced to cut staff, cease all elective surgeries, and allow certain equipment to go into disrepair.

It was usually moments like this, when the president saw what the American people *could* be getting—in this case, quality care for loved ones who came down with Covid-19—and realized that they *weren't* getting it, that he sprang into action. If the doctors didn't have him pinned down and quarantined, I'm sure he would have checked himself right out of the hospital.

Still in Walter Reed, President Trump turned his attention to the Abraham Accords. In the weeks following our official announcement of the deal, the press coverage had been largely positive. Even some of the more liberal outlets, whose business model seemed to include a few op-eds a week denouncing whatever the Trump administration happened to have done on the day before they went to press, had been forced to admit that the deal was a good one. They did it through gritted teeth, of course, but this time, their hatred of the president wasn't enough to obscure the facts.

In *Slate*, a war correspondent named Fred Kaplan called the deal "a notable achievement" that "possibly herald[ed] a geopolitical shift in the Middle East." He also referred to it as a "huge step forward" for countries in the region. In *Politico*, the signing ceremony was covered with the reverence and respect that I believed was due to an event of such enormous historical significance, which was a welcome change of pace, considering the tenor of their past coverage. The news story quoted the president as saying that the accords would "change the course of history" and allow "people of all faiths and backgrounds [to] live together in peace and prosperity," and it managed to do it without all the snarky subtext that usually accompanied stories from the magazine's news division.

I wasn't exactly printing out these clippings and putting them on my wall, but it was refreshing not to be lied about for a change. With expectations for peace in the region so high, future deals could undoubtedly receive negative nitpicking, but we were prepared for that.

The president had also seen the initial round of coverage and been pleased by it, though, in his way, he tried not to dwell on the success for too long. Despite what often seemed like a never-ending war with the mainstream media, President Trump did still read what they had to say about him, and he always

knew where we were in terms of their opinion of our performance. In fact, that briefcase I had carried over on Marine One
for him was partially full of clipped articles from all the papers
we professed to hate the most—*The New York Times*, the *Washington Post*, perhaps even the odd story from magazines like the
Atlantic and *The New Yorker*. Every morning, he would spend a
few minutes flipping through newspapers and magazines to get
a sense of where the country was, what was being said about
him, and what issues might move the needle in terms of public
opinion. That hadn't changed during his stay at Walter Reed.
On the table of his room, I could see a big stack of newspapers
that the Secret Service had brought in for him.

Typically, whenever the president saw a positive article,
he would have someone from the White House staff cut it out
so that he could write a note across the clipping in a big black
Sharpie and mail it to the person who wrote it. He also did
the same thing with negative articles, though not as often and
usually with notes that weren't quite as nice. But he was never
outwardly mean; most of the time, the notes to his haters
contained jokes or snarky comments. I'm sure that right now,
there are a few hundred of these news clippings, covered
in the president's unmistakable angular scrawl, framed and
hung in the offices of reporters, congressmen, and senators
all over the country. I know that I have several from my days
in Congress. The president got nothing from this. It was just
one of the many ways he had of reinforcing his message to the
people he was representing, whether they were on his side all
the time or not.

On the Abraham Accords, though, the president wanted
to keep the positive coverage coming. He saw the press's initial
burst of enthusiasm as a wave that we could ride to a complete

deal, which he hoped would eventually include participation from Sudan, Morocco, and Saudi Arabia. These were countries that were not in the original agreement but had expressed interest in joining in the future.

Now the future was here, and it was up to us to bring them into the fold. I knew that the effort was in good hands with Jared Kushner, Secretary Pompeo, and Avi Berkowitz.

We were making progress with Morocco and Sudan, but talks with one of the most the most important countries, Saudi Arabia, were moving more slowly. The boss knew that there had been back-channel negotiations that could normalize the relationship between Saudi Arabia and Israel, and he was eager to turn these into a public show of support.

I said that the team would work on it, and the president went back into his room to rest.

Toward the end of Saturday afternoon, when the final round of tests was done for the day, President Trump began asking what he could do to assure the country he was all right. He knew he couldn't go outside, but he wanted to do something.

That night, President Trump sat down at one of the large conference tables in the presidential suite and began addressing the American people. We had arranged for a few members of the White House video crew to come in and film him so that the message would be a professional-quality piece. The crew also brought along a massive television, which we installed in the president's room so that he could follow the news of the day without getting up to come into the conference room.

During his address, President Trump spoke without notes, which was impressive considering his condition. In the days

since our arrival, the president had been given Pepcid, mela-
tonin, zinc, and aspirin, in addition to the first round of Regeneron. We called this "the Covid cocktail." Covid itself usually
caused fatigue and drowsiness, yet while he was speaking, I
couldn't detect any.

"I want to begin by thanking all of the incredible medical
professionals," he said. "The doctors, the nurses, everyone, at
Walter Reed Medical Center. I think it's the finest in the world.
I came here and I wasn't feeling so good. I'm feeling much
better now. We're working hard to get me back because we
still have to make America great again. We've done an awfully
good job of that, but we still have steps to go . . . I'll be back—I
think I'll be back soon . . . This is something that happened
to millions of people, and I'm fighting for *them*, not just in the
US, but all around the world. We're going to beat this coronavirus, or whatever you want to call it, and we're going to beat it
soundly. If you look at the therapeutics, which I'm taking right
now, some of them, and others are coming. Frankly, they're
miracles. People criticize me when I say that. But they look like
they're miracles, coming down from God."

After the video Saturday, I met with Jared and Dan Scavino, who'd just arrived from the White House. We discussed
progress on Covid relief measures, the economy, and a few other
routine matters concerning Oval Office operations. Inside, the
president was busy signing a big stack of documents and executive memos that had been sent over by the White House staff
secretary. He also signed a number of FEMA requests, which
approved urgent relief in some states that were suffering the
most. I would bet that the president, who was being forced to
sit still for probably the first time in the roughly seven decades
he had spent on this earth, managed to sign as many executive

memos and orders during the three days he was at Walter Reed as, he would have in the Oval Office.

During my conversation with Dan and Jared, I looked down at my suit—the same one I had been wearing when we left the White House on Thursday evening—and realized it was probably safe to slip out so that I could go home and change, if only for the sake of the people who had to be in the same room with me over the next few days. I asked Dan if he could stay and hold down the fort, which he was more than happy to do, and I rode home with a Secret Service agent to change.

In the car, I spoke with Derek Lyons, who was one of the hardest-working people in the West Wing. For years, he had been the staff secretary, a job that few people even know exists. This is the position that vets and prepares every official document for signing. During the riots that summer, it was Derek who had prepared the papers that President Trump would have needed to invoke the Insurrection Act. The document was never implemented, of course, but we were only a few decision points away from doing so. Derek let me know that he was sending over more documents for President Trump the next day, and that things were moving well in the White House.

When I returned to Walter Reed in a few hours, freshly shaved and showered, I got the sense that we might finally be nearing the end of this terrible ordeal.

I whispered a prayer, hoping I was correct.

———

Outside, the crowd of supporters had continued to grow. It was moving to see these strong, burly motorcyclists down on their knees praying for their president. Every so often, the president would bemoan the fact that he couldn't walk out there and thank them for all their support. I saw him watch live TV streams more than once, look at the massive crowd, and walk away with a frustrated look on his face. All he wanted was to be back out there, among his supporters, showing them how much he appreciated them and telling them how much he wanted to be in the Oval Office fighting for them. And yet he—the leader of the free world, the man who was supposed to be able to get whatever he wanted with the snap of a finger or the push of a button—was being told that he couldn't do it.

Being told what he could or could not do was something the president was not accustomed to. And he didn't take well to it, that's for certain.

That Saturday, sick of the healthy hospital food they'd been trying to shove down his throat for two days, President Trump asked for some hamburgers and french fries from McDonald's. This had been his favorite meal during the campaign, and also one that he enjoyed from time to time in his private office off the Oval. The food at the hospital was fine, he said, but it had been a rough couple of days, and he could use a burger. A member of the president's Secret Service detail took a car out to the local McDonald's and came back with bags of Big Macs, Quarter Pounders, fries, and Filet-O-Fish sandwiches.

As usual, he came back with more than any one person could possibly eat.

By this point, Jared Kushner had stopped by again with get-well cards from his children. His eldest daughter had made a card for her grandfather, which included a picture of them together and some words of encouragement scrawled in crayon. Dan Scavino also joined us.

When the McDonald's arrived, Jared looked at it the way my kids used to look at the veggies Debbie would serve them with their dinner every night. You would think the Secret Service agent had just found them sitting in the toilet, fished them out, and plopped them down on the table. (Jared is not a burgers-and-fries kind of guy.)

When President Trump came out for dinner, he said hello to everyone, cracked a few jokes, and insisted we sit down for a meal with him. I was slightly taken aback. During the time we had been in the hospital, the president had never received a visitor in anything less than a dress shirt and jacket, or at least a polo. This time, he was wearing a T-shirt and a robe. The sight of it was strange to me, even though I had seen it before. It was a rare moment when I realized the president was, in fact, just a guy like the rest of us.

As he sat down at the table, he said, "How are things going," and motioned to the food that had just arrived to suggest he was ready for us to eat heartily, and gave me a quick pat on the shoulder. For the first time in a long while, there was no talk of work.

As we began taking the burgers out of the bag, I noticed that one of the president's doctors was watching reproachfully from the door.

Clearly, we were breaking protocol.

"If you're going to sit here," he said. "You'll have to put on face shields."

I could feel the president rolling his eyes. We were about as far apart as the room would allow, and besides, I had been sitting in small rooms with the president for the past forty-eight hours. If this thing was going to come for us, it would have done so already. But he kept going.

"You could get the virus through your eyes if you're not careful. Also, your skin. And you'll also want to make sure you're six feet apart."

So, there we sat—me, Dan, Jared, and the president, our giant plastic face shields steaming up from our burgers and fries, enjoying a meal together for the first time in weeks. I only wish we'd brought along a White House photographer to capture the moment. I'm sure that it would have looked great hanging in the Trump Presidential Library in fifty years, right above a plaque explaining what Covid-19 was, and how we beat it.

By Sunday morning October 4, President Trump was up and giving orders. He'd been doing that for the past few days, of course, but this was the first time that I had heard his full bark restored. In a way, it was good to hear him shouting orders again. It meant that my friend was on the mend, and that we were finally going to be able to get back to running the country full-time.

Late in the morning, the doctors came into the president's room and let him know that he would be able to get back to the White House within twenty-four hours. The president wasn't exactly thrilled about this—he wouldn't have been satisfied with anything short of walking out the door right that second—but I could tell he was relieved. A few hours later, we convened a small group of advisors to plan the president's return. The president was effusive in his praise for the hospital staff, the drugs he'd been given, and the people who had shown him support over the course of his illness.

"I swear, I feel better now than I did twenty years ago," he said. "I feel like I could walk out of here right now, like I'm Superman."

At some point during President Trump's stay, it was suggested, as a joke, that he get a Superman T-shirt to put under his clothes; the three or four of us who were in the hospital with him thought it might be funny if he ripped the top shirt off and revealed the big *S* when he got to the White House. This was a passing comment, obviously not intended to be taken seriously. I wouldn't have remembered it at all if it hadn't been for what happened next.

Clearly, someone who'd heard the conversation had run straight to the press a few minutes later to repeat everything that was said, including that little joke about the Superman shirt. I don't think this person did it maliciously. Every day, there were reporters calling staffers at the White House, especially the ones who were young, impressionable, and eager to prove that they were in the know. During my tenure as chief, I'm proud to say that the leaks from senior staff had been greatly reduced, so the reporters had gone hunting around in other departments for their quotes. This, I believe, included the White House medical unit, where we had found many leaks during the previous few months.

However it got out, this little joke ended up in a story by Jennifer Jacobs of Bloomberg News.

This was a silly leak, and it didn't do any lasting damage to the president. But it serves as a perfect example of how the media takes a real quote, strips it of context, throws it in a shaker, mixes it up with a few other fake quotes and half-truths, and then serves it up as a nice, cold Fake News martini. There really *was* a discussion about the president's health, and someone really did mention a Superman shirt. But were we ever serious about buying one? No. Would the president have actually considered doing such a thing? Also no.

So, the next time you read a story that's sourced anonymously and contains something that seems a little too bizarre to be true, that's probably because it is.

———————————

In the afternoon, as the president was making his final prepa-rations to leave the hospital, he went to the window, trying to see if the crowd was still there. This time, he wondered aloud whether there was anything we could do to let them know how much we appreciated them. We had already made a video and mentioned them in a few media appearances.

But for the president, this wasn't enough.

"I just wish there was some way we could take the Beast out there," he said. "I'd like to get as close as we can without putting anyone in danger."

It was a member of the Secret Service who suggested that a quick drive around the grounds for a wave was possible. The president considered it and decided he loved the idea. Contrary to reports that would come out in the days and months to come, there was no pushback to the idea within the hospital. The Secret Service, as always, was happy to go wherever the president asked them to go. They served at the pleasure of the commander in chief, and they would follow him anywhere. They were already in close contact with the president. It was their job.

We made sure that everyone who'd be in the car took proper precautions, then began planning a route. The car would go from the back door of Ward 71, where we'd come in, around to the front gate, and then back again. It would take only a few minutes. I would follow the president in what we called a control car, which would drive a few feet behind his car, taking the same route. The Secret Service would have drivers for both vehicles. This would be an "off-the-record" event, so the press would not be informed about it in advance. We didn't want any more complications than we already had, and we didn't think press alerts would do anyone any good. This was between the president and the hundreds of people who had come out to support him.

We loaded up the cars around three o'clock in the afternoon, when the crowd was at its apex. The people who usually went home at night were still there, and the evening crowd was beginning to arrive with their signs, cards, and candles. For the rest of my life, I will remember the looks on the faces of the people when they saw the president from the back window of his big black car. Since I was in the car immediately behind him, I had a birdseye view of them when they stopped rubbing their eyes, looked at one another, and realized that yes, that *was* really the president of the United States who had just waved at them from the car. Unlike the president, I was able to hear the words that passed between people in the crowd.

It's him!

Yes, I'm serious!

No, I don't need glasses. That was the president!

Some supporters even ran alongside the limo.

I recall one couple in particular who'd been there for the past two days. They had been holding up get-well signs almost the entire time. When the president first passed, they let the signs fall and said nothing. Then they looked at each other, as if to ask whether they had really just seen that happen. When they realized they had, they dropped their signs and started cheering, tears falling from their eyes and big smiles on their faces. To so many people out there who'd been following the news for updates, that ride in the car was a kind of confirmation not only that the president was going to be okay, but that the country was going to be okay, too. It was a validation of the love and appreciation they had shown for the president. He had felt their support for the past forty-eight hours during one of the darkest times of his life, and it was incredibly important to him that he acknowledge it somehow. The smiles on the faces of the people in the crowd made the absolute uproar that followed worth it.

Almost.

Within a few hours, the media was back to accusing the president of reckless endangerment, claiming that he was putting the lives of the Secret Service officers at risk when he asked them to go in the car with him. We decided not to comment on that, and we encouraged the members of the president's detail—who were as loyal to him as anyone—not to comment either. Of course, that's not to say that they needed any lessons in discretion from me.

Throughout history, with a few notable exceptions, the men and women of the Secret Service have served the president of the United States with honor and integrity, even when they may have disagreed with him politically. In the Trump White House, that didn't change.

Now all that was left to do was get back to the White House, fix Covid-19, broker peace in the Middle East, distribute money to hospitals, provide aid to cities that were still reeling from riots, reduce the prices of prescription drugs, speed up the production of therapeutics, come up with a plan to get vaccines to a hundred million people, and reopen the economy. Oh, and we had to win this little thing called an election, which was now less than thirty days away.

Piece of cake.

— THIRTEEN —

Back at It

WHEN HE STEPPED back onto the grounds of the White House, the first thing President Trump wanted to do was address the American people. He knew that they had watched him come down with Covid-19, the disease which we had all been living under the threat of for months, and they had been listening to pundits on television give their spin on the story. Many of these liberals had said he deserved it for not wearing a mask more often. Other haters predicted that he would almost certainly die because of his age, weight, and lifestyle. The media didn't care about his health but the American people certainly did.

Now it was time for the president to give *his* side of the story.

Around seven o'clock in the evening, President Trump disembarked from Marine One, this time with every ounce of his old strength back (and *then* some, it seemed), and saluted the Marines who'd been awaiting his return. He waved at the press, stopped for pictures, and then ascended the iron steps that led up to the lower balcony on the south side of the White House.

Interestingly, the balcony above where President Trump stood had been named for President Truman because he had been the one to build it. In the late 1940s, President Truman and his family had begun feeling cramped in their living quarters, and they believed that a balcony would provide some much-needed leisure space outside. So, they had commissioned architect William Delano to build it and released those plans to the public. Almost as soon as they made the plans public, there was an uproar over the supposed "damage" that Truman was going to do to the building. Critics argued that he was destroying the classical Greek style in which the White House was designed; newspapers suggested that the addition might cost him the 1948 election. In the end, Truman paid for the addition using funds from his own pocket, and it was completed in March 1948. A few years after it was completed, most of the people who opposed it wrote to President Truman to let him know how much they liked it. Today, the balcony is an integral part of the building's image. I, for one, can't picture the White House without it.

It's a perfect example of how every move a president makes—whether it's an executive order or a simple addition to the building he's living in—is questioned, attacked, and run through the ringer by his enemies. There is no move that he can make that isn't political. No matter what he does, he'll get opposition. The only option is to forge ahead, do what he thinks is right, and hope that he is vindicated by history.

But that's not a lesson that anyone ever needed to give President Trump. To him, opposition didn't matter one bit. He could smash through any obstacle, Covid-19 included.

As President Trump walked to the front of the balcony, standing strong for the cameras snapping pictures of him from the lawn below, he removed his mask so that his stern expression could be seen throughout the world. It was of great importance to him that he convey an image of strength, showing that he was willing to take on the world in these photos. Again, he knew that he stood for the entire country at that moment in history; the United States of America would be judged—by its friends and by its enemies—based on the impression he gave that afternoon.

Looking on from the White House Residence, I was once again impressed. While he spoke, I glanced over the address that the president was planning on delivering to the nation shortly. It had been largely written by President Trump himself during his final hours at the hospital. The president had gone over the final copy with his signature black Sharpie, making small fixes to words and phrases.

President Trump always treated every speech as if it was the most important one he'd ever give, but he seemed to pay special attention to this one.

When the photo op was over, the president prepared to address the country. This was his opportunity to deliver the message he had been holding on to since the moment he went into Walter Reed. That message was simple, and vital: although Covid-19 was dangerous, and in some cases life threatening, it was not something that most people in the country had to live in fear of. In most cases, even people who were at a high risk of having complications from the virus—which, as the media never seemed to tire of reminding us, the president did—had a good chance of recovery. When complications did occur, there were new treatments and therapeutics that could help. Anyone who wanted to fault the president for getting out on the trail and seeing his supporters, especially while Joe Biden cowered from the virus in his basement, was about to be sorely disappointed.

I believe his remarks, delivered straight to the camera just after dusk with the Washington Monument at his back, are worth printing here in full.

"I just left Walter Reed Medical Center," he said, "and it's really something very special. The doctors, the nurses, the first responders, and I learned so much about coronavirus. One thing that's for certain: *Don't let it dominate you.* Don't be afraid of it. You're going to beat it. We have the best medical equipment; we have the best medicines, all developed recently. You're going to beat it. I went—I didn't feel so good, and two days ago, I could have left. I felt great. Better than I have in a long time. I said just recently, better than twenty years ago. Don't let it dominate you. Don't let it take over your lives. We have the best country in the world. We're going back to work. We're going to be out front, and as your leader, I had to do that. I know there's danger to it, but I had to do that! I stood out front, and I led. Nobody that's a leader would not do what I did. I know there's a risk, there's a danger, but that's okay. Now I'm better, and maybe I'm immune! I don't know! But don't let it dominate your lives. Get out there, be careful. We have the best medicines in the world, and it all happened very shortly. And they're all getting approved. Vaccines are coming momentarily. Thank you very much. And Walter Reed, what a group of people. Thank you very much."

The speech, although it was short, contained everything that had put President Trump in the White House in the first place. It was direct, plainspoken, and shot through with the kind of humor, grace, and humility that people had come to expect from him. Although the prose wasn't quite as polished as the Gettysburg Address, delivered by President Abraham Lincoln after the bloodiest battle of the Civil War, it had the same compressed, forceful quality that had made President Lincoln's words so effective at the time they were delivered. This was the kind of direct, unpolished honesty that the country had been missing from President Trump, while he was sick. I dreaded to think of the results if we had to go without it after 2020.

The president came back into the Residence when he was finished speaking, and I walked with him through the halls. I explained the precautions we would need to take throughout the West Wing so that we could get back to work effectively. I had been in contact with the White House medical team, who were working to outfit the Oval Office with even more equipment to prevent the spread of Covid-19. When anyone stepped into the office, they would have to don a few layers of protective gear, do their business with the president, and then deposit that protective gear in a special bin at the door.

The president asked me to follow him as he sped down the hallway to the sitting room.

Clearly, the break, such as it was, had ended. It was time to get to work.

The first thing he asked about was the latest Covid-19 relief bill.

I felt a familiar pit beginning to open in my stomach.

In the months since negotiations on the second round of Covid-19 relief had begun, Nancy Pelosi and her team had been about as agreeable as a sack full of rattlesnakes. They had absolutely no intention of reaching an agreement with the Trump White House, and they were making it clear during the closed-door sessions we had been holding all summer. But they allowed the talks to drag on anyway. During a rare candid moment during one of our meetings, Nancy Pelosi had accidentally let the truth slip out—something she's been known to do on occasion—and told us her real motivation for letting the talks go for so long with no real progress.

"I will *not*," she said, narrowing her eyes, "have checks go out with that man's name on them before November 3."

I understood why. The $1,200 checks that had gone out to millions of Americans in April had been enormously popular, and they had gone out with President Trump's signature on the front. Once again, it was the president's way of letting the people of the United States know that he was there, that he cared, and that he was going to keep fighting for them no matter what happened. It worked. In some parts of the country, people had begun referring to their stimulus payments as "Trump checks." Pelosi knew that in the impending election, her party's candidate seemed to have given up campaigning altogether. There was certainly no enthusiasm for him at the time. The last thing she needed was more excitement about all the hard work that President Trump was doing for the country.

Her comment was never reported by the liberal media, which I found noteworthy considering that *someone* in that room had been leaking the details of our talks for months. Speaker Pelosi knew this. Right before the beginning of one meeting, she looked me and Steven Mnuchin up and down, then told us that we needed to deposit our phones in a small bowl at the door of the Speaker's conference room.

"I don't want you recording anything that is said here today," she said.

I didn't bother telling her that our phones had been issued by the federal government, which meant that they were *incapable* of taking recordings. Mnuchin and I couldn't use our phones to do crossword puzzles, let alone record the details of confidential meetings and leak them to the press.

After a few indignant moments, we obliged, tossing our phones into Speaker Pelosi's metal bowl, and then sitting down once again for hours of empty words and grandstanding on the part of the Speaker's office. She made claims that seemed geared toward an outside audience, which was suspicious, considering that no one other than those in the room was supposed to be listening. Pelosi played the part of tough negotiator like a bad actor in a soap opera. Nothing that she said that day was intended to get a bill passed for the American people.

As expected, shortly after that meeting, specific details of it leaked to *Politico* and *The New York Times*. Secretary Mnuchin and I were the only representatives from the Trump White House present, and we had both deposited our phones in a bowl before entering. Speaker Pelosi, on the other hand, had invited several representatives from her office, as well as Chuck Schumer, none of whom had to get rid of their devices before entering. I wouldn't be surprised if she still had a phone, too.

Now, I'm not saying that Speaker Pelosi and her team were leaking details to the press to put themselves in a favorable light during negotiations on a bill that was supposed to help those in need. But someone leaked it, and it wasn't Mnuchin or me.

Time and time again, confidential details of our talks would end up in news reports all over the world. What was interesting, although not surprising, was that every single one of these reports seemed designed to make the Democrats look good and the White House look bad. And by this point, making the Democrats in the House look good was not an easy task. Even though they were not in control of the White House, they controlled the House of Representatives, which put them in a strong negotiating position. All they had to do was lob shots from the cheap seats, delay the bill until after the election, and throw their hands up about why we couldn't get something done. By design, they managed to bungle the negotiations.

Democrats in the House had begun by asking for a $2.4 trillion package, which was a massive number, several times the size of any relief bill that had ever been passed. We had countered with several smaller bills that kept the important Covid-19 relief elements but jettisoned some of the unrelated pet projects that Democrats were trying to stuff into the legislation under cover of darkness. When we agreed to move up closer to her number, Speaker Pelosi and her team went up even further, putting forward a $2.9 trillion bill. Clearly, these were not the actions of a group who wanted to reach a deal. In fact, every time we seemed to be within shouting distance of a deal, they did something to make sure it could never happen. Either that, or they really were as bad at negotiating as they seemed to be. In any case, the results were the same.

Since the beginning of the negotiations in July, I had been issuing stern warnings to Pelosi and her team. The longer they waited, I said, the less money they were going to get. That's not because Republicans are cheap or "heartless," as Nancy Pelosi once described us in the press; it's only because we are prudent and realistic about the way the world works. We knew that eventually, someone was going to end up paying for all this money we were throwing around, and that it was inevitably going to be the taxpayers. Democrats were content to kick the can down the road, spending trillions now and then raising taxes in a few years to pay for it. Republicans were not okay with that.

When negotiations began, the need for government intervention to prop up the economy was great; without it, people would suffer. But we also understood that the fundamentals of the economy were strong, largely due to the work of President Trump and his advisors, and that with each day that passed, the situation would improve. Every day, the need for the government to step in and throw money at the problems—which, for Democrats, is the answer to everything—would decrease sharply. As the weeks wore on, we were proven right. The economy was recovering faster than any of our models had predicted, and the need for government intervention was shrinking every day. If they continued to delay, and insist on bailing out poorly run democrat cities, I said, they were going to get only half of what we were currently offering, which was $1.7 trillion.

For Pelosi, that didn't move the needle an inch. She didn't want to see the bill succeed because, if it did, the American people would see it as a victory for the Trump White House. That was something that she simply would not allow.

She had rejected every offer that we made her, always finding a reason to delay rather than make a deal.

By the morning of Tuesday, October 6, just one day after his release from Walter Reed, the president was at the end of his rope. I'm not sure whether it was the time that he had spent in the hospital thinking or the sudden realization that the election was approaching, but I do know that something in him seemed to click that morning. We had delayed too long, and people were suffering. It was time to take another route.

The plan, as he explained it to me, was to cut off negotiations on a large stimulus package. At the rate we were moving, there was no way to get Nancy Pelosi to a deal. Instead, we were going to isolate the provisions that actually mattered to the American people—most importantly the direct payments—and try to pass them as stand-alone bills. During the impasse over the summer, the president had taken executive action to provide immediate relief.

It seemed like a workable way to get our agenda passed without having it distorted by the pesky projects of the Democrats.

By the time we hit the campaign trail again in October, I had been to around twenty Trump rallies. Whenever I attended one of these, I was struck all over again by the intensity of the support for President Trump across the country and by the media's steadfast refusal to cover the events for what they were: huge, energetic seas of excitement—celebrations of prosperity and patriotism, held in honor of the man who believed in America and believed in them. They were always a great time. But I had never seen *anything* like the rallies that occurred when we got back on the road after the president's battle with Covid-19 had ended.

At the time, there was certainly a lot to celebrate.

In the months since we instituted Operation Legend and cracked down on looting and rioting, the streets of our cities were on their way to becoming safe again. There were still scattered outbreaks of violence, mostly in liberal strongholds like Portland and New York City, but for the most part, the federal government had helped to regain control. As long as we could keep President Trump in the White House and halt the spread of crazy ideas like "defund the police" and Critical Race Theory, we could stop more damage from occurring to our cities. The sad irony was that a large portion of the damage that had been done during this period of racial unrest had been done to the African American community.

Often, when the riots were over, the young liberal kids who had shown up to break windows and burn things down usually went home to their safe communities, leaving many black Americans they claimed to be so concerned about to clean up the mess. Out on the trail, the president had heard from countless African American constituents about the detrimental impact that the riots had had on their communities; they wanted him to know that some of the loudest voice in the Democrat Party did not represent them, and that they were going to turn out in record numbers for him on Election Day.

Anyone who doubted this obviously wasn't at the White House on October 10, when we arranged a rally hosted by a foundation called Blexit, a group of Black and Latino citizens who had seen the light, so to speak, and wanted their fellow people of color to get on the Trump Train with them. It was a remarkable day. Members of the group and its supporters gathered outside on the South Lawn behind a rope line, waving Trump flags and signs and cheering for the president, who was about to give his first major speech since recovering from Covid-19.

When the president got up to the microphone on the lower balcony, there was uproarious applause. Even out on the lawn, where you don't typically get the kind of acoustics that are available in an auditorium, it was a formidable sound.

Inside, after the rally was over, I met with the president to update him on several issues. Before entering the Oval Office, I donned my surgical smock, face mask, and a pair of gloves, which had become standard operating procedure after the president's infection. During the time we were at Walter Reed, we had set up stations in the Outer Oval, which also included a few hand sanitizing stations with never-ending supplies of gel. I doused my hands, which, at this point, were about as dry as old firewood from all the hand sanitizer I was using, and walked inside. I must have looked like I was going in to perform open heart surgery rather than brief the president. But I was relieved to have him behind the Resolute Desk where he belonged. I would have dressed in a giant penguin suit if it meant having him back in the Oval, running the country.

I was also pleased to tell the president that, thanks to some hard work on the part of Jared Kushner and Avi Berkowitz's team, we were going to be able to bring Sudan into the Abraham Accords. Soon, they would agree to normalize relations with Israel, and we would arrange a meeting in the Oval Office to celebrate. This would happen over the phone, of course, but it would be a major step in the negotiations, and a clear signal to the world that we were indeed open for business. He had a certain raising of his eyebrows and a subtle nodding of the head that let me know he was pleased.

We also discussed some of the rallies that the president had coming up. I remarked on how energizing it had been to see him up at the microphone again, giving a speech like it was 2016 and he was taking on the whole world—which, as always, he was.

"If people turn out in those kinds of numbers on Election Day," I said, "we'll have absolutely nothing to worry about."

The president wasn't so sure.

"It's these mail-in ballots," he would say. "This isn't going to be right. You can't have all these mail-in ballots, most of them going to voters who don't have any energy and enthusiasm, and not know where they're coming from. I don't know what's going to happen here. But it is not going to be good."

The rest of October was a whirlwind. Even though we were less than a month out from an election that we had every expectation of winning, President Trump did not let up for even a second on passing key elements of his agenda. If anything, that invisible clock in the White House that kept us all on Trump Time sped up rather than slowing down.

Amy Coney Barrett was confirmed to the Supreme Court. She showed the senators who tried to trip her up what we already knew: that she could handle absolutely anything that was thrown at her. Obviously, she wasn't kidding when she told President Trump during her first interview that she was ready for the attacks. She brushed them off like they were nothing.

By the time the election arrived, we would have fulfilled almost all of President Trump's campaign promises. The economy was rebounding, we were bringing peace to the Middle East, and the southern border was finally under control.

Had it not been for the China Virus, we could have spent the past months reaching more voters and running up our historic vote totals even higher.

— FOURTEEN —

Election Night

WHEN THE NIGHT of the election finally arrived, spirits in the White House were high. The staff in the West Wing, most of whom had arrived that morning dressed in bright red ties and party dresses, had hung around at their desks after work. At the end of the day, when the returns began coming in, they went out to the shops around the White House for pizzas, beer, and party favors. Every television in the building was tuned to a different news network, and there was music playing from small speakers in some of the West Wing offices.

By around six o'clock, the place looked like we were holding a big party rather than watching the election results come in, and it felt like it, too. But there was an underlying tension.

There would be an official celebration in the East Room, where President Trump would stop by later in the evening to make a speech. This room was directly downstairs from the Residence, and it was often used to greet diplomats and hold private celebrations on behalf of the First Family. Everything served that evening was paid for by President Trump or the RNC, not the American taxpayer. From what I witnessed, there were also smaller celebrations breaking out all over the West Wing. By most accounts, we were going to win easily. The polls were leaning our way, and the online traffic was all trending in the right direction. It seemed that all we had to do was sit around, wait for the results to roll in, and celebrate when the time came.

But I was in no mood for a party.

I had spent most of the day helping the campaign team set up an election command center in the East Wing of the building. Our primary headquarters were going to be in the Map Room, a small space on the first floor of the East Wing that sits directly below President Trump's bedroom. It was in this room that President Franklin Delano Roosevelt, who served as president before there was anything like the modern Situation Room, made key military decisions during the first days of World War II. From a small desk that he set up in the middle of the room, he corresponded with generals, gave orders about supplies, and tracked the progress of the Allied Army on several large maps of Europe that hung on every wall. Every day, President Roosevelt would head over to this room from the Oval Office, sit back, and slowly find out whether our soldiers—a band of young, freedom-loving men from all over the United States—were going to prevail against the most evil socialists in the world. Now I walked inside and prepared to do something that felt somewhat similar.

On tables spread throughout the room, we had set up laptop computers and television screens, manned by some of the best political minds. These people were mostly workers from the campaign who had demonstrated an aptitude for electoral math and knowing which way the wind was blowing during prior elections. They were the ones who knew, for instance, that we should not trust the polls that were predicting our demise back in 2016. They had told us that the polls were inherently skewed against the Trump campaign, and they had found ways to get at the truth of the situation. Now they were using those same methods again, and we were ahead in almost every key area. For the next hours, these people would be our official link to the outside world. Whatever the tweets and news reports began to say, we were going to trust the data that was coming from the Map Room. And no one was allowed in the Map Room who was not on the list. Jared Kushner, Bill Stepien, Jason Miller, and Justin Clark, ran point on the room.

In the final days of the campaign, Bill Stepien had proven himself an effective campaign manager. He answered questions directly, didn't sugarcoat bad news, and possessed a thorough understanding of key battleground states. He understood where our weaknesses were, and he did an excellent job coordinating with people on the ground to ensure that those weaknesses were fixed. Now he and Jared Kushner were bringing their expertise to the war room, running the whole thing in the manner of Jack Webb: *Just the facts, ma'am.*

We had a feeling that things were going to go well, but we weren't counting on it. For the past year, Democrats had been pushing to get just about everyone in the country signed up for mail-in voting. President Trump had alerted us to the strong possibility that there would be fraud connected to these mail-in ballots, and we wanted to be on the lookout for it.

So, elsewhere in the White House complex, we had set up an internal brain room that provided information to the campaign team, and we wanted to approach any potential challenges with the utmost seriousness.

From there, we were looking at raw election data using an army of lawyers, state coordinators, and IT professionals who were pulling in numbers from all over the country in real time. They would feed this information into the Map Room, where it would be compiled and analyzed to detect any hints of unexpected results.

If our analysts *did* find fraud. We would take legal action right away. That's why we had lawyers ready to file suits or challenge results. It turned out to be not nearly enough. In the days to come, credible tips from all over the country poured in, so much in fact that even our computer team was overwhelmed by the sheer volume.

Walking around the building, I noticed that there is something unsettling about election night. Standing in the campaign headquarters—in this case, the White House—on that day makes you feel slightly powerless. For years, all you've been thinking about is what you can do to win the election, and during that time, the answer was never "nothing." There was always a call to make, a television hit to do, or one last rally to get on the books. But when it comes down to the last few hours, with the voters on their way to the polling places, there really isn't much beyond making sure that their votes are counted properly, and that the only votes that *are* counted are the ones cast by living people who are registered to vote. That last part would turn out to be a problem, but there was nothing we could do about it on the day of the election.

At the time, all we could do was wait.

Standing in the East Wing that afternoon, I watched as the television screens around the room came slowly alive. On the left-hand side of the room, fittingly, we had MSNBC and CNN, both of which seemed gleeful at the possibility that this might be President Trump's final term in the White House. I couldn't help but think back to the programming that they had aired on November 8, 2016, which I watched from a gathering in Asheville, North Carolina, after I had won my own reelection to Congress. The sight of those anchors slowly realizing what was happening, their faces falling more with each passing second, is something that I am not likely ever to forget. If it was physically possible to frame video footage, I might have those few minutes running on a constant loop on my bookshelf.

Farther down the wall, we had coverage from the rest of the news networks. I looked from ABC, CBS, and NBC, then to a few smaller networks. Finally, I came around to the forty-eight-inch television screen on the far end of the room that was playing a live feed from Fox News. Brett Baier and Martha McCallum were anchoring the network's coverage. At least it wasn't Chris Wallace, the man who had so thoroughly bungled his first shot at moderating a presidential debate. I felt a flash of irritation, which lasted only for a second.

Which is good, considering what was coming for us that evening.

I had been reading several news reports about a man named Arnon Mishkin, the head of the "decision desk" at Fox News. According to reports, Mishkin and his team were going to be the ones calling the shots on election night for Fox, analyzing the returns as they came in and then deciding which states to call for which candidate. For the past few months, Mishkin and his team had also been in charge of Fox News's polling, which was showing President Trump trailing behind Joe Biden by a significant amount, something that seemed to defy all reason and logic.

In the various profiles that were published of him during the early months of election season, Mishkin was portrayed

as some kind of liberal savior within Fox News. In an article for *The New York Times,* media columnist Ben Smith wrote
that he would be "the last bulwark against the most frightening
prophecies of electoral insanity." The article was called "Trump
Wants to Discredit the Election. This Nerd Could Stop Him."

For most of my time in the West Wing, Fox News was one
of the rare networks that would cover us accurately. They were
certainly the only major network that was willing to report on
the administration's accomplishments rather than spending
their time hunting for the next gossip-column scoop on who
was getting fired, what the president's mood was like, and how
many Russian operatives were working in the White House.
That's why when we got requests from the network for interviews with senior officials, we would usually try to oblige. We
needed to get an accurate message about what was going on in
the White House out to the public, and there was only so much
the president could do from his Twitter feed.

But during the later months of the campaign, something had
begun to change. Fox's coverage of the Trump White House
had taken a distinctly negative turn, and it had nothing to do
with what we were actually doing. Remember, this is during a
period when we had just signed the Abraham Accords, brought
the country through a once-in-a-generation pandemic, effectively sealed the border, and were restoring a strong economy.
From what I could tell, this change came straight from the top.

As usual, it was President Trump who saw this coming
before anyone else. In the early months of Covid-19, back
when most people probably thought Wuhan was a little-known
Chinese takeout dish, he had called me into his private office
off the Oval, where the evening coverage on Fox News was
playing.

"Something is going on here," he said. "They are swinging way to the left. This is going to be a problem."

I wasn't so sure about it, but it would become clear that he was absolutely correct. Whenever I went on some of the news shows on Fox, the hosts would cut me off a little quicker, asking questions that had less and less to do with the topic at hand. While we could always count on the support of straight-shooting commentators like Sean Hannity, Lou Dobbs, Maria Bartiromo, Tucker Carlson, and Laura Ingraham, the so-called real journalists in the news division were beginning to turn on us. President Trump always seemed to be able to sense these things coming a mile away. Just as he talked about the lab leak hypothesis long before anyone believed it was possible, once again, he was right on the money when it came to Fox News.

The change in the Fox's coverage was never clearer to me than it was one afternoon in late October, when President Trump held a rally in Tampa, Florida. The heat in Tampa that day was sweltering, seeming hotter than it had ever been during the time I had spent living there as a young man. We had arranged for President Trump and First Lady Melania Trump to go onstage for a joint speech. This was a unique event. Even during the final months of the campaign, the First Lady rarely took to the stage with the president. It was the kind of thing that any objective news network would have covered.

A few miles away, the Biden campaign had organized a rally—if you can call it that—in the parking lot of an office building. Against a backdrop of absolutely nothing, the former vice president spoke to an audience of about a dozen cars that had all lined up to hear him. The level of excitement was lower than I had even thought possible. It was as if they were holding a funeral at the DMV. I wouldn't be surprised if the Biden campaign had lured the cars into the parking lot with a promise of free ice cream, then locked the gates so that no one could get out until their candidate was finished speaking. I could not think of any other reason that someone would sit and listen to that man speak for just under twenty minutes, which is about how long he had been droning on by the time President and Mrs. Trump were preparing to go onstage.

But to the major networks, this humdrum event warranted coverage. CNN and MSNBC both aired it in full, which we had been expecting. We were not expecting Fox News to follow suit, especially with the election only days away.

As the rally got underway, someone came up to me with a phone in his hand to let me know that Fox News had shifted to coverage of the Joe Biden "rally." Apparently, they were reverting to some arcane rules about "equal time" regardless of what their viewers actually wanted to see. Someone at the news division was making the call that a Trump rally that was being watched by tens of thousands of people was as important as Joe Biden talking to himself in a parking lot while a couple of people fell asleep in their cars. That, to them, was "fair and balanced."

I pulled out my phone and dialed Bill Sammon, the managing editor of Fox News's Washington division, who was making the decisions about the network's election coverage. I knew that Sammon was no great fan of President Trump. He had made his career writing favorable books about the administration of President George W. Bush, including one called *At Any Cost: How Al Gore Tried to Steal the Election*. He might have written a whole book about the last time Democrats tried to steal a presidential election, but he was ignoring that it was happening again right under his nose.

I got him on the phone and told him my problem. His response was not only curt, but revealing.

"Well," he said. "I do not answer to the president's chief of staff, and your opinion on Fox's programming is not important to me."

I said nothing, waiting to see if he wanted to change direction slightly. He did.

"You know, it's really—it's really the producers of the individual shows who make these play calls."

I knew that at the time of the rally, Dana Perino's show was supposed to be on Fox News. They were airing the Joe Biden rally instead.

"One," I said. "I do not believe that this decision was made by an individual producer at the Dana Perino show. And two, if it was, I will make sure that not a single White House official shows up on the Dana Perino show from now until the election. And three, if you have no more concern about what is fair and balanced, then you have lost your target audience, and I can't believe that your viewers are going to want to watch Joe Biden when the president and the First Lady are at a rally. If anything would be newsworthy, it would be the First Lady making an appearance in the battleground state of Florida."

From there, Sammon mumbled a few things and then hung up the phone.

I was angry about the call, but I didn't have much time to follow up. I didn't know who had made the decision, or who was really in charge of the most-watched cable news network in the country. All I knew was that these calls were coming straight from the top, and that if things kept going in this direction, Fox was in big trouble.

———————————

Around ten o'clock on election night, I went up to see President Trump in the Residence. He was planning to stay there most of the night with Melania and his family, trying to re-create the circumstances of his historic victory in 2016. That night, he had watched the returns from his penthouse apartment in Trump Tower, only coming down to celebrate when his victory was all but assured.

"We're looking good," he said. "I think we're in pretty good shape here."

By eleven o'clock things were looking even better for the Trump campaign. We were ahead in most key states, and the returns from Florida were showing lots of promise. One day earlier, we had heard from Susie Wiles that the state of Florida would be an easy win for the president. Susie had done a great deal of work in Florida during the election of 2016, She had been willing to deliver both good and bad news to the campaign team, so I took Susie at her word. If there was anyone I trusted to handle the numbers, it was her. I wished we could have one of her in every state.

As I watched the numbers on the red side of the screen climbing in several of Florida's counties, I was feeling hopeful as well.

Looking back, I had every reason to believe that the state of Florida was going to us. I had been there on October 15, when President Trump participated in a town hall event with Savannah Guthrie, a journalist from NBC News who had never shown anything but outright contempt for him. I'm sure that she was chosen on the assumption that she was going to rake President Trump over the coals on national television, and that he wouldn't respond in kind because he didn't want to appear too bullish after his first subpar debate performance. They were totally wrong about that but it didn't stop Savannah Guthrie from trying.

For several minutes, Guthrie tried and failed to trip up the president with questions about everything from foreign policy and the Supreme Court to a little-known online conspiracy theory known as QAnon. His answers were properly combative without seeming too mean-spirited. I watched from the sidelines with David Bossie, one of the president's advisors on the 2020 campaign who had helped President Trump with guidance on laws, policies, and the inclinations of Republican voters all over the country.

What amazed me was that no matter what Savannah Guthrie said, no matter how hard she attempted to pander to the liberal viewers crowded around their televisions at home, the audience never wavered in their support for President Trump. Behind him, I heard several people letting out cheers of "Latinos for Trump." At one point, a woman dressed in red and white stepped up to the foot of the stage with a microphone. We had a feeling backstage that she was going to ask a negative question, which was true. But first, she took a pause and told President Trump that he had a nice smile.

"You're so handsome when you smile," she said.

That moment quickly went viral on Twitter, much to the dismay of the networks that were broadcasting the townhall. It seemed that, for all their efforts, they could not make President Trump look bad. I noticed, for instance, that right behind President Trump, visible to viewers at home, there was a young Hispanic woman—a recent immigrant from Venezuela—who smiled and nodded along with just about everything President Trump said. I understood why. I had spent much of my early life in the Tampa Bay area, and I still had friends there. I knew that many of the people who lived there had chosen to come to the United States because of political turmoil in their home countries. In most cases, these people had been alive when a charismatic leader had taken power, promising a worker's utopia with socialist policies. Then, they had seen their countries devolve into poverty, chaos, and instability. Unlike many of the liberal media journalists who were attacking President Trump from their penthouses in Manhattan, these people had *chosen* the United States as their home. They knew how fragile democracy and capitalism could be.

After the townhall was over, I walked over to where this supportive woman was sitting in the stands and gave her my card. "My name is Mark Meadows," I said. "I'm the White House chief of staff. Any event you want to get into, you just give me a call. You've got a free ticket."

She laughed and talked with me for a few minutes. President Trump also came over to say hello.

No matter what happened, I thought, we had Florida locked down.

Around ten thirty on election night, President Trump got a call from Karl Rove, the architect of George W. Bush's successful campaigns, congratulating him on his victory, which seemed all but assured. I stood there in the Residence with him while they spoke about the future of the Trump White House.

By this point, most presidents would have begun writing an acceptance speech. But not President Trump. He retained his conviction about writing speeches before the outcome was officially declared, and he did not want to go out there until every news network in the country had made the call.

I walked back down to the Map Room, where our analysts were reporting good news from social media. The Twitter traffic was all trending in the right direction. Then, out of nowhere, I heard a loud series of screams and expletives from the next room.

Fox News had called Arizona for Joe Biden.

Not only was this infuriating, but it was also mathematically impossible to determine at this early hour. With the information that Fox News had at the time, they could not possibly have been able to legitimately make the call that they did. My worst fears—that there was a liberal contingent within the network trying to sabotage President Trump in the name of objectivity—had been realized. I dialed Bill Sammon once again, tapping the numbers with such force that I'm surprised I didn't crack the screen of my iPhone.

"I don't see how you could have called it," I told him. "There is no information that you could have at this time that would make this call possible."

"Our models say that President Trump is going to lose Arizona," he said.

"It may well be that President Trump loses Arizona," I said. "But if he does, it's going to be by fewer than ten thousand votes, and there is *no way* you could know that right now."

The next answer was similar to the one I had gotten a few weeks earlier during President Trump's rally in Tampa. He said that Fox News did not care what we in the White House thought about their coverage, and that they were going to air whatever they damn well pleased. I knew in my heart— and my head, which, unlike Fox's election team, was capable of performing basic math—that their call was wrong, or, at the least, premature. But the call wasn't going to change. That much was certain. It didn't matter what happened now or how many votes ended up coming in for President Trump. Fox News couldn't just make a call like that and then take it back.

From there, it only got worse.

Somewhere around three a.m., the tide began to turn, but no one on our team could quite explain how. There were thousands of votes for Biden popping up all over the country, coming so quickly that it seemed to have been engineered that way. We learned about boxes of ballots being found in trucks, vote totals changing, and election workers being ushered out of rooms while the numbers shifted. If you looked at the social media traffic from that night—which I did, constantly—there was no doubt about it: President Trump was going to be reelected by a healthy margin. But what played out on the ground was much different.

By the time the sun came up, it was clear that we had a fight on our hands, and no one knew if we were ready for it.

— FIFTEEN —

The Long Con

I KNEW HE DIDN'T LOSE.

On the morning after the election, I came back to the White House and found President Trump sitting at his desk. It was clear that he'd been up most of the night, probably getting even less than his usual four or five hours of sleep. I knew that the situation was dire, and so did he. We were down a few votes in Arizona at the time, and the votes were still being counted in Georgia, Pennsylvania, and my home state of North Carolina. The campaign team was hard at work across town coming up with a plan of action. They were speaking with teams of lawyers on the ground, deciding how best to deal with the results as they came in. But President Trump knew that the numbers we were seeing weren't accurate.

They couldn't be.

For weeks, we had been campaigning at a herculean pace. President Trump had delivered more speeches during the last days of the campaign than any other period in his life, and the excitement of the people was palpable. In the last two days, we did a total of eleven rallies. Even with the seemingly impossible array of misfortunes we had suffered as a nation over the course of the past year, the crowds had continued to turn up in record numbers, excited as ever to get a glimpse of President Trump and to hear one of his speeches in person. There was just as much electricity as there had been in 2016, if not more.

I had spoken with dozens of people during those rallies, and I had heard some inspiring things from them. They were thrilled to be together, which is something you simply cannot fake. Some had turned up to hear President Trump speak for the first time; others had spent the last five or so years attending every rally that was held within a hundred miles of their home. Every time President Trump came to a city, some supporters would line up many hours in advance, often setting up camps and forming small communities to pass the time until Air Force One finally touched down on the tarmac.

In general, I found them to be some of the kindest, most generous people I had ever met. Many of them had met one another at Trump rallies in the past. There was a kinship in the MAGA movement that is almost never reported on, and it includes people from all walks of life. In the months that I had been traveling to rallies with of President Trump, I had spent time with carpenters, computer programmers, business owners, and used car salesmen, all of whom seemed like the best of friends as soon as the MAGA hats came out. I saw bartenders milling about with medical doctors, and groups of young people mixing with retirees like it was the most natural thing in the world.

These people were united by a common purpose—not so much by a love and respect for President Trump, although there *was* plenty of that, but by their shared sense of America as something that we should actually be proud of. (A crazy idea, I know.) When it seemed like the whole country was full of people who wanted to see this country torn down and rebuilt from the ground up, claiming that it was nothing more than a support system for the worst kind of racism in the world, you could come to a Trump rally and experience a renewed sense of pride in the United States of America, a country that most Americans love and respect.

For that, these people were routinely mocked by the mainstream media. They were referred to as "low-IQ voters," and "non-college-educated whites." They were routinely featured in newspaper columns about what "people in the middle of the country"—read: *stupid people*—really think about what this country needs. In June 2019, a pundit on MSNBC's *The 11th Hour with Brian Williams*, mocked every attendee at a Trump rally in Florida, saying that they were probably wearing "formal flip-flops and dress cargo pants."

In his rollicking Fake News account of the Trump campaign, Mike Bender of *The Wall Street Journal* follows a group of these devoted Trump fans who call themselves the Front Row Joes, attempting to subtly make the point that everyone in the group meets some dreadful end as a result of their support for the president. In a particularly troubling passage near the end of the book, he seems to mock one of these people for dying in a car accident on his way home from a Trump rally, then insults another one by saying that she lost her life savings by flying around the country to see the president speak. These sincere, trusting people let a reporter into their close circle of friends because, I'm sure, he acted like a friend and a confidant. He probably spoke with them as if he understood what they were going through. Meanwhile, he mocked them for their support of President Trump, convicting them in print for the *"crime"* of not having been born in the right place or educated at the right universities or worst of all, not being "woke."

When you think about it, these mocking portrayals of your average Trump voter all shared something in common, and that was *fear.* The mainstream media, which had been in control of the political narrative for the last hundred years, had finally come up against a group of people who simply would not swallow their elite leftist propaganda. For the first time, they encountered a sizable portion of the country who didn't need the biased information that they were selling.

So, they turned to mockery.

They mocked President Trump for just about anything they could think of, and when that didn't work, they turned their sights on his supporters. When conservatives raised questions about the Russia hoax or the impeachment, both of which were baseless and fraudulent from the beginning, they were mocked by the media. When they granted interviews to reporters outside of rallies in their home cities, expressing joy and hope at the prospect of Trump's second term, their words were chopped up, rearranged, and then shown on nightly comedy shows for the hosts to make fun of. For four years, the mainstream media sent a message to their viewers that anyone wearing a MAGA hat was willing to believe anything. They were accused of conspiracy thinking and hero worship, and compared at various points to the helpless adherents of a cult.

This would come in handy, of course, when the media wanted to deny any irregularities or fraud in an election.

———————

In the Oval Office, the first thing that President Trump wanted to discuss was Georgia.

He asked Kellyanne Conway, who had just suggested we come out with a weak statement about "making sure all votes were counted," whether the numbers we were seeing were even plausible. Yes, she said. In fact, they were quite plausible. President Trump was losing, and she didn't seem all that broken up about it.

"How can we be losing Georgia?" President Trump asked, seeming exasperated by the notion that the state was even up for grabs. "We were supposed to win Georgia by a landslide."

He was right. During a rally on November 1 in Rome, Georgia, a small city in the foothills, we saw more excitement for President Trump than we had seen in the last three cities combined. The morning after the rally, we had received estimates that more than thirty thousand people had attended—a massive number, even by the high standards of the Trump campaign. In fact, our support in the state was so strong that we hadn't even thought to schedule a rally there until a few days before it actually happened. And even then, we had scheduled it only as a favor to Senator David Perdue, who was running against a liberal media darling named Jon Ossoff.

The result was astounding. As soon as those Trump supporters left the parking lot and piled into the arena to hear their president speak, the roar of the crowd came at us with such force that it nearly knocked me over. It was like a rock concert, a game-winning touchdown, and the stroke of midnight on New Year's Eve all rolled into one. Yet within that wall of sound, I could have sworn that I could hear each of those thirty thousand voices speaking with perfect clarity, each one with its own story and history. It seemed that there were a million reasons that the people of Rome would want President Trump back in the White House, and they were all on full display that night. Whether it was the freedom to be proud of America again, the record-breaking economy that President Trump had provided, the extra money in their paychecks, or the thousands of soldiers who were preparing to come home from war thanks to President Trump's decision to safely end our endless wars in the Middle East, these people all had reasons to want four more years of Trump.

Over the course of my years in politics, I've run four campaigns. I've also seen a few hundred more up close, working with candidates as they wrote their speeches and greeted voters on the rope lines. And in that time I've become familiar with the malaise that comes over crowds in the late days of a losing campaign, the general sense that no matter how much excitement there seems to be, it's not going to be enough to win the votes that are needed on Election Day.

But that is *not* the feeling I got during the final days of President Trump's campaign. If anything, it was exactly the opposite.

So, I didn't know what to say to him, standing there in front of the Resolute Desk with some of the campaign's top advisors, when he asked me what had put us so far behind in states that we were sure—as in *dead certain*—that we could win. As we spoke, there were more mail-in ballots being counted, more boxes of Democrat ballots being located in trucks and basements all over key swing states. But we didn't know that at the time. All we knew was that something was not right, and that we weren't going to quit until we found out what it was.

Over the next few days, President Trump enlisted the help of a few top election lawyers. Right in the middle of all of this, two days after the election, I learned that I had come down with Covid-19. After just one day at home, and an immediate dose of hydroxychloroquine and a Z-Pak, I was feeling normal. The president told me it was not a convenient time for me to get sick. Still I had to work from home.

Physically fine, that was. Mentally, I was about as disturbed as I had ever been. During the days that I spent sitting in my home, I received calls from people all over the country who had troubling stories to tell.

After only a few days, they had found videos and evidence that was shocking and remains shocking to this day. In summary, we found that in the lead-up to the election, Democrats had followed a simple playbook. They worked tirelessly in the key battleground states of Arizona, Michigan, Nevada, Georgia, Pennsylvania, and Wisconsin to flood the system with ballots, many of which were mail-in. Using Covid-19 as an excuse, the governors of many of these states altered election procedures, which is a job that was supposed to be left to the legislatures. Then, because of the new flood of mail-in ballots, they lowered the standards for determining which ballots could be considered valid. If the signature on a ballot didn't match the one that the state had on file for an individual (which is something that should set off alarm bells for fraud), they went ahead and counted it anyway. That was if they ever bothered to check the signatures.

They were teed up for a Biden victory before a single vote was even cast.

But once election night arrived, and it became clear that President Trump was performing better than anyone—even those on his campaign team—had expected, they had to get creative. In Pennsylvania, a state where the Supreme Court had already ruled to extend the deadline for accepting mail-in ballots to well past Election Day, there were reports and tips of vans backing into a Philadelphia counting center with boxes full of ballots. In Georgia, there was video of a room full of vote counters leaving after a "water main break," then coming back to resume the count with boxes of ballots that they "found" under tables. I'm sure that these kinds of small-time frauds have been relatively common for years, and that they were allowed to occur only because no presidential candidate had ever taken the time to look for them. But this time, there seemed to be far too many to simply ignore them. Three or four instances of fraud would have been nothing. Even a few dozen would have seemed like little more than a rounding error. But we were finding hundreds and often thousands of allegations of widespread fraud. They just kept on coming.

If we were going to get to the bottom of this and ensure that our elections were truly free and fair, as our founders had intended, it was going to take much longer than a few days. Contrary to what the media reported, we never asked for an automatic victory for President Trump. All we wanted was time—time to sort through the ballots, root out the illegal ones, and count every single one of the valid ones. The president believed he had won and that any proper reconciliation of the legitimate votes was sure to demonstrate that.

Anyone who believed in American democracy should have wanted exactly the same thing.

———————

Around the country, the liberal media was ecstatic. They were following the vote counts in swing states as if their lives and careers depended on it, anxiously seeking any sign that President Trump was headed for the loss that they had been telling us was imminent. Every time President Trump or one of his allies would bring up clear evidence of electoral misconduct, their misinformation machine would kick into high gear, pouncing on the video or the document before it ever had any chance of seeing the light of day. Any article or video that suggested something shady had occurred at a polling place—even those that simply asked questions about it—was immediately taken down. Soon, it became impossible to find these videos on Google or Twitter. Big Tech was slowly continuing their attempts at erasing President Trump and his administration from history, and they weren't even trying to hide it.

Meanwhile, the Fake News was instituting a full-court press against President Trump. Before the so-called counting of the ballots was even done, they were labeling him a lunatic and a dictator for daring to question the outcome of the election. It was as if they had prewritten the headlines a few weeks in advance, then begun deploying them as soon as the polls opened on November 3.

Reading the coverage, I couldn't help but think of Stacey Abrams, a frighteningly radical liberal who had organized a big voter registration drive in Georgia. In the media, she was written about as some kind of hero who had turned Georgia, a state that was hotly contested for days, over to the Democrats on a silver platter. No one was quite sure *how* she had been able to do it, but they wrote the stories anyway, giving Abrams full credit for registering *just* enough Democrat voters to flip the state for Joe Biden. Few of them mentioned, however, that in 2018, Abrams had run for governor of Georgia and lost to Brian Kemp. For months afterward, she had gone around shouting to anyone who would listen that she had, in fact, *won* the election, saying that it was racism and gerrymandering that had cost her the race.

But did the Trump-hating media call *her* a lunatic or a conspiracy theorist? Of course not. She was on their team. Instead, they wrote about her in fawning magazine profiles, asking questions about the romance novels she was writing and the brave moves she had made to declare victory despite all available evidence to the contrary. In one particularly ridiculous story, titled "Why Stacey Abrams Is Still Saying She Won," the magazine spent a good portion of the interview asking the losing candidate her opinions about *Star Trek*.

I could not even imagine President Trump, who had never done anything but raise legitimate concerns about the way our elections are run, receiving similar treatment.

Obviously, President Trump had learned over the last four years that the deck was stacked against him, so he made plans to air his challenges to the official vote counts in court. He assembled a team of lawyers with Rudy Giuliani, Pam Bondi, Jenna Ellis, Cleta Mitchell, and others to tell the country about all of it—the mail-in ballots, the fraud, and the dirty tricks on election night.

I was well aware that this sounded like a conspiracy theory. In a sense, that was all part of the Democrats' game. The people who rigged this election knew that eventually, these irregularities would come to light. It simply was not possible, given this age of camera phones and constant social media surveillance, to carry out an operation like that in complete darkness. They knew that they wouldn't be able to get away with it by hiding their actions, at least not in the traditional sense. Instead, they conducted the operation, then attacked anyone who dared ask questions about what they had done.

Thanks to their allies in the liberal media, this was easy. For years, the media had been writing stories about Trump supporters that portrayed them as crazy, unhinged, or moronic. When your average CNN viewer heard "Trump supporter," they tended to think in cartoonish extremes rather than anything based in reality. I imagine that upon hearing the phrase, most liberals pictured a middle-aged white man with a big Pepe the Frog tattoo on his chest, probably shouting racist epithets and telling anyone who would listen that the aliens were coming back to get him at any moment.

This, like so much else, was intentional.

Even major newspapers like *The New York Times* and *The Wall Street Journal* devoted thousands of column inches to fringe conspiracy movements like QAnon, attempting to impute the bizarre ideas of that movement onto the average men and women all over the country who simply wanted President Trump back in the White House. The fake news machine painted with one broad brush, and they were not going to stop until they had covered more than 50 percent of the country. Their job was not to report the news, but rather to flatten all nuance, making it so that the phrase *Trump supporter* became politically and socially toxic.

This might have seemed harmless at the time, but as usual, there was a method to their madness. Thanks to their constant barrage of misleading news stories, whenever a supporter of President Trump raised concerns about a real issue—say, the fact that the Trump campaign had been illegally spied on by our intelligence agencies in an operation that was based entirely on a dossier full of lies—it became all too easy to label them "crazy," "paranoid," or, their favorite, a "conspiracy theorist." When people heard these terms, their brains drew on the years and years of negative stories that the media had been writing about Trump supporters. These epithets conjured images of lonely people stuck in their basements with bulletin boards and various clippings from magazines, tying the pieces of their insane theory together with pushpins and lengths of string. But in reality, the people asking questions about the election were only reacting to what they were seeing—actual evidence of fraud, right there in plain sight for anyone to access and analyze. I could not believe that more outlets were not writing about what was going on. I suppose that even with all the abuse that I had seen President Trump suffer at the hands of the Fake News, I was still relatively naive when it came to plumbing the true depths of their depravity.

In time, it became clear that the media's plan—the "long con"—had worked. Soon, anyone who had questions about the election was labeled a nutcase. And as anyone who's ever seen an Alfred Hitchcock film knows, trying to prove you're *not* insane once someone has already told the world that you are, only serves to make you look . . . well, like an insane person. It didn't matter how often we presented the facts, or how many signed affidavits we produced. The media, Big Tech, and the political establishment, a group that comprised both Democrats and Republicans, had finally seen the payoff on a four-year disinformation campaign, and it had resulted in victory for them.

Certainly, a once-in-a-century pandemic had helped them out, meaning that the number of mail-in ballots would explode far beyond anyone's control. Irregularities—of which there were many—could simply be blamed on Covid-19. They could say that the massive uptick in mail-in ballots was due to the increased number of people who didn't want to vote in person. They could say that the extremely low rate at which ballots were rejected for being fraudulent—which, in Georgia alone, decreased dramatically—was also due, somehow, to the pandemic. But all you had to do was scratch the surface to see that almost none of these inconsistencies had anything to do with Covid-19.

They ignored the fact that President Trump, who was supposedly losing support left and right, got 12 million more votes on election night than he had in 2016, or that despite being, in the words of *The New York Times*, "a racist" who "talks about and treats people differently based on their race," President Trump saw an enormous surge in his support among Black and Latino voters and a *decrease* in his support among the white men who were supposedly his main supporters.

The Fake News also touted, for about ten seconds, the fact that Joe Biden, a candidate with all the charisma of an old, rusty coin collection, had (supposedly) managed to rack up 81 million votes, more than any candidate in the history of American politics. Then, in what seemed like the blink of an eye, they stopped talking about it. I have a suspicion this if that number were *real*, you wouldn't have been able to open a newspaper without seeing it. Brian Stelter and Don Lemon would have gotten matching "81 million!" tattoos on their foreheads. But it's not a real number, and they knew it. It was one thing for them to rig the election and get away with it, but even for them, bragging about the theft would be a bridge too far. It would, to adapt an analogy favored by President Trump, be like a thief getting away with a whole bag of loot from Tiffany, then showing up to the store the next day wearing three brand-new diamond necklaces. So, they got quiet, secure in the knowledge that no one was going to catch them.

When we brought these credible accusations of voter fraud to court, however, they were dismissed quickly, before anyone even reviewed the evidence. For the most part, the cases were dismissed because the judges believed that states had no "standing" to bring the cases. The facts of fraud were not looked at by the judges and courts. In the middle of December, the Supreme Court dealt us the final blow, ruling that they would not hear any of President Trump's many challenges to the election results. In the court's opinion, the president of the United States had no standing to bring a challenge to an election that he was running in—one that was unfairly decided against him. If he didn't have standing, I wondered, who did? Would they have made the decision if things had gone the other way, and Joe Biden was the one bringing the challenge?

If you've been paying attention, I'm sure you know the answer to that.

To this day, I don't think I've ever seen President Trump quite as despondent as he was when I walked into the Oval Office in late December. My head hanging low, I informed him that the Supreme Court would not be hearing our challenges to the election results.

For a moment, he said nothing. Then, finally, after a few seconds, he looked up from the desk at the ceiling and folded his arms.

"Can you believe that?" he asked.

"No sir," I said. "No, I can't."

I don't think that was quite true. Considering what had occurred during the last four years, it was sadly believable.

Over the course of the next weeks, President Trump went through various stages of grief and anger. He was livid that the election had been stolen from him and eager to do something that would give us more to prove that he had, in fact, gotten enough votes to hold the White House for another four years. Contrary to the slew of false allegations made against him, not once during these weeks did he suggest that we invade another country, set off a nuclear bomb, or deploy the United States military to remain in power. All he wanted was time to get to the bottom of what really happened and get a fair count. But the political establishment, up to and including the United States Supreme Court, would not give him the chance.

During those last months, we kept getting tips from all around the country from people who claimed to have witnessed fraud right in front of their eyes. At the time, we took these reports seriously, knowing that if there had been one credible instance of fraud that we knew about—and there were many—there were probably hundreds, even thousands, more that we *didn't* know about. The media alleged that President Trump was trying to "disrupt the Democratic process" by objecting to the results of the presidential election. They could not be more wrong.

In fact, President Trump was among the people who wanted to *uphold* the Democratic process. Everyone else seemed content to ignore credible allegations of fraud and simply move on, happy to turn a blind eye to the evidence around them.

It didn't surprise me that our many referrals to the Department of Justice were not seriously investigated. I never believed that they would, given the weak track record of that department in President Trump's first term.

But that didn't stop President Trump from making a last formal address to his supporters, which would be held on a fifty-two-acre plot of land on the south side of the White House called the Ellipse. The idea to gather on January 6 was organic and it wasn't until the president said that he wanted to address the various groups that the plans came together. Before the final word came down from Congress that the election was settled, he wanted to make sure that all those people he had met over his four years—the ones who had shown up to every rally, listened to his speeches, and written him letters about their frustrations with the establishment—would have one more chance to come together, make their voices heard, and encourage each other. He did not call for violence, and he did not expect that anyone would enter the Capitol Building.

I was with him in the motorcade on the way to the speech, which had been scheduled for early in the afternoon. The sky was gray, and the weather was cold, even for January. President Trump wore a black overcoat and black gloves, almost as if he was in mourning for the second term that he had been unfairly denied. When he mounted the podium that afternoon, it was not ranting demands that came out of his mouth; if anything, he was more subdued than usual, simply stating his points and letting the crowd know that he was not going to give up on America, or on them.

"Our media is not free," he said. "It's not fair. It suppresses thought. It suppresses speech, and it's become the enemy of the people. It's the biggest problem we have in this country. No third world countries would even attempt to do what we caught them doing."

A few sentences later, President Trump ad-libbed a line that no one had seen before, saying, "Now it is up to Congress to confront this egregious assault on our democracy. After this, we're going to walk down—and I'll be there with you. We're going to walk down to the Capitol, and we're going to cheer on our brave senators and congressmen and women. We're probably not going to be cheering so much for some of them, because you'll never take back our country with weakness. You have to show strength; you have to be strong."

When he got offstage, President Trump let me know that he had been speaking metaphorically about the walk to the Capitol. He knew as well as anyone that we couldn't organize a trip like that on such short notice. It was clear the whole time that he didn't actually intend to walk down Pennsylvania Avenue with the crowd. In the end, most of the hundreds of thousands there didn't walk down, either.

To this day, no one is quite sure how many people were standing in the Ellipse listening to him speak those words. In the immediate aftermath, President Trump would guess a million, which is probably slightly above the mark, although it certainly did look like there were around that many from where I was standing. If I had to bet, I would say there were about at least 250,000 people there that day, which is astounding, considering that most of them did not live anywhere near our nation's capital.

But no one would be focused on the actions of those hundreds of thousands of people in the months to come—all those peaceful supporters of President Trump who came without hate in their hearts or any bad intentions. Instead, they would laser in on the actions of a handful of fanatics across town who had decided—all on their own, by the way, with absolutely no urging from President Trump—to break into the Capitol Building and try to wreak havoc. These people were not representative of the crowd that was there that day any more than the hundreds of people who had broken windows, assaulted police officers, and ripped down statues during the George Floyd protests were representative of the millions of Americans who believed in Martin Luther King Jr's dream of a nation where men would not be judged by the color of their skin. Yet the same networks who had covered for those Antifa and BLM criminals and rioters all summer soon jumped right onto the narrative that the people who breached the Capitol were indicative of all concerned Trump supporters.

Now they could equate anyone who suggested that the election had been stolen with the people who had breached the Capitol. They could now produce their so-called proof, shaky and nonsensical though it was, that President Trump supposedly wanted to incite a violent overthrow of the country. And perhaps most significantly, they finally had their reason to remove him from Twitter, the medium that he had used to cut through their lies and false narratives for four years, effectively putting him on the road, they believed, to irrelevance.

Finally, the long con was complete.

Yet if you really study what occurred, you'll find that these people who broke in were on their way to the Capitol Building long before President Trump uttered his ad-libbed line about walking down to "cheer on our senators and congressmen and women." They didn't need instructions from anyone to do what they did.

The real question—the one that should be investigated by Congress—is why, despite several offers from the White House and DoD to send 10,000 National Guard into our nation's capital before the January 6 rally, Mayor Muriel Bowser refused to accept their help. Over and over again, President Trump said that the crowd was going to be huge and that a great deal of help would be required. He said that he would be happy to provide this help, if the mayor would only take it. But again, she refused. In fact, the response time, which has been largely criticized, was only possible because the National Guard had been put on alert at the president's direction.

What occurred that day was shameful. Nobody doubts that. But the regrettable actions of a small group of people do not invalidate the genuine concerns of the other hundreds of thousands of people who had gathered peacefully that afternoon, or of the millions more who were showing their support on Twitter and other social media networks. In the aftermath of the attack, President Trump was mortified. He knew that the media would take this terrible incident and twist it around. He also knew that his days on Twitter were probably numbered; even so, he sent out a few final messages to his supporters.

But his enthusiasm for getting things done never wavered. As the staff continued to leave around him, he was still asking about the last-minute executive orders we could sign before we left the White House. He was always concerned for the forgotten men and women of the United States—the ones who had lined up every time he came into town, eagerly hoping to get a glimpse of him, or to catch one of the signed hats that he threw out at the end of his rallies. They were the ones he was thinking of when he organized the Rally to Save America in the first place, and they are the ones he still thinks about to this day.

"Mark," he would say to me. "Look, if I lost, I would have no problem admitting it. I would sit back and retire and probably have a much easier life. But I *didn't* lose. People need me to get back to work. We're not done yet."

He was absolutely correct. There was so much more to be done, and we had so little time. And when you considered all the time that we had to waste defending ourselves against the baseless accusations of Congress and the Fake News, we had barely even started.

— SIXTEEN —

The Ride Out

AROUND SIX THIRTY in the morning on Inauguration Day, my phone rang. It was President Trump, who was calling me from the White House for the last time. I put down the Bible that I'd been reading and answered the phone. By the sound of his voice, he seemed to have been up for a few hours already.

"Mr. President," I said. "Good morning."

I knew that there were a few hundred things we could discuss. There was so much we hadn't done. For about two weeks or so, we had been moving at a speed that was astounding, even for the Trump White House. First, we had been preparing documents that would allow us to issue pardons to more than 144 Americans who, President Trump believed, needed to have their records expunged. We had been working to declassify various documents related to the Russia hoax, ensuring that the egregious crimes that the United States intelligence community had committed against President Trump were entered into the public record once and for all. We created the 1776 Commission that would focus on teaching our nation's real history. Finally, we had been preparing a team to defend President Trump against yet another impeachment inquiry, which Democrats in Congress were pursuing even though he would no longer be the president.

With less than five hours left in his historic presidency, at a time when most outgoing presidents would be quietly making notes for their memoirs and taking stock of their time in the White House, President Trump was being forced to defend his legacy yet again.

"How do we look in Congress?" he said. "I've heard that there are some Republicans who might be turning against us. That would be a very unwise thing for them to do."

I assured President Trump that our allies in Congress were still with us. No matter what was said during the impeachment trial, anyone in the chamber with half a brain would know that he was absolutely innocent of the charges against him—which, to my genuine surprise, included "inciting an insurrection."

It was amazing, I thought, their use of that word *insurrection*. During the riots that had been occurring all summer, these same Democrats and their allies in the Fake News had balked at President Trump's use of the term. Even when the basement of St. John's Episcopal Church was on fire and the violent crowds were inching closer and closer to the White House, many of them armed with weapons and other projectiles, the liberals insisted that all we had on our hands was a bunch of "peaceful protests." In recent months, several books have gleefully recounted a story—which, like anything else contained in these books, may or may not be apocryphal—about General Mark Milley, who supposedly sat in the Oval Office, pointed at a portrait of President Lincoln, and said "*that* guy had an insurrection; what we have, Mr. President, is a protest."

In the end, those "peaceful protests" and the criminals who participated in them did millions of dollars of damage to property all over the country. In Portland, they tried to burn down a federal courthouse and attempted to take over city hall, *literally* overthrowing our federal government there. In Seattle, they organized zones where police and other law enforcement officers were not permitted to go, causing the deaths of two people over the course of several months. If burning a federal courthouse and establishing a separate "autonomous zone" within the borders of the United States is not an insurrection, then I'm really not sure what is.

But I assured President Trump once again that all would be well with the impeachment trial, and we discussed what my role in the proceedings would be after we left the White House. I told him that I would be with him, as always, until he no longer needed my assistance. It didn't matter whether he was sitting behind the Resolute Desk, a dinner table at Mar-a-Lago, or the massive, magazine-covered desk in Trump Tower. He was my president, and I would serve at his pleasure for as long as he needed me.

When we finished speaking about impeachment, President Trump began turning to other things. For a moment, I felt as if this bright, clear morning was the beginning of just another day—as if I was about to wash up, put on any old suit, and head into the office, where I would find President Trump seated in the Oval Office where he so rightly belonged.

But I wasn't.

Instead, in about two hours, President Trump would walk out of the White House for the last time, striding across the south lawn with First Lady Melania Trump by his side. Behind them would be Dan Scavino and Melania Trump's chief of staff. A few days earlier, President Trump had approached me after a meeting in the Oval Office to ask if I wanted to be the one to accompany him on his last ride out of the White House. I was moved beyond words to have been asked. But I decided that Dan, who had been with President Trump since he worked at one of the Trump golf courses in the early 2000s, then by his side during the campaign and his entire four-year stretch in the White House, should be the one walking beside him on his way out. I know that Dan was honored when President Trump asked him to go.

On the phone, President Trump spoke as if he wasn't planning to go anywhere. He mentioned the long list of pardons we hadn't been able to complete, largely due to the slowness on the part of various attorneys in the federal government. He wondered again about the precise details of the impeachment trial, including how much money the new lawyers would charge and how we could best defend him against the Democrats' attacks.

"This was nothing," he said. "They are impeaching me over—"

"Mr. President," I said, cutting him off for the first time since I had taken the job nearly one year earlier. "I hate to cut you off, but it's almost seven o'clock. I have to meet you down at Andrews Air Force Base in one hour and . . . well, sir, I haven't even showered yet."

President Trump paused. It was as if, for a moment at least, we had slipped into the same pleasant alternate reality—one in which we weren't going anywhere, and we had all the time in the world to continue the business of running the country, fighting the Fake News, and making life better for every single person in the United States—even, in the words of President Trump, for the "haters and losers" who attacked us day in and day out. After a moment, he laughed, although not in the hearty, feel-good way that he usually did. This one was solemn, almost defeated.

"Alright, Mark. I'll see you there."

I put the phone down, showered, and headed out to Joint Base Andrews with Debbie a little after seven, my Secret Service detail driving. One of my detail members had flattered us by saying that of all the people he had protected—West Wing staffers and their families, even several presidents themselves—we were the easiest ones to get along with. Our Secret Service agents had become as close as most friends. One even told us, in confidence, that today, the final day of President Trump's time in office, would be what he referred to as a "heavy day" for many of the men and women of the Secret Service. There was not a glimmer of partisan bias in the statement. Just a kind word for a difficult day. Despite what you might be reading in books and the press, there was no group of people who loved and respected President Trump more than the brave people who kept him safe every day.

We arrived at the airport shortly before President Trump and gathered on the tarmac, where Air Force One sat waiting to take President Trump and the First Lady down to Mar-a-Lago. They were planning to spend winters in Florida for the foreseeable future—at least until they came back to Washington, triumphant, the winter of 2025. We saw Jared Kushner and Ivanka Trump, who were there with their children. Over the years, Debbie had developed a friendship with Arabella, Jared and Ivanka's eldest daughter, which began when Debbie gave her some *Little House on the Prairie* books as a gift. Arabella had proudly reported that she'd finished the first book, and that she was moving on to the rest, staying up late some nights to finish the whole series.

I also saw Donald Trump Jr., who had become a good friend throughout the last four years. In 2016, as the first campaign was hitting its stride in my home state of North Carolina, Don Jr. was a surrogate for his father. He came to my district in the western part of North Carolina to address a small group of farmers. The Trump kids were never shy about helping their father on the campaign trail, but Don Jr. surprised me by jumping on to the flatbed of a pickup truck with a John Deere tractor in the background, a few hay bales on each side, to speak to a group of less than one hundred people. The time that he took to get there, driving for hours through small towns over one-lane roads, let the people know that he—and, by extension, his father—cared about them. Don Jr. was also uniquely positioned to speak about guns and ammo, something that flowed off his tongue with ease.

By 2020, Don Jr. still carried the Trump name, but his connection was no longer just to his father. He was his own man, and he spoke to his own audience—one that loved freedom, loved guns, loved America's greatness, stood for our flag and hated the swamp. No one connected with the base better than Don Jr. He was a bit edgy, and perhaps too edgy to ever run for office. Of course, that was said about his dad as well.

In the chilly, breezy morning, the mood of the crowd was somber in a way that it probably wouldn't have been if we had been holding the ceremony after eight years in the White House rather than four—or if we believed that Joe Biden was the rightful winner of the 2020 election. As President Trump has said often, he would have had no problem admitting that he lost the race. If he really did believe that the American people had gone to the polls on Election Day, cast one ballot each, and come together in a show of support for Joe Biden just as they had done for him four years earlier, he would have been the first to admit that it was time to go. He would have called to congratulate the Biden campaign, invited the new president to the White House, and then cheerfully resumed the wonderful life of luxury that he had given up to serve as our president in the first place.

But that is *not* what he believed happened. The election had been rigged, and his primary means of getting that message out to the American people—the president's Twitter feed— had been taken away.

Even so, it was inspiring to watch President Trump step off Marine One for the last time, waving to his supporters and saluting the two United States Marines who waited at the door of the helicopter. It was hard not to feel slightly uplifted as he ascended to a small stage that his team had set up in front of the plane that would take him away in a few minutes. He took to the podium for the last time as president, thanking me and the rest of his team for our four years of hard work. From there, he ran through a short list of what he had been able to accomplish as president. I knew that every sentence he spoke represented hundreds, even thousands of hours of backbreaking work on the part of his administration.

What we've done has been amazing by any standard. We rebuilt the United States military. We created a new force called the Space Force. That in itself would be a major achievement for a regular administration. We were not a regular administration . . . We took care of the vets, ninety-one percent approval rating. They've never had that before . . . They were very badly treated before we came along. And as you know, we get them great service and we pick up the bill and they can go out and they can see a doctor if they have to wait long periods of time . . . We also got tax cuts, the largest tax cut and reform in the history of our country by far. I hope they don't raise your taxes. But if they do, I told you so . . . And if you look at the regulations, which I consider the regulation cuts to be maybe even more important. That's why we have such good and have had such good job numbers. The job numbers have been absolutely incredible.

I'm sure he could have spoken for another four hours, just listing all the things he had been able to accomplish, even in the face of seemingly insurmountable opposition. In fact, a notebook we produced in the final weeks turned out to have one thousand of the most amazing accomplishments of the first term of any president. But instead, he wrapped things up after a few minutes, finishing with these moving lines:

I will always fight for you. I will be watching. I will be listening. And I will tell you that the future of this country has never been better. I wish the new adminis- tration great luck and great success. I think they'll have great success. They have the foundation to do some- thing really spectacular. And again, we put it in a posi- tion like it's never been before, despite the worst plague to hit since, I guess you'd say, 1917—over one hundred years ago. And despite that, despite that the things that we've done have been just incredible and I couldn't have done them, done it without you.

So just a goodbye. We love you. We will be back in some form.

After a prolonged applause, President Trump left the stage and walked toward the plane. As he walked, I thought briefly of all that we might have been able to accomplish if we only had four more years. Despite the long list of accomplishments that he had just read—which was only a small percentage of what he had been able to do—there was so much work left to be done.

As we were finishing things up at the White House, Debbie had reminded me of a story from the Old Testament, which recounts how Joshua, right-hand man to Moses and his successor as the leader of the Israelites, had prayed to God for aid during a battle. Then, as a sign that God was on the side of Joshua and the Israelites, He had made the sun and the moon stand still for a full day, giving them twenty-four hours of light to prevail over their enemies, the Amorites. Standing at Joint Base Andrews that morning, watching President Trump board his final flight as president of the United States, I found myself wishing for something similar. If we could get only one more day, one more hour, the things we could accomplish would make all that we had done so far seem minor by comparison. Truly, we were just getting started.

Just before he got on the plane, the boss turned around and looked my way. I gave him a thumbs-up and he started walking back to me, leaving Melania steps away from Air Force One. So I met him halfway.

President Trump pulled me in and whispered into my ear, "You've done a terrific job, Mark," he said. "I wish I'd gotten you earlier."

"I'm proud of you," he said. "Now go get 'em."

Emotions flooded over me as he turned to board Air Force One and I walked away.

By this point, I had spent enough time around President Trump to know that he did not give compliments freely—at least not directly to the person he was talking about. That was part of his style. He'd always give a shout out to a staffer or two in the beginnings of his speeches, or maybe start a meeting by saying what a terrific job someone had done on a project or a bill. When you worked with him, you were expected to come to work, do your job, and to do it with some small percentage of the energy that President Trump brought to his own job. If you were in it for pats on the back or compliments, you were working in the wrong White House.

I walked back to Debbie, still fighting back tears, secure in the knowledge that when Joe Biden took his oath of office at noon, it would not signal the end of an era, as some pundits were predicting. It would not deal a deathblow to the America First agenda that President Trump had worked so incredibly hard on for the past four years. If anything, it would be a brief time to rest, gather our strength, and prepare for the campaign of the century.

Our work, I thought to myself, was not done. Far from it.

Then I remembered that my work—as in the things that I still had left to do that day as chief of staff—was not done either. I walked briskly back to my car and headed straight for the White House.

We sped down the parade route set up for Joe Biden. It was around ten o'clock in the morning, and the sidewalks were nearly empty. I remarked briefly that President Trump had managed to bring out a bigger crowd when he was sitting in Walter Reed sick with Covid-19 than Biden had drawn for his inauguration. Those people had seemed ten times as excited when he drove by as any of these people looked now. Somehow, the president who had supposedly won millions more votes than any candidate in the history of this country was about to speak to a mostly empty National Mall, and his crowd looked like they were in one giant waiting room at the dentist.

I wasn't buying it.

But for now, the election wasn't my focus. Back at the White House, I had several documents to pick up, and only about two hours to do it. For weeks, we had been attempting to declassify several key papers that would unravel the full story of how the United States intelligence community had targeted President Trump, spied on his campaign, and attempted to bring him down—which, by the way, is the only "coup" that ever occurred during President Trump's years in the White House. For months and months, the President would ask, "Where's Durham? What has happened to the Durham report? How can it possibly be taking that long? We will NEVER see anything come from it." The West Wing had no visibility into this investigation being conducted by the Department of Justice and could only wait, along with the rest of America, for the verdict. It was not only the President that had these valid questions but nearly every Trump supporter that I ran into would ask the same thing. They had seen nothing come from the years of Capitol Hill hearings. They heard James Comey say that Hillary was only reckless despite their chants of "Lock Her Up". They had heard Attorney General Bill Barr confirm that the President's campaign was indeed spied upon and yet, like most things in Washington DC, the urgency for reform and transparency moved at a snail's pace. Wait, that is unfair to the snail.

The President had declassified some documents before I became Chief of Staff, but several key documents remained classified despite his direct orders to declassify a list of relevant notes, memos and emails. The DOJ or the FBI would consistently push back when he asked for the remaining documents to be declassified. In these final weeks, when the President's request was once again ignored, he demanded that these documents be brought to the White House and I personally went through every page, to make sure that the President's declassification would not inadvertently disclose sources and methods. DOJ had finally allowed key documents to be declassified and yet minutes before Joe Biden would be sworn in, they were trying to redact information they had just provided. I am confident that President Trump's order will provide much needed clarity and remove any excuse for the final Durham report to remain in a classified vault.

But the clock was ticking. At the stroke of noon, the Biden administration would officially be in control of the building. At 12:01, Trump Time would stop. I would cease to be an employee of the building, and would, technically, become a trespasser on government property.

On my way out, I stopped into my old office to see Ron Klain, who was taking over the job of chief of staff. At the president's request, I had worked with Ron and his team to assist with transition briefings as well as coordinating the daily intel briefings that the Biden team had been receiving even before January 20.

As was the custom, Ron and I had a brief but cordial conversation. The whole time I was in the room, he wore two masks and wouldn't come within ten feet of me. I did not envy the job that he was about to begin. But I knew that no matter who was in the Oval Office, this job was sacred. I'm sure that Ron had a similar respect for Biden as I had for my president, and I wished him the best.

On my way out, I noticed that they were also setting up plexiglass on two sides of every desk. Not *all* sides, just two. The air was still free to flow into the face of whoever was sitting down at all of these desks.

I left the building around eleven forty-five, just in time to avoid the "Chief of Staff Refused to Leave the White House" headline in the next day's *New York Times*.

My heart was heavy, but I walked with my head held high, secure in the knowledge that my colleagues and I had, as President Trump had put it so beautifully that morning "left it all on the field."

Over the next few days, Debbie and I worked to readjust to civilian life. I had turned in my government phone, which was probably full of enough Chinese and Russian viruses to make it physically heavier. I felt like telling the guys in the White House tech shop to just give it the old Hillary Clinton treatment, washing it out with bleach and crushing it under the wheels of a car. The next day, we went down to the garage and kicked the tires on my old BMW, wondering if it would start after ten months of sitting idle.

It didn't.

During a dinner in a small restaurant near our condo, a waiter recognized me and leaned down just before taking our order.

"I just can't believe we lost," he whispered. I said the same thing, and a frown came across his face. Soon, we were eating some special dishes compliments of the house. It turned out that he *and* the owner were huge fans of our president, though they were always careful not to say it publicly, lest some blue-haired BLM terrorist throw a brick through their window in the night.

Something similar happened when we went to buy a new car to replace my old BMW, which clearly wasn't going to come back from the dead this time. As soon as we walked onto the showroom floor, the owner of the dealership recognized me and pulled me aside.

"We're huge Trump fans here!" he said. "All of us!"

He wanted his picture taken with me. I think it made him feel like he'd gotten close to Trump himself. When we came back to pick the car up a few days later, Debbie brought him a bag of some Trump swag we had saved—hats, candles, small boxes of candies for the kids. We told him that half the bag was for him and the other half was for the rest of the sales staff, but we later saw him throwing the whole thing in the trunk of his car. Then he came back to let me know that he'd gotten a haircut that made him look *much* better, and asked if we could take another picture, which we did.

It didn't end there. I was stopped almost everywhere I went. I would meet people who seemed to be utterly baffled that President Trump had lost the election.

Whenever I got discouraged, though, I would usually get a call from President Trump. The first one came when he had been out of office for only about three hours, and it was to Debbie's phone. He'd gotten a new phone number, and he didn't know my new number yet. We missed the call, but the message, which we still have, went something like: "Hi Deb. It's Donald Trump, your favorite president. I saw you out there during the speech. Kind of sad, but it's okay. Anyway, tell Mark to give me a call. Try this number . . . no, wait, not that number. Use this one." I talked to him that afternoon.

The next morning, we got a call from Molly Michael, who gave us one of the boss's new numbers. President Trump called a few hours later, asking if I could recommend a new accountant for him. I promised to keep an ear out.

And just like that, we fell into a new rhythm. It was nothing like working in the White House. There was a little more time to comply with requests. One afternoon, he called to let me know that he had a brand-new phone number—one that the head of Verizon, who was a friend, had gotten him. Apparently, it ended with a special series of numbers. When I told him that I couldn't see it, and that his number still came up "private" when he called me, he was amused.

"Well, look at that. This thing is worth a million dollars, and now no one is going to know."

Aside from the jokes, there was something comforting about hearing President Trump's voice every day again. All throughout the impeachment trial, which ended in his quick acquittal, as everyone expected, we spoke about the frightening direction that the country was taking. We discussed how desperate the Democrats must be for attention if they were still bringing him up, and still trying to impeach him when he was out of office. But once that was concluded, our discussions turned to the future of America, and to what role President Trump might play in it.

Make no mistake. Our work is not done.

President Trump will be back.

American Carnage

BY THE TIME President Trump touched down in Cull-man, Alabama, a hard rain had been falling for hours. Earlier that afternoon, the first winds of a tropical storm had begun blowing in the Northeast, nearly forcing the small private plane President Trump was traveling in to remain on the runway in Bedminster, New Jersey.

Even the weather, it seemed, was against him.

But once again, President Trump and his team had taken off just in time, hitting the runway in Alabama with about one hour to spare. On the sprawling fields of a local business called York Family Farms, there were around 20,000 people waiting in the rain to hear him speak. Many of them had been stand-ing in line all day, holding their homemade signs facedown to keep the ink from running in the rain, turning the brims of their MAGA hats against the weather until seven o'clock, when President Trump was set to arrive. Unfortunately, I was not able to attend the rally. Neither were the dozen or so women from my home state of North Carolina whom the pres-ident called his "rally ladies." Since his first campaign, these hardworking and enthusiastic women had traveled to several states where President Trump had scheduled rallies, often showing up hours early to work before the speech began. To date, they have worked more than sixty rallies, coordinating with the campaign's logistics teams, verifying credentials, and making sure the VIPs got to their reserved places. Once that was all done, they would sit right in the front row, cheering and showing their support for President Trump.

In all my years attending events with President Trump, I don't think I had ever seen a crowd more in need of a few words from their president—their *real* president—than this one. I watched closely from home, as anxious to hear from President Trump as anyone else in the country. In the weeks leading up to the rally, the forgotten men and women of this country had been dealt more blows than it seemed possible to bear. In the middle of a summer that had already included rising inflation, extremely high gas prices, and hundreds of thousands of illegal immigrants pouring into our country from the south (many of whom were almost certainly infected with Covid-19), the Biden administration had managed to create a crisis of such magnitude that everything else seemed minor by comparison.

It began on July 6, when, acting on explicit orders from Joe Biden, United States soldiers shut off the lights at Bagram Air Base for the last time, slipping out in the dead of night without even telling the base's new Afghan commander. For years, Bagram Air Base had been the center of the United States' effort to wage the War on Terror in Afghanistan. From there, we had driven the repressive, radical Islamic regime known as the Taliban from power and hunted down several members of the terror group Al-Qaeda. In the years since, Bagram Air Base had served as a bulwark against the Taliban; as long as there was still an American flag flying overhead, they knew that their return to power was impossible.

President Biden knew this—although it might be more accurate to say that he *used to* know it, back when his critical thinking skills were still semi-intact, before his brain was reduced to a pile of half-formed sentences and stories about his old pal Corn Pop. He was also aware, surely, of how crucial this air base was to the Afghan Army. When the United States pulled its troops out, they would be left to face the Taliban— or, as Biden insisted on mispronouncing it, the *TAL-ee-bon*— alone. Any competent general might have told him that without American air support, the Afghan Army was nothing more than a bunch of guys standing around in the sand, holding their expensive American rifles and waiting to die.

Biden knew this, and he ordered the base to be shut down anyway. For the Afghan Army, and for the Americans who had been in the country for years supporting them, this was a potential death sentence. Biden knew it, and so did General Mark Milley, who had stayed on as Biden's chairman of the Joint Chiefs. Possibly, Milley might have missed a few intelligence briefings during those months, given how busy he seemed to be granting long interviews to Trump-hating writers and brushing up on the latest works of antiracism, gender studies, and textbooks on white rage. As I was watching the devastation unfolding in Afghanistan, it was difficult for me not to think about the testimony that General Milley had given before Congress a few months earlier, during which he professed a strong desire to study Critical Race Theory so that he could understand "white rage." I saw plenty of rage during the debacle in Afghanistan—with reports of ritual killings, public executions, and the abject subjugation of Afghanistan's women—and none of it, as far as I could tell, was coming from the angry white people that General Milley had seemed so concerned with. Rather, it was coming from a band of deranged radical Islamists, all of them freshly emboldened by the knowledge that weak-willed, self-serving, supposed leaders like him were now fully in charge of the world's greatest fighting force.

When he was in charge, President Trump also had allies willing to execute his military objectives. One of them was Robert O'Brien, who served as the national security advisor after John Bolton. Robert became a key ally in the West Wing, making sure that our military and national security objectives were addressed and reviewed with urgency. In last year of the Trump administration, it was Ambassador O'Brien who would step in when secretary of Defense Mark Esper went AWOL. In truth, there were only a few times when Secretary Esper was personally unavailable, but they were crucial. Once, I tried to reach out to him while he was snorkeling in the Pacific and his staff indicated that he was not to be interrupted. In the weeks following that incident, Secretary Esper would claim he had no knowledge of operational decisions that had long been discussed, saying that it was "the first [he was] hearing" of the decisions. It was the typical "defer and delay" tactic response that was all too common with him in his last six months.

After he returned from his trip, on a video conference with several of our top national security team in attendance, Secretary Esper's "first I am hearing of this" comment struck a nerve. My response was direct and to the point. "Perhaps," I said, "if you spent less time snorkeling in the Pacific and more time doing your job, you wouldn't be surprised. Just get it done." Esper was effective at making small decisions on canceling clergy in California or authorizing the latest woke training material, but when it came to critical decisions that affected our national security, it was Robert O'Brien whom I relied on.

A little more than one year earlier, I had been with President Trump while he negotiated with the Taliban. I heard the way he spoke to these enemies. I can tell you that today they would be acting much differently if President Trump was still calling the shots. I witnessed firsthand how President Trump would send air support to specific regions to help the Afghan Army ward off advancing Taliban fighters. I was with O'Brien and Pompeo when President Trump made it clear that any withdrawal would not be done "Saigon style." Instead, he would make sure that all Americans were evacuated first, that all interpreters were brought to safety, and that all our army equipment was removed. He expressed a clear desire to hold Bagram Air Base, where he had landed on a previous Thanksgiving to express his deep appreciation to our men and women in uniform. I was also with him when he received "the best military advice," which said that we could reduce our troop count from 4,500 to 2,500, keeping them safe while a transitional power government was formed.

In early 2020, President Trump and a small group of his national security advisors gathered for a call with Abdul Ghani Baradar, the chief negotiator for the Taliban. During his reign, Mullah Baradar had ruled Afghanistan with cruelty and terror, stoning women and executing men in soccer stadiums for minor offenses against Islam. President Trump was dead set on not allowing that to happen again.

During the various calls that made up our negotiations, President Trump spoke with a calm authority that carried just a hint of menace, not unlike General George Patton during his famous speeches. He clearly stated the conditions that would need to be met before a single American soldier came home. Under President Trump's supervision, the Taliban would not be permitted to simply run roughshod over the Afghan coun-tryside as they had done in the years prior to the US invasion. Instead, they would have to form a joint interim government with the democratically elected officials who were already in power, attempting to form a representative government that would maintain diplomatic ties to the United States. Together, this group would have to forcefully condemn the terror group Al-Qaeda. They would also have to consent to a small special operations force remaining in the country to prevent terror attacks. It would be a slow, methodical withdrawal, one that would be delayed any number of times, but when it came to the safety of our service members, we were willing to wait.

According to President Trump, the final withdrawal would begin once those conditions had been met—and *only* when those conditions had been met. We did begin reducing the number of troops from 4,500 to about 2,500 as planned, but we did it safely.

Toward the end of the meeting, President Trump leaned closer to the speakerphone on the edge of his desk in the Oval Office, delivering an ultimatum that would make the hairs on the back of your neck stand up. I'm sure that somewhere Mullah Baradar is still thinking about it too, sweating under that jet-black turban of his every time the words come back to him.

"Before we start this withdrawal," President Trump said, "I want to make something clear. Let me just tell you right now that if anything bad happens to Americans or America inter-ests, or if you ever come over to our land, we will hit you with a force that no country has ever been hit with before—a force so great that you won't even believe it. And your village, Mullah? We know where it is. We know it's the Weetmak village. If you dare lay hands on a single American, that will be the first thing that I destroy. I will not hesitate."

There was dead silence in the room after President Trump said this. Everyone listening knew that he meant it. In 2018, he had ordered the killing of Abu Bakr al-Baghdadi, a high-ranking member of ISIS, not wavering for a moment when he knew that we could take out this murdering terrorist. A few months later, he had blown Qasem Soleimani—an Iranian general who had personally ordered the deaths of hundreds of US servicemembers—right off the face of the earth with a drone strike. In both cases, President Trump had been acting against the wishes of some of his top advisors, who insisted that he "remain calm" and respond to the monstrous acts of these two men with "patience and understanding."

But he had ordered them both eliminated, and he would do it again in a second.

Judging by the quiet on the other end of the line, it was clear that Mullah Baradar knew it. One wrong move, and his home, along with everyone he had ever known and loved, would be reduced to rubble and ash. After years of presidents who had spoken to him in nice, sanitized diplomatic language, he was finally talking to one who wouldn't think twice about leveling his village if he felt it was necessary.

Then, less than one year later, President Joe Biden, a man who probably has trouble remembering where his *own* home is, let alone the village of a foreign terrorist, took to a podium in the White House for a press conference. Reading off a script that had been carefully written for him, he said that things in

Afghanistan were going just fine. When the reporters to whom he was speaking began asking him questions, as in *real* questions that were about something other than the weather back home in Delaware or his favorite flavor of ice cream, he seemed genuinely surprised.

Asked about the likelihood that the Taliban would take over the country, he was about as direct—and as wrong—as humanly possible.

"Do I trust the Taliban?" he asked, repeating a piece of the question. "No. But I trust the capacity of the Afghan military, who is better trained, better equipped, and more re—more competent in terms of conducting war."

This, as Biden must have known, was verifiably false. Thanks to his actions the previous day, the Afghan Army was devastated. Without our air support, they didn't stand a chance.

Asked whether he saw any similarities between the end of this conflict and the horrendous end of the Vietnam War—something that Biden himself had witnessed as a senator, back when his ability to ruin things was mitigated by 99 other senators—he said, "None whatsoever. Zero. What you had is, you had entire brigades breaking through the gates of our embassy, six, if I'm not mistaken. The Taliban is not the south—the North Vietnamese army. They're not—they're not remotely comparable in terms of capability. There's going to be no circumstance where you see people being lifted off the roof of an embassy in the—of the United States from Afghanistan."

Almost exactly one month later, on August 15, American diplomats were airlifted off the roof of the American embassy in Kabul. On the streets below, the Taliban had surrounded the embassy on all sides, driving around with their US military AK-47s held high, shooting dead any Afghans who were even rumored to have supported the United States during the twenty years we were in the country. In a matter of days, the city of Kabul—which, according to the guesswork of General Milley, was not going to fall to the Taliban—was overrun. All of it could have been avoided. In fact, it *was* avoided by President Trump, who was president under the same conditions that Biden inherited in January 2021.

Suddenly, women who had been allowed to attend universities while the United States had troops in the country were turned away at the gates of their schools, told to return home immediately or face horrible consequences. Thanks to Joe Biden, a supposed #MeToo hero and defender of women's rights everywhere, Afghan women who had been just a few years, even months, from gaining a college degree were forced to go back to their homes, allowed to come out only when they were covered head to toe in a burka and accompanied by a male relative. In Kabul and other provinces, girls as young as fifteen were told that they would be taken as "wives" for Taliban fighters. In many cases, their male relatives were killed in front of them when they tried to intervene.

In a matter of days, the airport at Kabul was flooded by people desperate to escape the country. Many of them were American citizens. They, much like the commander of Bagram Air Base, hadn't been warned that the United States was going to disappear from Afghanistan in the night. Either Joe Biden hadn't thought about getting these people out of the country before he began his disastrous withdrawal, or he *had* thought about them and decided that he would let them fend for themselves. Either way, he had left Americans behind, to be murdered in a foreign country—an impeachable offense if there ever was one.

By August 17, when we saw footage of an American C-17 taking off from the airport in Kabul with several doomed Afghan citizens hanging off the wheels and wings, most of whom would fall to their deaths minutes later, even Biden's most strident defenders had abandoned him. During his disastrous withdrawal from Afghanistan, the liberal media were almost forced to admit that Joe Biden was, in fact, everything they had been pretending that Donald Trump was for four years: mentally unfit, unwilling to listen to the intelligence, and, most importantly, more concerned with optics than keeping Americans safe. I say *almost*, of course, because it will only be a matter of time before they get back to defending him.

But, the damage was just beginning. Thanks to Biden's incompetence, the credibility of the United States was destroyed. For twenty years, the American government had been asking people to risk their lives in order to help the United States fight the Taliban and terrorism. We assured them that when things went wrong, the United States would be there to protect them. We promised the same protection to them that we offered to our men and women in uniform and to all American citizens: no man would be left behind. It was a promise that President Trump had upheld in October 2020, when he oversaw a special forces operation to rescue a kidnapped American citizen being held hostage in Nigeria, killing all but one of the people who had taken the American hostage. On that evening, the world watched while President Trump sent a clear message: No American or ally of America would be harmed while he was in the White House; anyone who dared would be dealt with in the harshest possible terms. The president safely rescued this American, with no US casualties, even though Secretary Esper attempted to delay and/or abort the mission. I have no doubt that if he had been allowed to stay in the White House for another four years, he would have been constantly vigilant in protecting every American citizen.

Joe Biden didn't even try.

In the days following the debacle of Afghanistan, there would be whispers in the press from President Biden's advisors, who were now saying that they had been "too afraid to tell him that he was wrong" about the consequences of a withdrawal. As a former chief of staff in the White House, I am tempted to question the competence and influence of Ron Klain, Biden's double-masked chief of staff. It was his job, after all, to be the last line of defense against Biden doing something absolutely disastrous.

But I also know that when you work in the White House, your whole team is only as good as the man sitting behind the Resolute Desk. When it comes to the big calls, all the hard work and raw intelligence in the world can't make the president of the United States do something that he doesn't want to do. No matter what you tell someone in that position, you can't make him act against his character. Thankfully for me, the nature of the person who occupied the Oval Office during my time in the White House had more strength of character than the last ten presidents combined. He would sooner have sliced off one of his arms than carried out the kind of horrific withdrawal that the Biden administration implemented during the month of August 2021, and he would never—as in *never, not under any circumstances*—have left American citizens in a foreign country to die.

As of this writing, the stage seems set for a Biden impeachment. The appalling news reports from Afghanistan are coming in at an alarming rate, and Biden is embarrassing himself every time he steps up to the podium. If there was always justice in the world, he would resign by the arbitrary 9/11 deadline he'd set for our withdrawal.

Sadly, though, I know how things work in Washington, DC. The newspapers and cable networks have memories like goldfish, and the American public isn't much better. That's especially true when it comes to foreign policy. I'm sure that by the time this book comes out, the media will be defending Biden all over again, insisting that if you *really* looked at the whole picture, his shameful handling of the situation in Afghanistan was a success. We'll have Don Lemon telling us that Biden is doing a great job, and that any talk of impeachment is reactionary and purely political.

When he got up to the podium in Cullman, Alabama, on August 21, President Trump had a lot to say about Joe Biden's devastating handling of the Afghanistan situation. He told the audience members, most of whom were unusually quiet for a Trump rally, what a horrible plan it had been from the beginning, why it was never going to work, and what he would have done differently had he still been in charge.

"This will go down as one of the great military defeats of all time," he said. "This is such a great stain on the reputation of our country."

For a moment, I'm sure the sound of President Trump speaking those words was comforting. It allowed all those present to recall, if only for a moment, what it had been like to have a president who was willing to stand up for us, fight on our behalf, and keep us safe from all enemies, foreign and domestic. But as with every dream, it ended. As soon as the applause (which had come only when President Trump discussed what *he* would have done if he were in charge) died down, the crowd seemed to remember where they were and what they were facing: The rain was still falling, Joe Biden was still in the White House, and our country had been thoroughly embarrassed on the world stage. The stage had been set for another serious attack on the United States, and the man in charge was clearly not prepared to deal it.

At that exact moment, according to intelligence reports from the ground, the United States military was attempting to find alternate routes from major cities into the airport in Kabul because ISIS—the terror group that President Trump had absolutely annihilated during his four years in the White House—was returning to its former strength, and its members were out for American blood. Sensing that the American military was no longer going to put up a fight, and that the commander in chief who had blown them out of existence was no longer in the White House, they were once again preparing to cover the provinces of Afghanistan with their black flags. President Trump's worst fear was about to become a reality.

When Joe Biden pulled out of Afghanistan, he left an enormous amount of military equipment behind, including four C-130 transport aircraft, twenty-three ground-attack aircraft, 109 helicopters, and just over 22,000 Humvees, along with billions of dollars of weapons. In fact, Biden's decision gave the Taliban control of one of the best equipped military forces in the world, in ways better than Australia and New Zealand. Soon, we would see members of ISIS and the Taliban riding around Afghanistan in the backs of American-made pickup trucks with their flags flying, shooting people on a whim using American rifles, and standing beside American missiles as they declared jihad on the West once more.

Even President Trump, who, exactly one year before his rally in Alabama, had warned us about the danger of allowing Joe Biden to get within whispering distance of the White House, seemed shocked by how quickly things had deteriorated in his absence. From the podium, he attempted to lighten the spirits of the people who'd turned out in such massive numbers to see him. There were certainly high points, such as when President Trump mocked Joe Biden's terrible press conferences, or when he reminded the crowd of all that he had been able to accomplish during his four years in office.

But in the end, the rally ended on a somber note. People were confused. They didn't know where to turn for leadership, and President Trump had not yet announced that he was going to run in 2024. It was as if heavy black clouds had appeared over the United States of America, and they showed no signs of letting up anytime soon. Even the momentary ray of light—a message from President Trump, a rally, or a good speech—was not enough to make that darkness go away. The American people needed a leader, and there was only one man in the country who had proven he could do the job.

Still, the whole world was against him. The day after the rally, it was as if nothing had occurred at all, at least if you checked Twitter or Facebook. Almost as soon as the videos of President Trump speaking hit the web, they were buried under a mountain of other hashtags and links to articles. I don't know what technological tricks of algorithms there are in Big Tech companies that keep President Trump out of the public consciousness, but I know that they must have been working overtime at the end of August. In a matter of days, it was as if all record of President Trump's address to his supporters disappeared from the internet, fading from history along with all of his old Facebook and Twitter posts.

Back when he was in the White House, or even when he was out on the campaign trail in 2016, President Trump would have been able to counter this obvious bias with tweets of his own, reaching an audience of nearly 100 million with the push of a button. It was his way of letting the men and women of the United States know that he was there, listening to them, and willing to fight. But thanks to Twitter's decision to ban him over the so-called coup that had occurred on January 6, he couldn't do that.

Meanwhile, representatives of the Taliban—who, it should be noted, had just carried out an *actual* coup against the government, this time with rifles and other weapons—were tweeting out messages like this one: "Afghanistan is conquered, and Islam has won!"

It was further proof of what we had known all along: Big Tech's quest to ban President Trump had nothing to do with the safety of American citizens, as they had claimed. It had nothing to do with the so-called coup that never really occurred. It was only ever about one thing, and that was fear.

These tech companies, along with some of the US intelligence community, the Chinese Communist Party, and the seemingly bottomless swamp of establishment politicians in Washington, have wanted President Trump gone for years because they are deeply *afraid* of him. He is the only politician in American history that they have been unable to control. He is the only one who, faced with every possible attack they could think of, not only to his administration, but also to his character, his family, and his business, stood up and said *Keep it coming; I can do this all day long.* As of this writing, despite being banned by most major tech platforms, he still manages to get his press releases out by posting daily to Telegram, a new social media tool. Other platforms, like Parler and Rumble are also stepping up to fill the void caused by Big Tech censorship. As we have seen, there is truly nothing that can get between President Trump and his supporters.

That is why he was the right person to bring this country back from the brink in 2016, and it's why he is the right person to do it again.

When I spoke with President Trump on the phone after the rally, he seemed to have a renewed sense of mission, as if watching Joe Biden woefully mismanage our country's attempt to get out of Afghanistan was the final straw that he needed to get back into the race for the presidency. During our conversation, I realized that there was a different tone to President Trump's voice—almost somber.

Given the state of the country at that time, this was understandable. President Trump could not seem to get his mind off all the Americans who were stranded in Afghanistan as we were speaking. They didn't have a way to get home or even a way to get to the airport. During our conversation, which occurred on the evening of August 25, President Trump reminded me of what it had been like when he was still in office.

"Mark," he said, "you were there for multiple conversations with the Taliban. You remember how clear I was with them that they needed to respect America, and how I warned them that they couldn't harm one American soldier."

"Yes, sir," I answered. "And I remember you saying you didn't want our enemy driving around in our Humvees with an ISIS flag either."

"Eighty-three billion dollars, Mark, eighty-three billion dollars. Can you even imagine how much money that is, and we gave it away to these bums? Americans working hard every day to pay their taxes, and Joe Biden just leaves it there and takes out our military before getting our people home. It just shows real weakness. No one wanted out of Afghanistan more than me, but you can't just retreat without making sure Americans are protected. Can you believe that it has gotten this bad this quickly? Seven months and it seems like everything has turned upside down."

President Trump fell silent for a moment. Finally, he said, "Mark, I don't know that America can survive another three years of Biden."

Tragically, the following morning, the headlines put an exclamation point on what the president told me less than fourteen hours earlier. Two explosions went off outside the airport at Kabul, killing more than two hundred civilians and twelve United States Marines and one Navy corpsmen, nearly all of whom were in their early twenties. A splinter group of ISIS claimed responsibility. This was something that never would have happened if President Trump had still been in office. We both knew it.

Yet we, along with everyone else in the country, were facing three more years of Biden, and things were looking bleaker than ever. Already, we had gone from energy dominance to begging OPEC to lower gas prices, from a robust economy and rising wages to government handouts, and from a secure border to millions of immigrants flooding our cities, communities, and hospitals. Overseas, the Biden administration was begging the Taliban for US citizens' safety while turning a blind eye to the violence in Democrat-controlled cities.

On another call a few days later, he also reminded me that it was strength, not weakness, that had allowed him to wipe out the ISIS Caliphate. He recalled some of our conversations about a potential withdrawal.

"Can you believe all the people and equipment Biden has left behind?" he said. "Weak, sad and dumb. The Democrats will try to change the subject, watch them. And remember, when 'Yesper'"—his nickname for Mark Esper—"who always said yes to the wrong people, and Milley, who looked tough but wasn't tough, said we should leave equipment behind?"

"Yes sir" I replied.

"I told them not one bolt, not one nut should be left for them. That crazy Milley said, 'Sir, It is cheaper if with leave it all there.' I said, 'You mean it is cheaper to leave millions of dollars of airplanes, helicopters and humvees than to gas them up and fly them back? That has got to be the stupidest f**king thing that I have ever heard, General.'"

During our conversation, President Trump said the words that I had been waiting to hear for seven months.

"We have to be ready," he said. "We have to do it again for the sake of our great country."

Clearly, the time for "hanging around" was over. When President Trump said we had to "do it again," he was not simply stating some abstract idea. The message was clear: We had to prepare for the second term that had been denied him. We needed four more years. That's four more years to reverse the damage that Biden had managed to inflict on our country in just seven short months; four more years to truly drain the swamp; four more years to remind America that our country *is* truly great, no matter what anyone on the left has to say about it.

We have the playbook. All we have to do now is run the plays again.

President Trump has demonstrated that he is a man of action, not just words. And clearly, the time for action is once again here. During our frequent phone calls, he often tells me that he wishes he knew then what we know now, namely that when you're running the White House, personnel is key. He says that he wishes he could go back and root out all the political appointees who worked privately to undermine his agenda. We can't do that. But we can make sure that we don't make the same mistake the second time around.

When I hung up the phone that night, I had an assignment. Find people for his second four years who will fully support the America First Agenda: people who will not quietly try to sabotage that agenda, who are not afraid to fight against China and support American workers and their families, who want to secure borders and safe communities, who are willing to support a strong military, who will focus on our greatness and not our flaws, who will stand for our flag and support our law enforcement, who will stop the march of socialism and cancel culture. In short, I was given the task of finding secretaries and undersecretaries who wouldn't undercut the president. It is a challenge that I look forward to tackling.

I'm sure that in the months to come, there will be "Draft Trump" movements, large rallies, and boat parades that would make the naval fleets of some countries seem small by comparison. There will be lots of chatter about President Trump's running mate, and about what he will do when he is once again back in the Oval Office. And I have no doubt that the efforts will all reach the same conclusion. It's time for more historic accomplishments, and . . .

Four more years.

— INDEX —